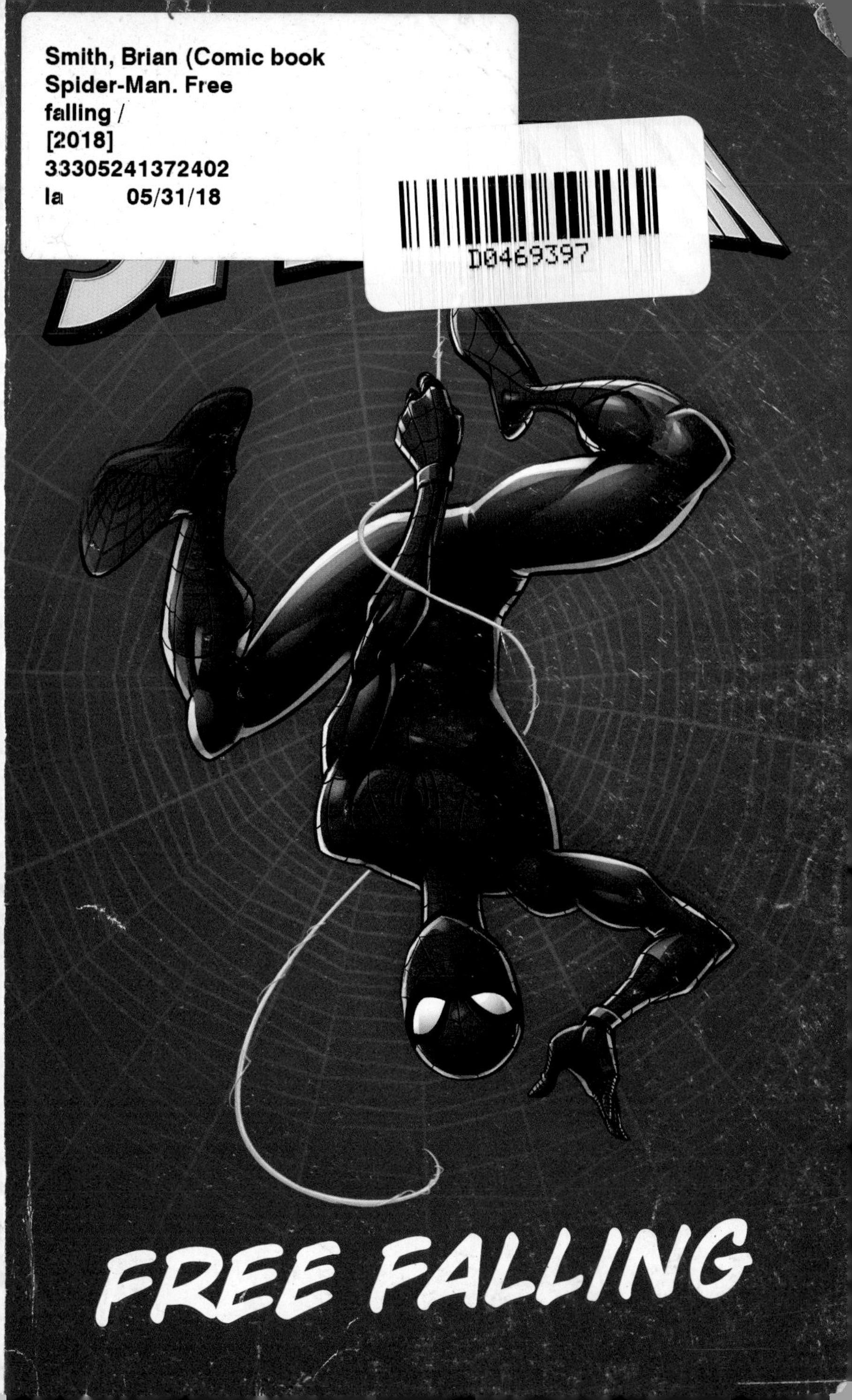
FREE FALLING

MARVEL

SPIDER-MAN
FREE FALLING

Brian Smith
WRITER

Mario Del Pennino
ARTIST

Carlos Lopez
COLORIST

VC's Joe Sabino (Chap. 1-7) & Travis Lanham (Chap. 8)
LETTERERS

Katherine Brown
PROJECT MANAGER

Darren Sanchez
EDITOR

Spider-Man created by **Stan Lee** & **Steve Ditko**

COLLECTION EDITOR: **JENNIFER GRÜNWALD**
ASSISTANT EDITOR: **CAITLIN O'CONNELL**
ASSOCIATE MANAGING EDITOR: **KATERI WOODY**
EDITOR, SPECIAL PROJECTS: **MARK D. BEAZLEY**

VP PRODUCTION & SPECIAL PROJECTS: **JEFF YOUNGQUIST**
SVP PRINT, SALES & MARKETING: **DAVID GABRIEL**
BOOK DESIGNER: **ADAM DEL RE**

EDITOR IN CHIEF: **C.B. CEBULSKI**
CHIEF CREATIVE OFFICER: **JOE QUESADA**
PRESIDENT: **DAN BUCKLEY**
EXECUTIVE PRODUCER: **ALAN FINE**

SPIDER-MAN: FREE FALLING. First printing 2018. ISBN 978-1-302-91221-5. Published by MARVEL WORLDWIDE, INC., a subsidiary of MARVEL ENTERTAINMENT, LLC. OFFICE OF PUBLICATION: 135 West 50th Street, New York, NY 10020. Copyright © 2018 MARVEL No similarity between any of the names, characters, persons, and/or institutions in this magazine with those of any living or dead person or institution is intended, and any such similarity which may exist is purely coincidental. **Printed in the U.S.A.** DAN BUCKLEY, President, Marvel Entertainment; JOHN NEE, Publisher; JOE QUESADA, Chief Creative Officer; TOM BREVOORT, SVP of Publishing; DAVID BOGART, SVP of Business Affairs & Operations, Publishing & Partnership; DAVID GABRIEL, SVP of Sales & Marketing, Publishing; JEFF YOUNGQUIST, VP of Production & Special Projects; DAN CARR, Executive Director of Publishing Technology; ALEX MORALES, Director of Publishing Operations; SUSAN CRESPI, Production Manager; STAN LEE, Chairman Emeritus. For information regarding advertising in Marvel Comics or on Marvel.com, please contact Vit DeBellis, Custom Solutions & Integrated Advertising Manager, at vdebellis@marvel.com. For Marvel subscription inquiries, please call 888-511-5480. **Manufactured between 3/9/2018 and 4/10/2018** by SHERIDAN, CHELSEA, MI, USA.

10 9 8 7 6 5 4 3 2 1

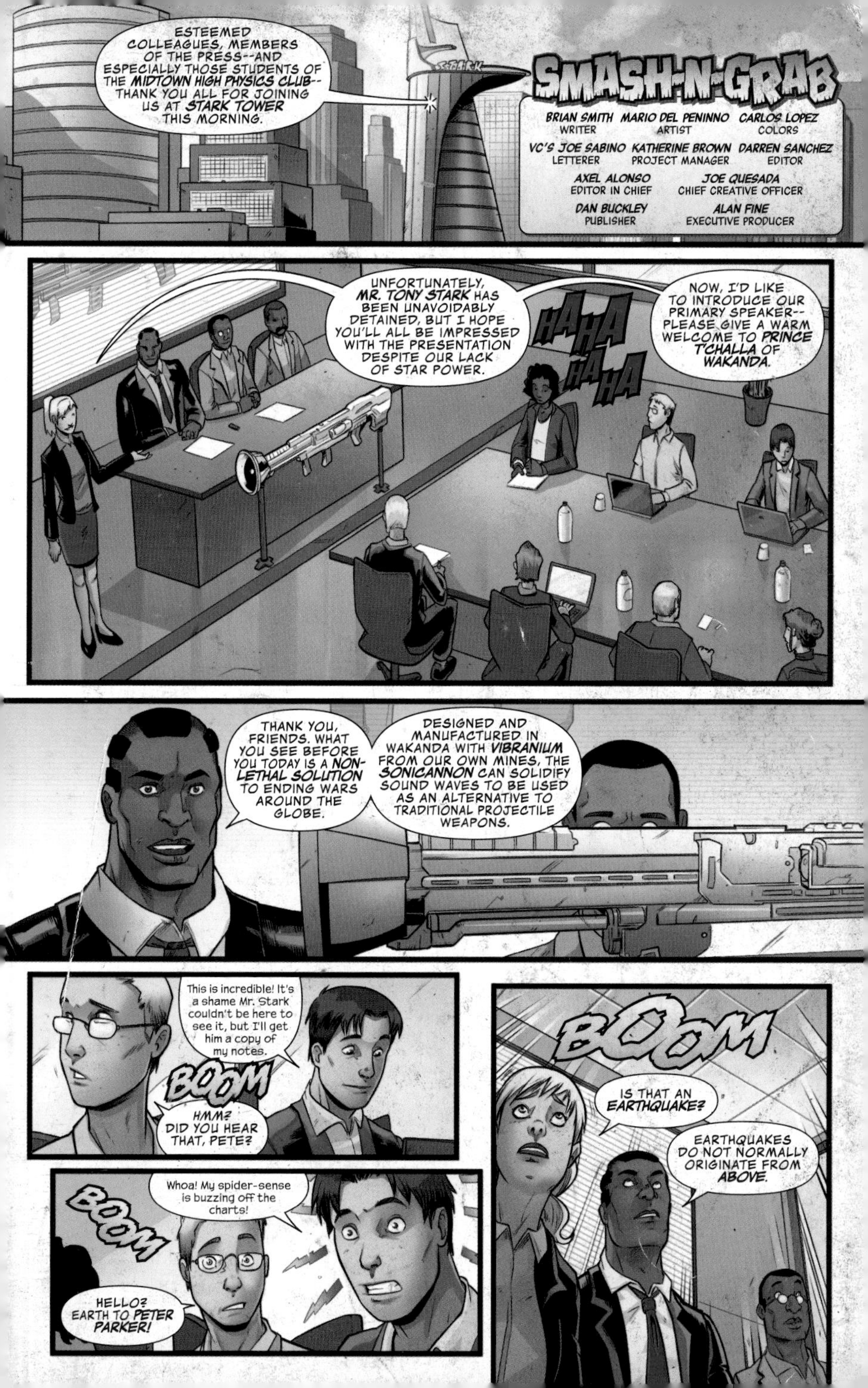

ESTEEMED COLLEAGUES, MEMBERS OF THE PRESS--AND ESPECIALLY THOSE STUDENTS OF THE MIDTOWN HIGH PHYSICS CLUB--THANK YOU ALL FOR JOINING US AT STARK TOWER THIS MORNING.
STARK
SMASH-N-GRAB
BRIAN SMITH WRITER
MARIO DEL PENINNO ARTIST
CARLOS LOPEZ COLORS
VC'S JOE SABINO LETTERER
KATHERINE BROWN PROJECT MANAGER
DARREN SANCHEZ EDITOR
AXEL ALONSO EDITOR IN CHIEF
JOE QUESADA CHIEF CREATIVE OFFICER
DAN BUCKLEY PUBLISHER
ALAN FINE EXECUTIVE PRODUCER
UNFORTUNATELY, MR. TONY STARK HAS BEEN UNAVOIDABLY DETAINED, BUT I HOPE YOU'LL ALL BE IMPRESSED WITH THE PRESENTATION DESPITE OUR LACK OF STAR POWER.
HA HA HA HA HA
NOW, I'D LIKE TO INTRODUCE OUR PRIMARY SPEAKER--PLEASE GIVE A WARM WELCOME TO PRINCE T'CHALLA OF WAKANDA.
THANK YOU, FRIENDS. WHAT YOU SEE BEFORE YOU TODAY IS A NON-LETHAL SOLUTION TO ENDING WARS AROUND THE GLOBE.
DESIGNED AND MANUFACTURED IN WAKANDA WITH VIBRANIUM FROM OUR OWN MINES, THE SONICANNON CAN SOLIDIFY SOUND WAVES TO BE USED AS AN ALTERNATIVE TO TRADITIONAL PROJECTILE WEAPONS.
This is incredible! It's a shame Mr. Stark couldn't be here to see it, but I'll get him a copy of my notes.
BOOM
HMM? DID YOU HEAR THAT, PETE?
BOOM
Whoa! My spider-sense is buzzing off the charts!
HELLO? EARTH TO PETER PARKER!
BOOM
IS THAT AN EARTHQUAKE?
EARTHQUAKES DO NOT NORMALLY ORIGINATE FROM ABOVE.

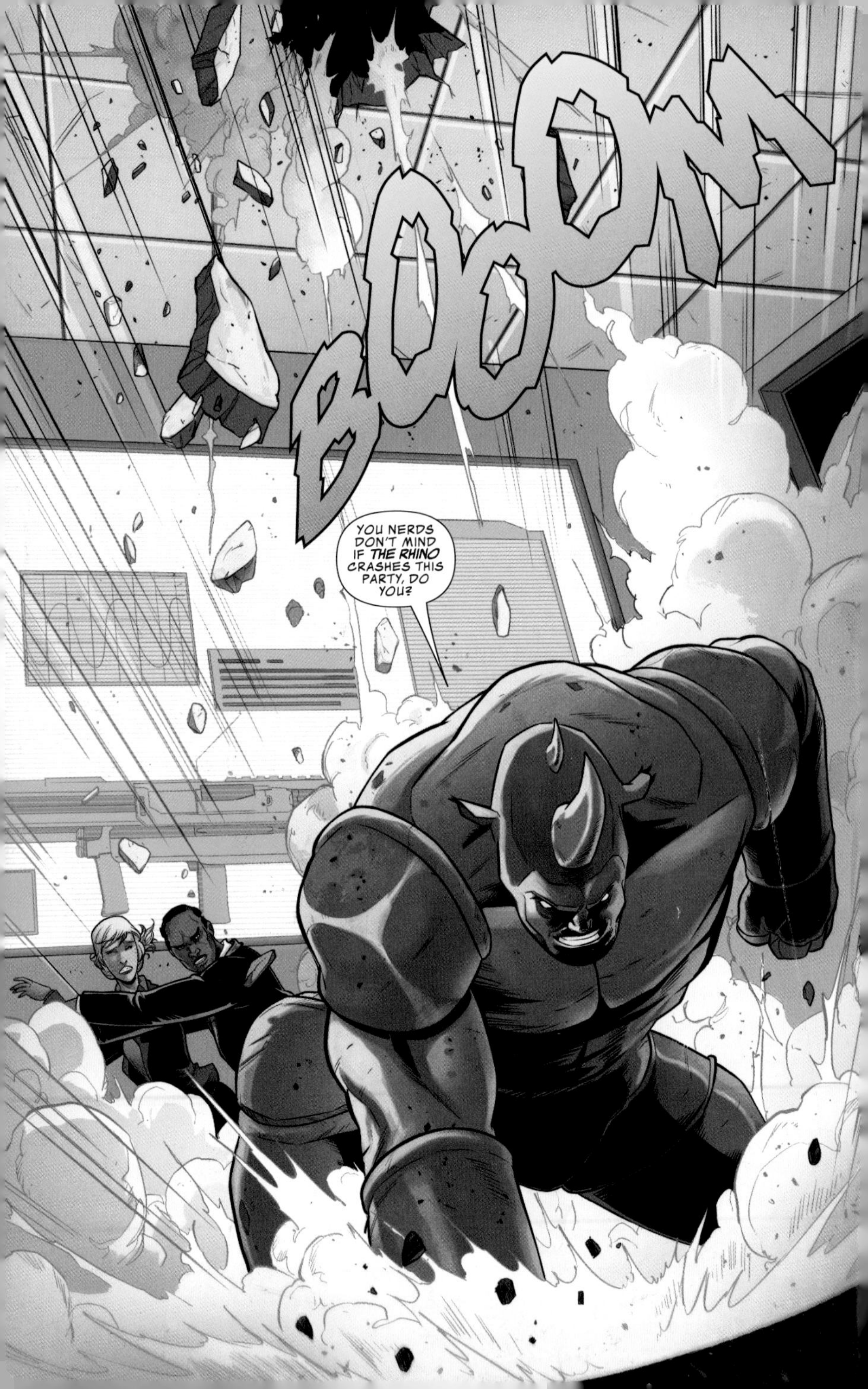
BOOOM
YOU NERDS DON'T MIND IF THE RHINO CRASHES THIS PARTY, DO YOU?

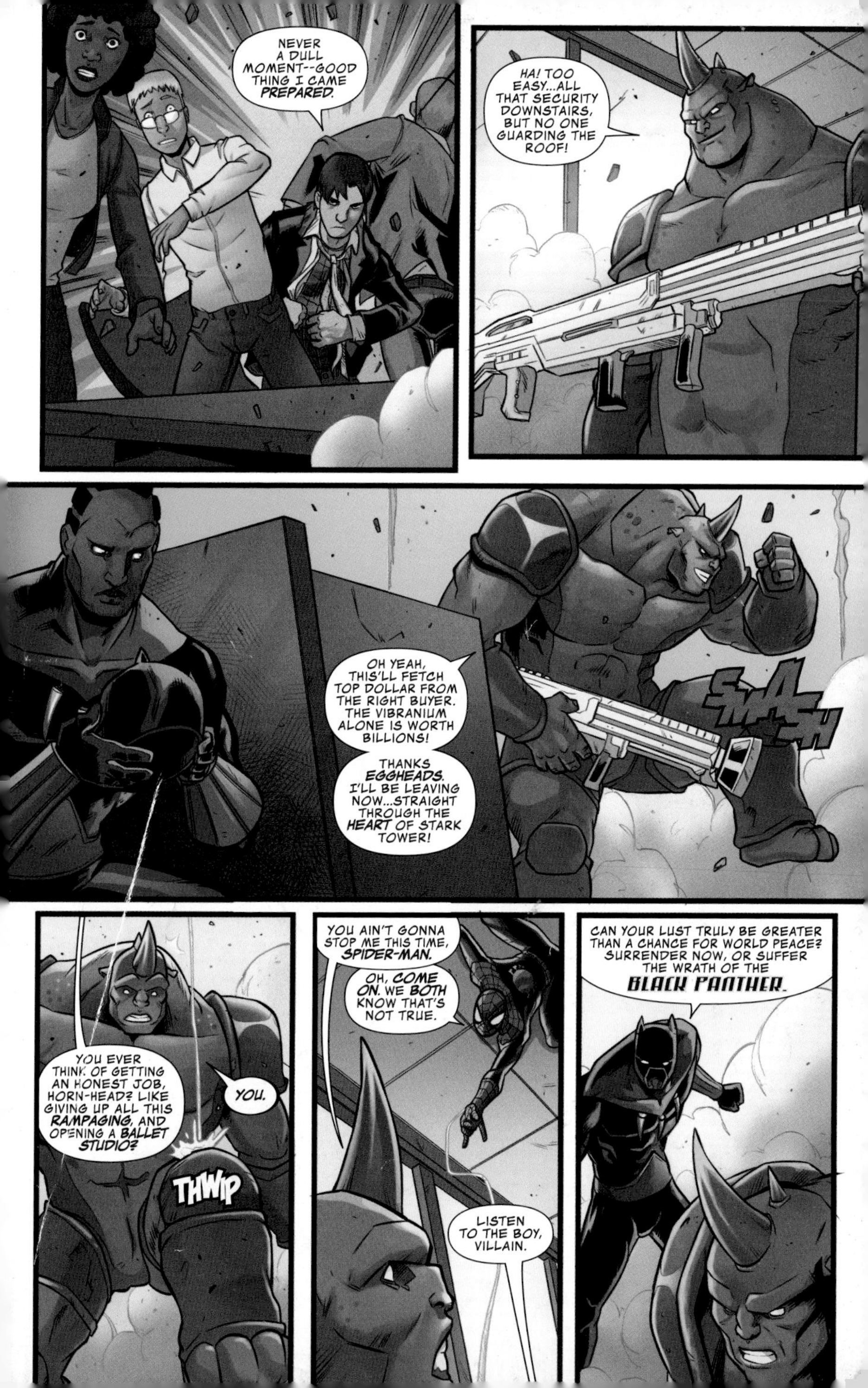
NEVER A DULL MOMENT--GOOD THING I CAME PREPARED.
HA! TOO EASY...ALL THAT SECURITY DOWNSTAIRS, BUT NO ONE GUARDING THE ROOF!
OH YEAH, THIS'LL FETCH TOP DOLLAR FROM THE RIGHT BUYER. THE VIBRANIUM ALONE IS WORTH BILLIONS!
THANKS EGGHEADS. I'LL BE LEAVING NOW...STRAIGHT THROUGH THE HEART OF STARK TOWER!
SMASH
YOU EVER THINK OF GETTING AN HONEST JOB, HORN-HEAD? LIKE GIVING UP ALL THIS RAMPAGING, AND OPENING A BALLET STUDIO?
YOU.
THWIP
YOU AIN'T GONNA STOP ME THIS TIME, SPIDER-MAN.
OH, COME ON. WE BOTH KNOW THAT'S NOT TRUE.
LISTEN TO THE BOY, VILLAIN.
CAN YOUR LUST TRULY BE GREATER THAN A CHANCE FOR WORLD PEACE? SURRENDER NOW, OR SUFFER THE WRATH OF THE BLACK PANTHER.

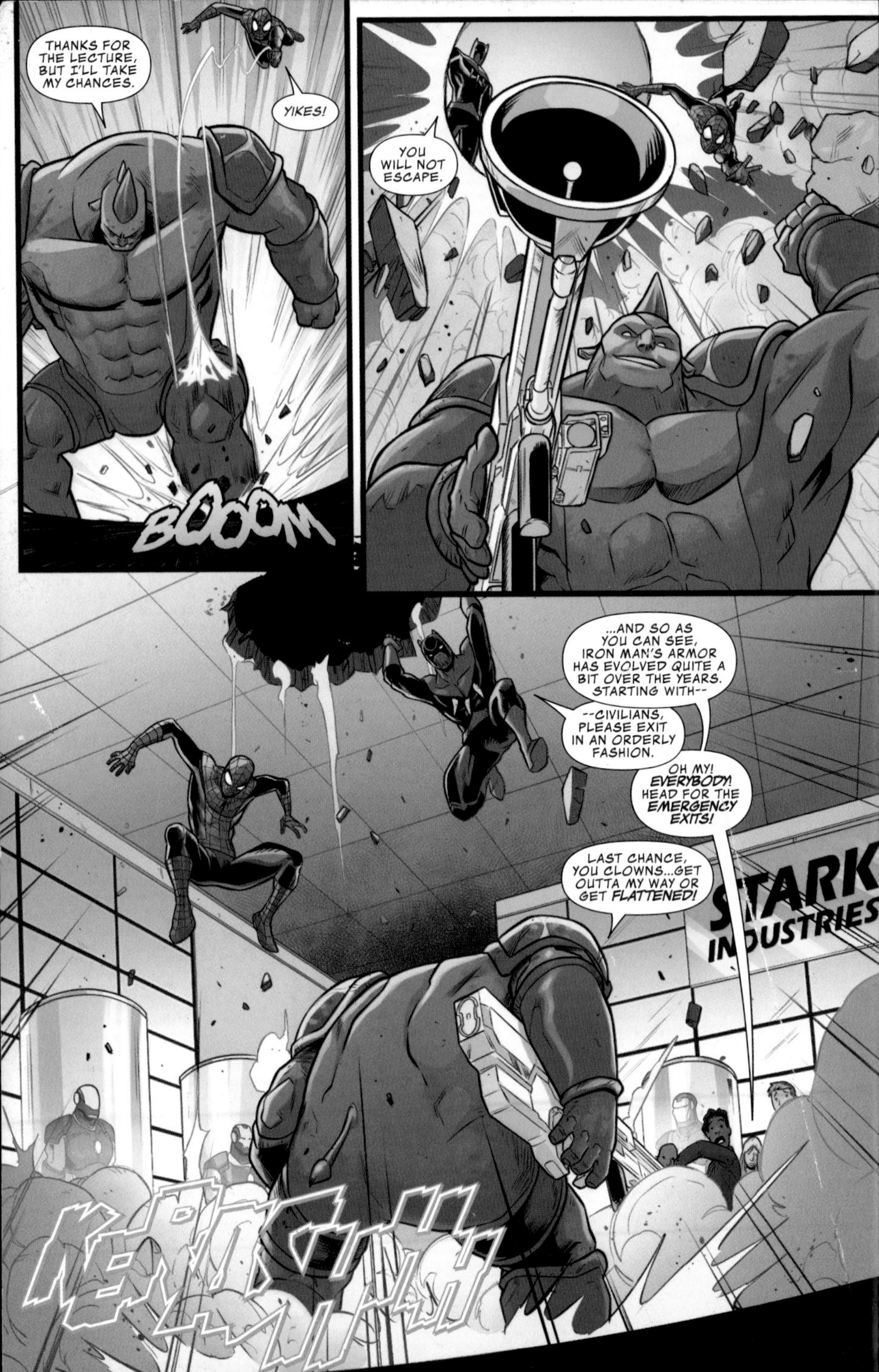
THANKS FOR THE LECTURE, BUT I'LL TAKE MY CHANCES.
YIKES!
BOOOM
YOU WILL NOT ESCAPE.
...AND SO AS YOU CAN SEE, IRON MAN'S ARMOR HAS EVOLVED QUITE A BIT OVER THE YEARS. STARTING WITH--
--CIVILIANS, PLEASE EXIT IN AN ORDERLY FASHION.
OH MY! EVERYBODY! HEAD FOR THE EMERGENCY EXITS!
LAST CHANCE, YOU CLOWNS...GET OUTTA MY WAY OR GET FLATTENED!
STARK INDUSTRIES

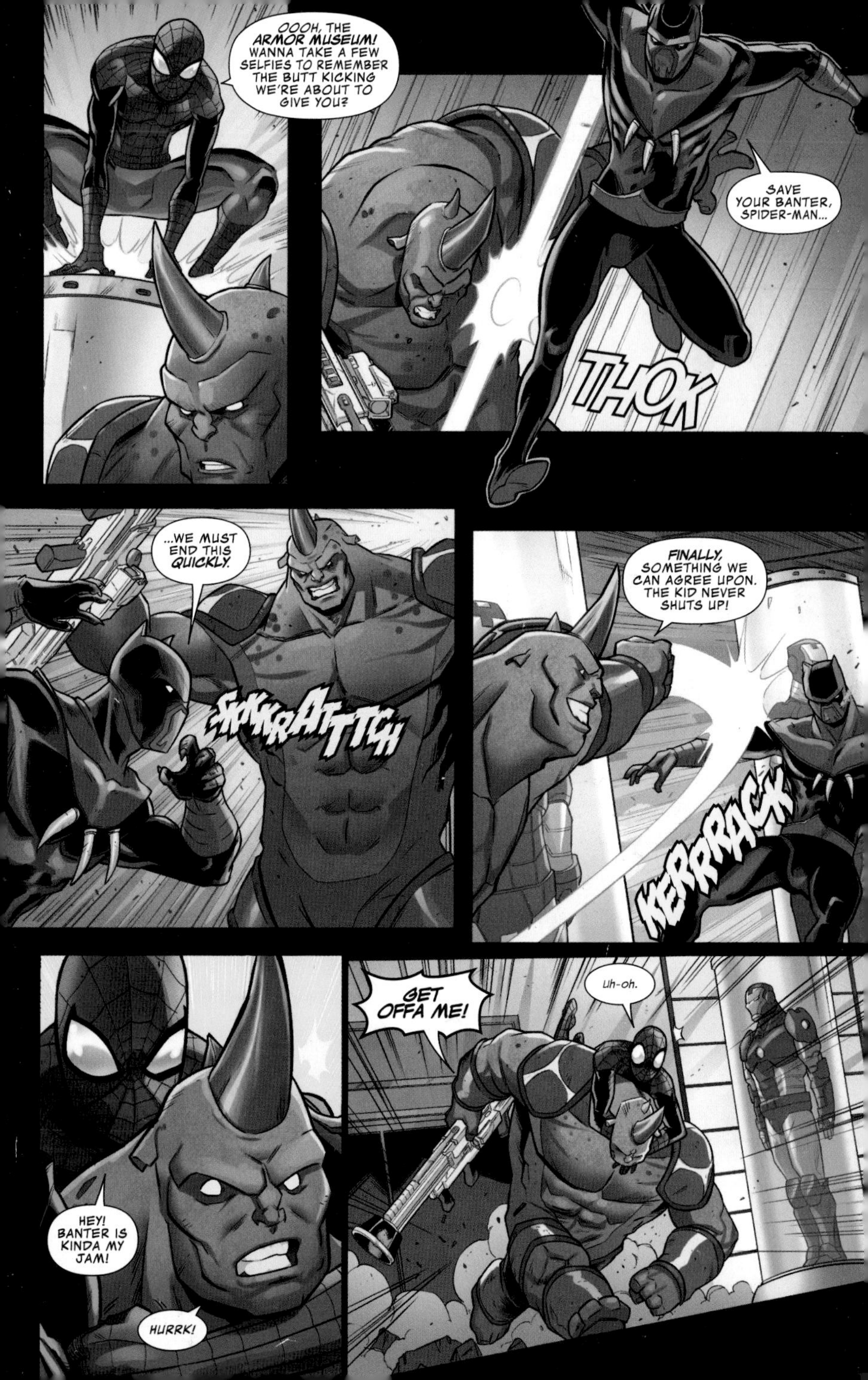
OOOH, THE ARMOR MUSEUM! WANNA TAKE A FEW SELFIES TO REMEMBER THE BUTT KICKING WE'RE ABOUT TO GIVE YOU?
SAVE YOUR BANTER, SPIDER-MAN...
THOK
...WE MUST END THIS QUICKLY.
SKKRATTTCH
FINALLY, SOMETHING WE CAN AGREE UPON. THE KID NEVER SHUTS UP!
KERRACK
HEY! BANTER IS KINDA MY JAM!
HURRK!
GET OFFA ME!
Uh-oh.

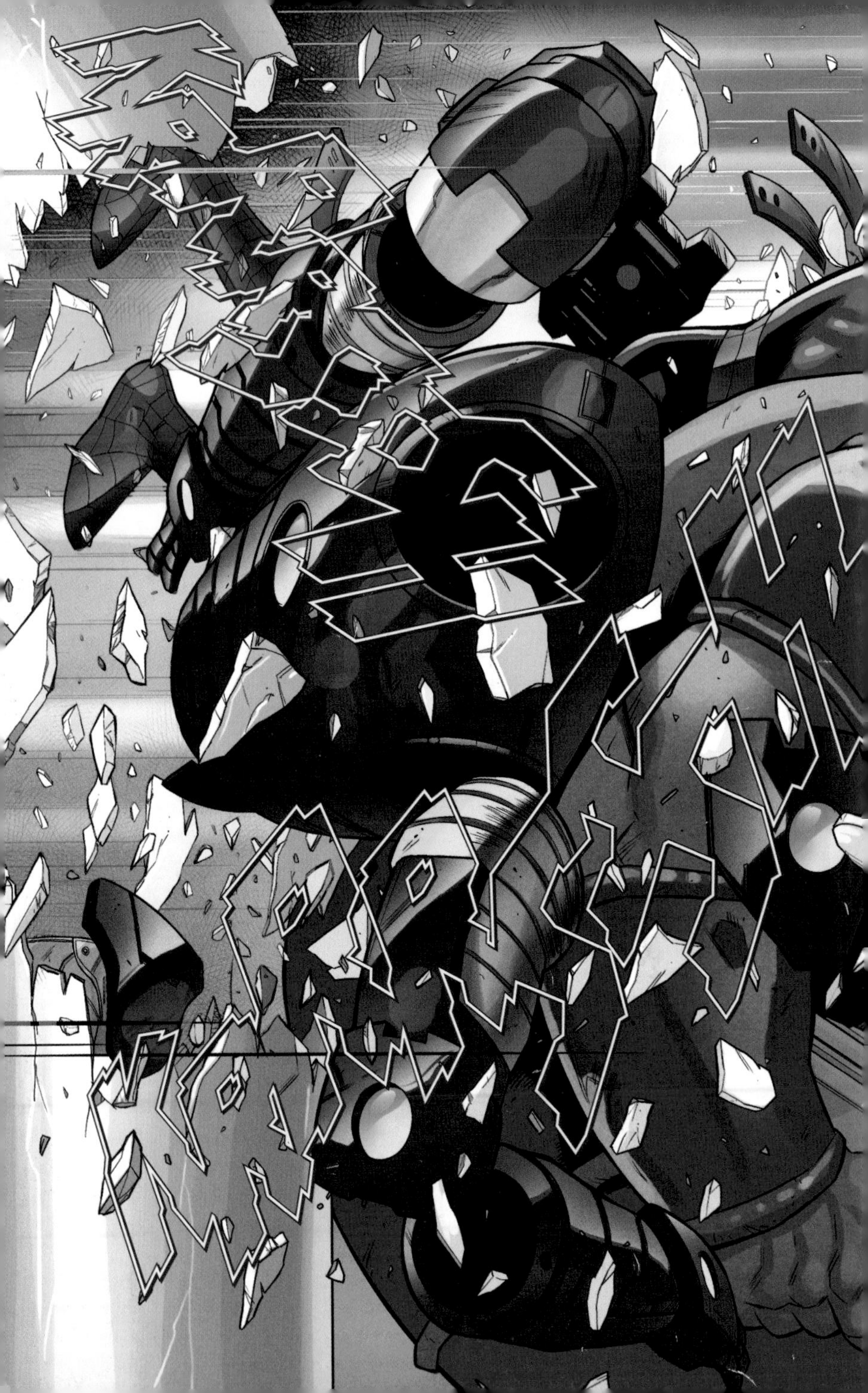

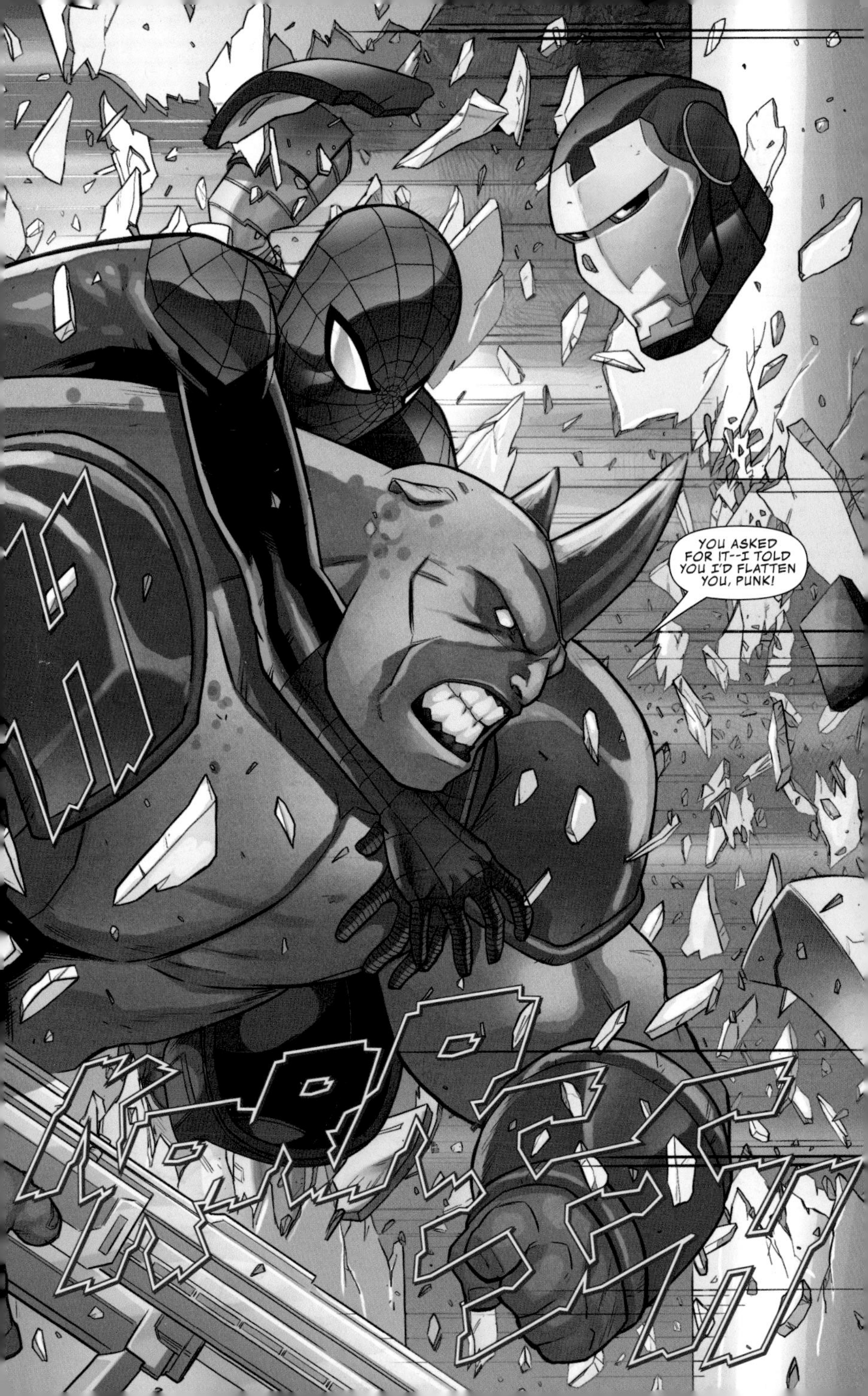
YOU ASKED FOR IT--I TOLD YOU I'D FLATTEN YOU, PUNK!

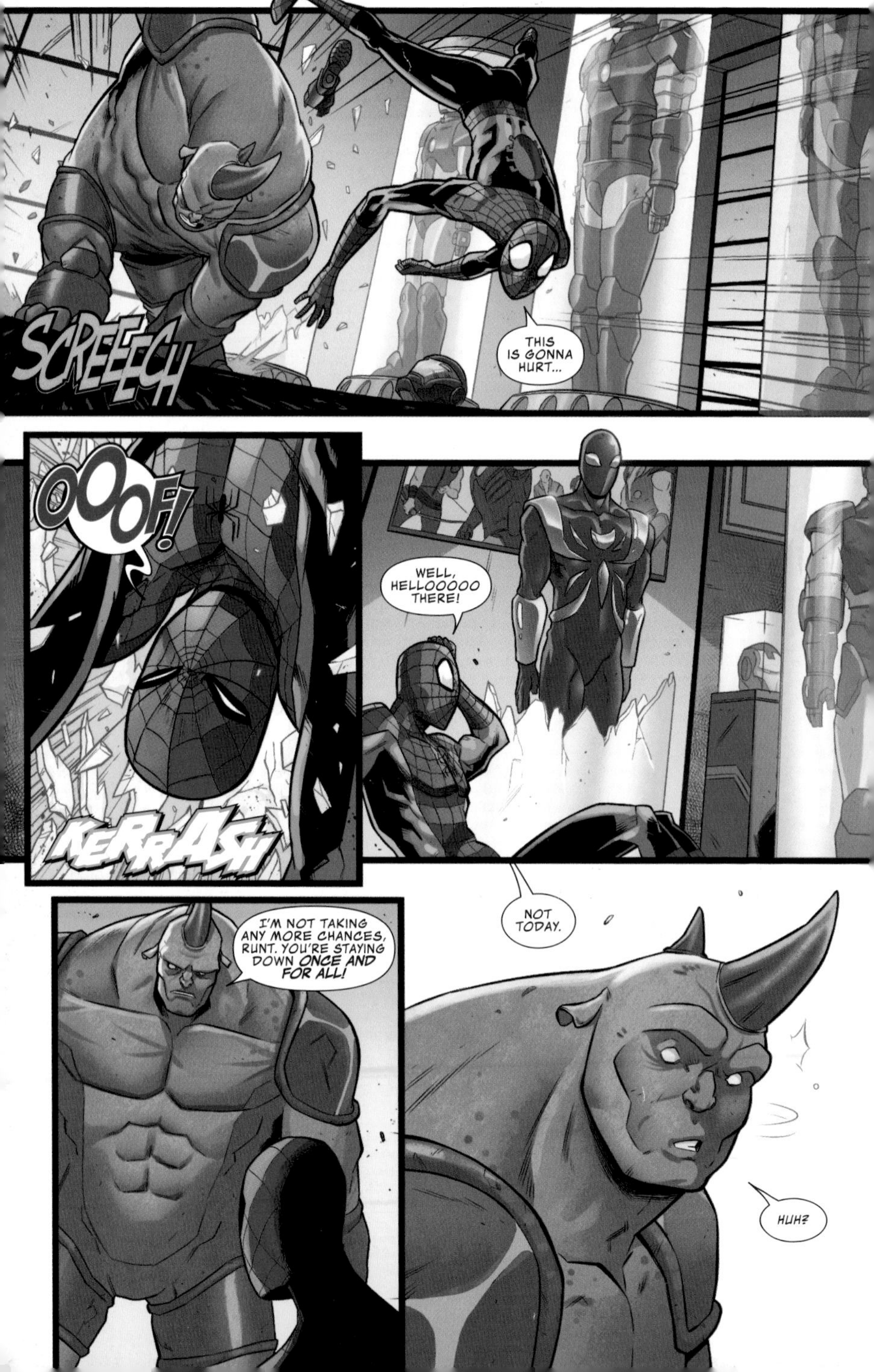
SCREEECH
THIS IS GONNA HURT...
OOOF!
KERRASH
WELL, HELLOOOOO THERE!
I'M NOT TAKING ANY MORE CHANCES, RUNT. YOU'RE STAYING DOWN ONCE AND FOR ALL!
NOT TODAY.
HUH?

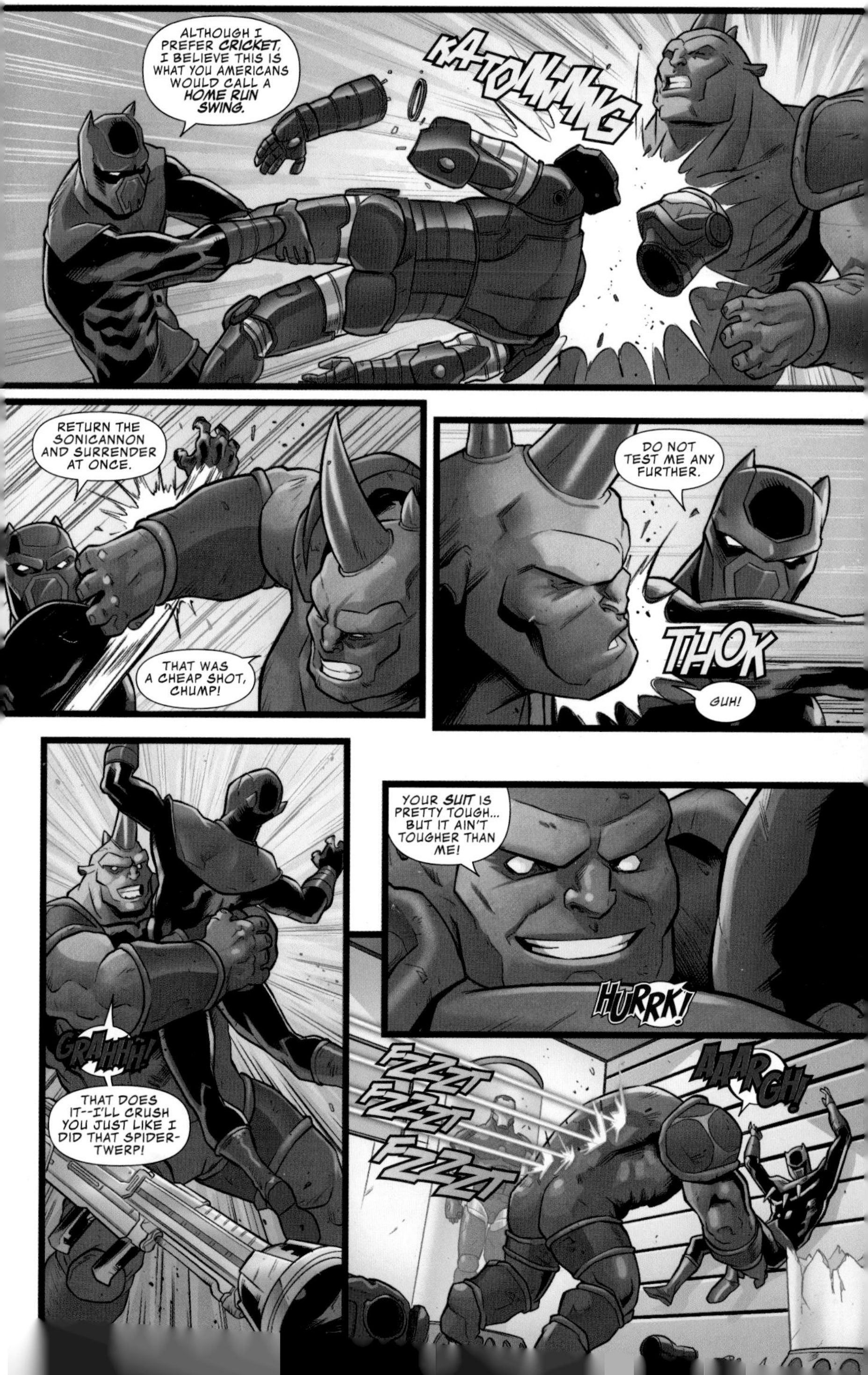
ALTHOUGH I PREFER CRICKET, I BELIEVE THIS IS WHAT YOU AMERICANS WOULD CALL A HOME RUN SWING.
KA-TONNNG
RETURN THE SONICANNON AND SURRENDER AT ONCE.
THAT WAS A CHEAP SHOT, CHUMP!
DO NOT TEST ME ANY FURTHER.
THOK
GUH!
GRAHHH!
THAT DOES IT--I'LL CRUSH YOU JUST LIKE I DID THAT SPIDER-TWERP!
YOUR SUIT IS PRETTY TOUGH... BUT IT AIN'T TOUGHER THAN ME!
HURRK!
FZZZT
FZZZT
FZZZT
AAARGH!

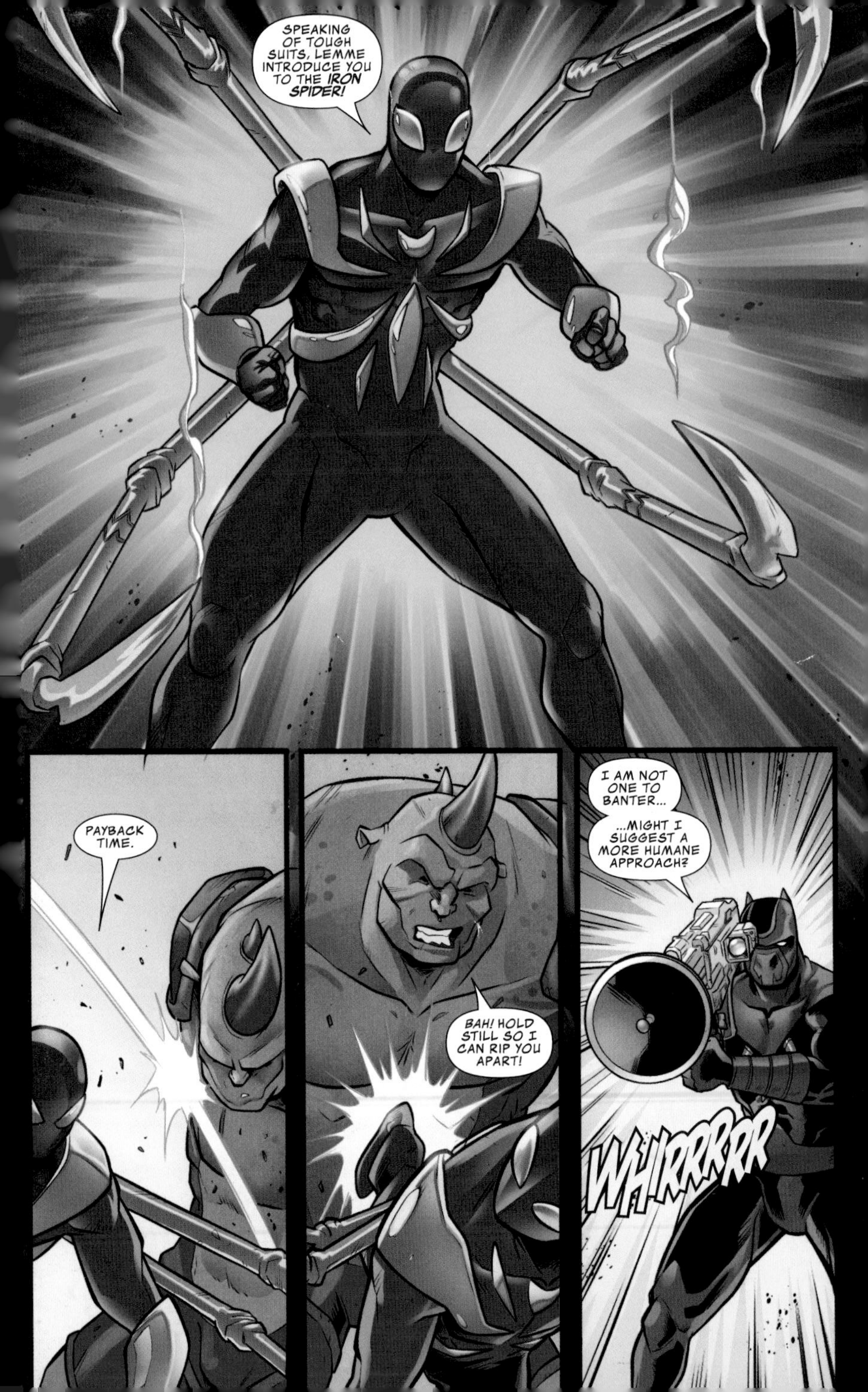
SPEAKING OF TOUGH SUITS, LEMME INTRODUCE YOU TO THE IRON SPIDER!
PAYBACK TIME.
BAH! HOLD STILL SO I CAN RIP YOU APART!
I AM NOT ONE TO BANTER...
...MIGHT I SUGGEST A MORE HUMANE APPROACH?
WHIRRRRR

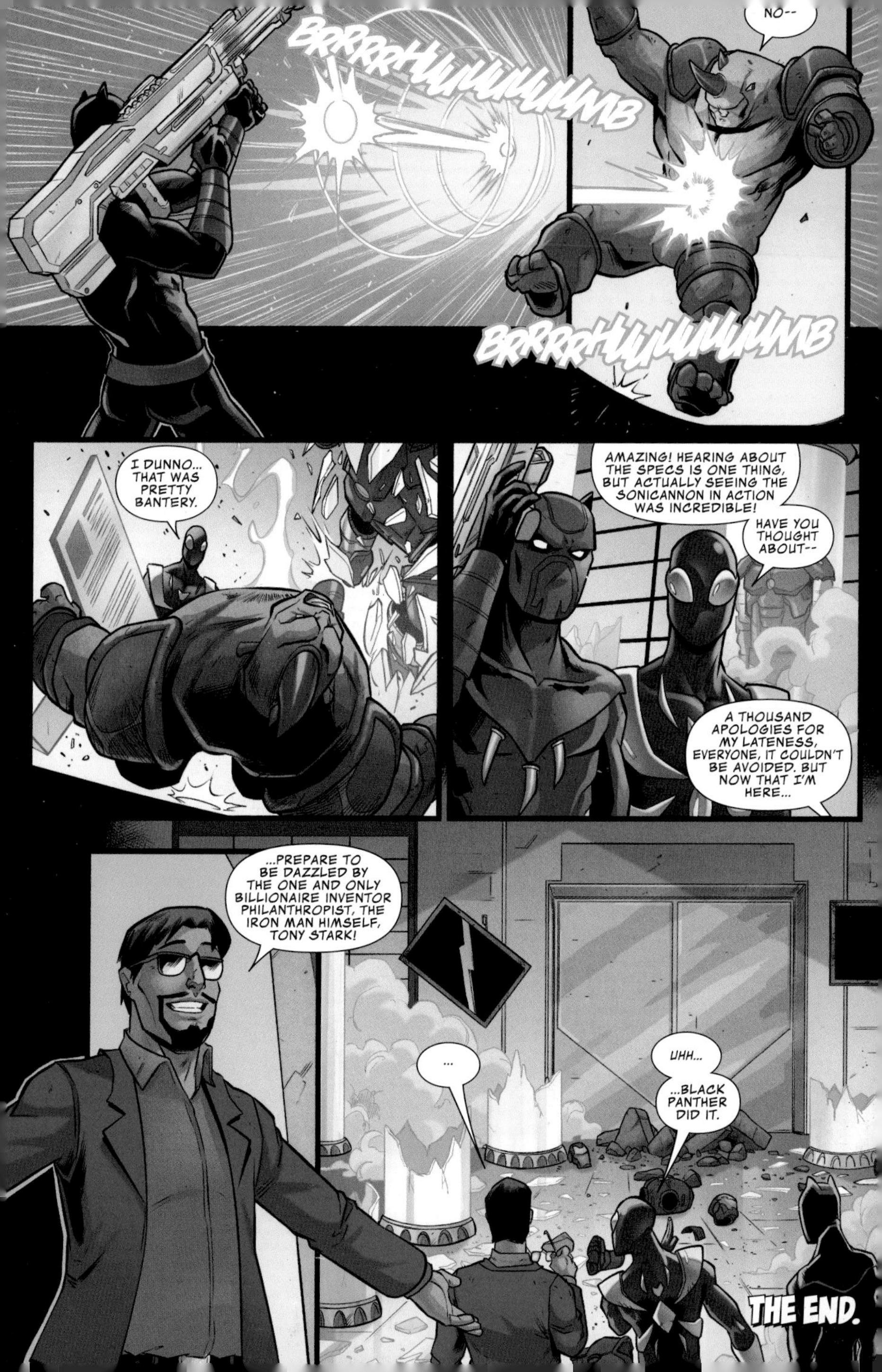
BRRRRHUUUUUUUMB
NO--
BRRRRHUUUUUUUMB
I DUNNO... THAT WAS PRETTY BANTERY.
AMAZING! HEARING ABOUT THE SPECS IS ONE THING, BUT ACTUALLY SEEING THE SONICANNON IN ACTION WAS INCREDIBLE!
HAVE YOU THOUGHT ABOUT--
A THOUSAND APOLOGIES FOR MY LATENESS, EVERYONE, IT COULDN'T BE AVOIDED. BUT NOW THAT I'M HERE...
...PREPARE TO BE DAZZLED BY THE ONE AND ONLY BILLIONAIRE INVENTOR PHILANTHROPIST, THE IRON MAN HIMSELF, TONY STARK!
...
UHH...
...BLACK PANTHER DID IT.
THE END.

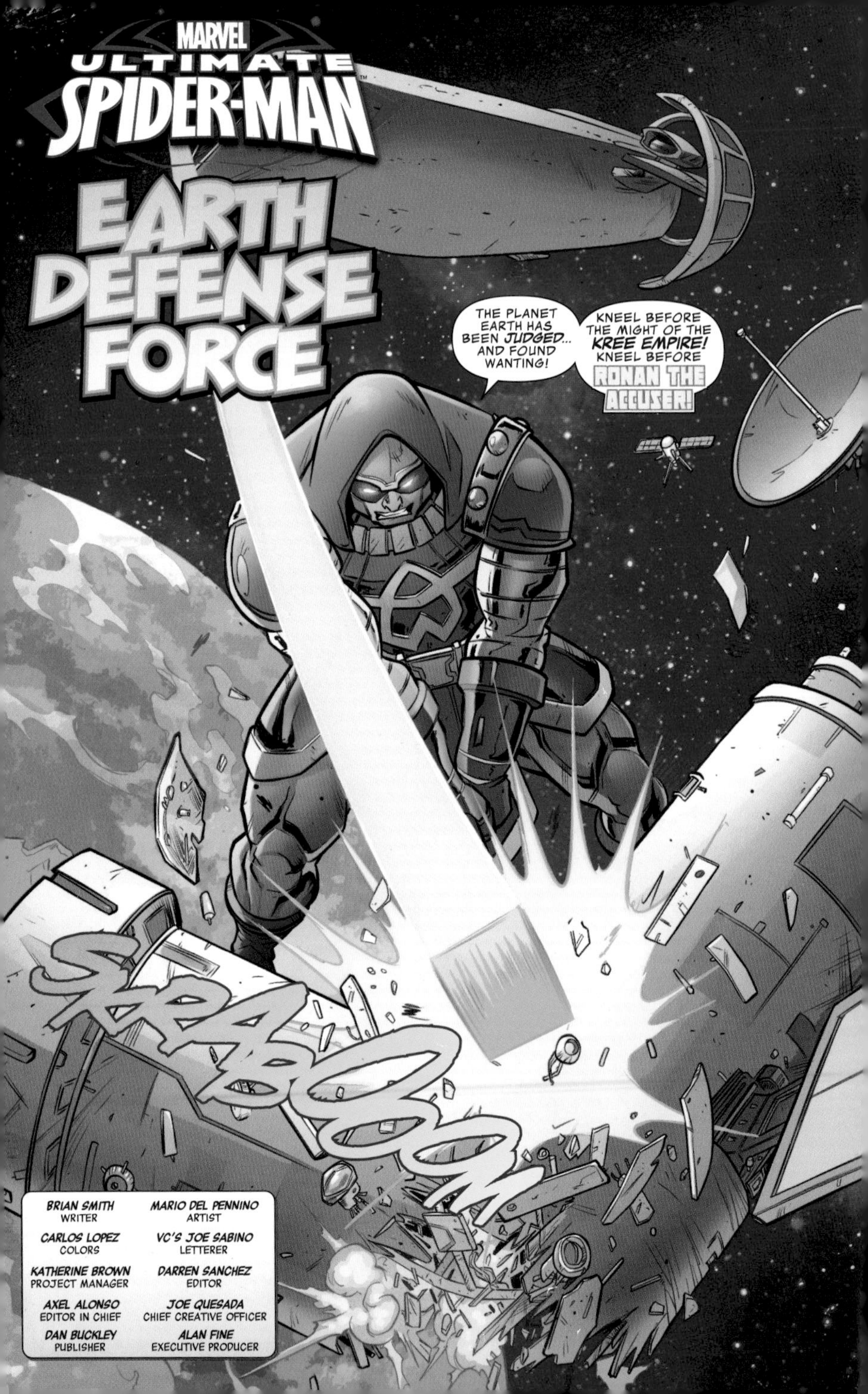
MARVEL
ULTIMATE
SPIDER-MAN
EARTH DEFENSE FORCE
THE PLANET EARTH HAS BEEN JUDGED... AND FOUND WANTING!
KNEEL BEFORE THE MIGHT OF THE KREE EMPIRE! KNEEL BEFORE RONAN THE ACCUSER!
SKRABOOOM
BRIAN SMITH WRITER
MARIO DEL PENNINO ARTIST
CARLOS LOPEZ COLORS
VC'S JOE SABINO LETTERER
KATHERINE BROWN PROJECT MANAGER
DARREN SANCHEZ EDITOR
AXEL ALONSO EDITOR IN CHIEF
JOE QUESADA CHIEF CREATIVE OFFICER
DAN BUCKLEY PUBLISHER
ALAN FINE EXECUTIVE PRODUCER

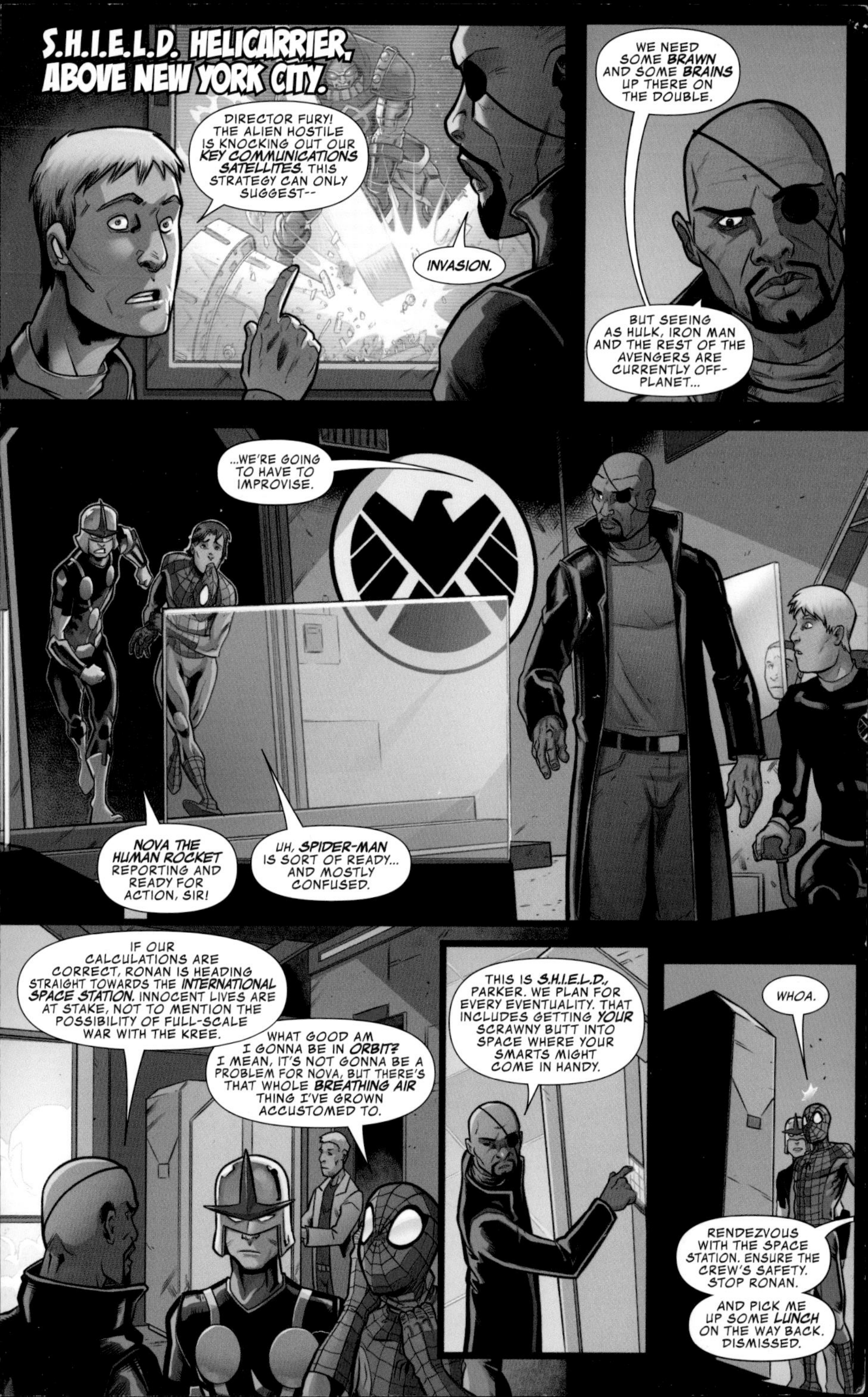
S.H.I.E.L.D. HELICARRIER, ABOVE NEW YORK CITY.
DIRECTOR FURY! THE ALIEN HOSTILE IS KNOCKING OUT OUR KEY COMMUNICATIONS SATELLITES. THIS STRATEGY CAN ONLY SUGGEST--
INVASION.
WE NEED SOME BRAWN AND SOME BRAINS UP THERE ON THE DOUBLE.
BUT SEEING AS HULK, IRON MAN AND THE REST OF THE AVENGERS ARE CURRENTLY OFF-PLANET...
...WE'RE GOING TO HAVE TO IMPROVISE.
NOVA THE HUMAN ROCKET REPORTING AND READY FOR ACTION, SIR!
UH, SPIDER-MAN IS SORT OF READY... AND MOSTLY CONFUSED.
IF OUR CALCULATIONS ARE CORRECT, RONAN IS HEADING STRAIGHT TOWARDS THE INTERNATIONAL SPACE STATION. INNOCENT LIVES ARE AT STAKE, NOT TO MENTION THE POSSIBILITY OF FULL-SCALE WAR WITH THE KREE.
WHAT GOOD AM I GONNA BE IN ORBIT? I MEAN, IT'S NOT GONNA BE A PROBLEM FOR NOVA, BUT THERE'S THAT WHOLE BREATHING AIR THING I'VE GROWN ACCUSTOMED TO.
THIS IS S.H.I.E.L.D., PARKER. WE PLAN FOR EVERY EVENTUALITY. THAT INCLUDES GETTING YOUR SCRAWNY BUTT INTO SPACE WHERE YOUR SMARTS MIGHT COME IN HANDY.
WHOA.
RENDEZVOUS WITH THE SPACE STATION. ENSURE THE CREW'S SAFETY. STOP RONAN.
AND PICK ME UP SOME LUNCH ON THE WAY BACK. DISMISSED.

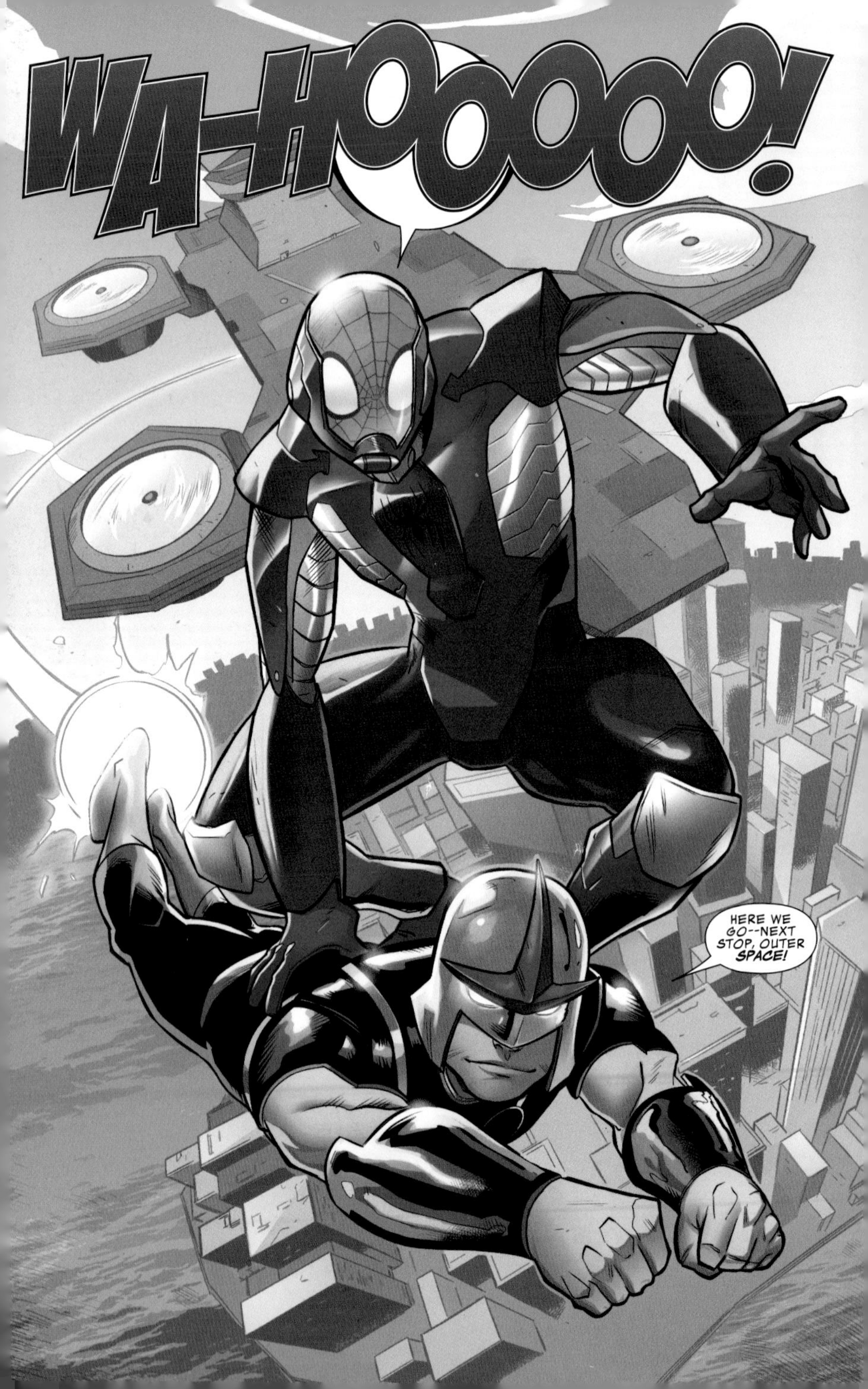
WA-HOOOOOO!
HERE WE GO--NEXT STOP, OUTER SPACE!

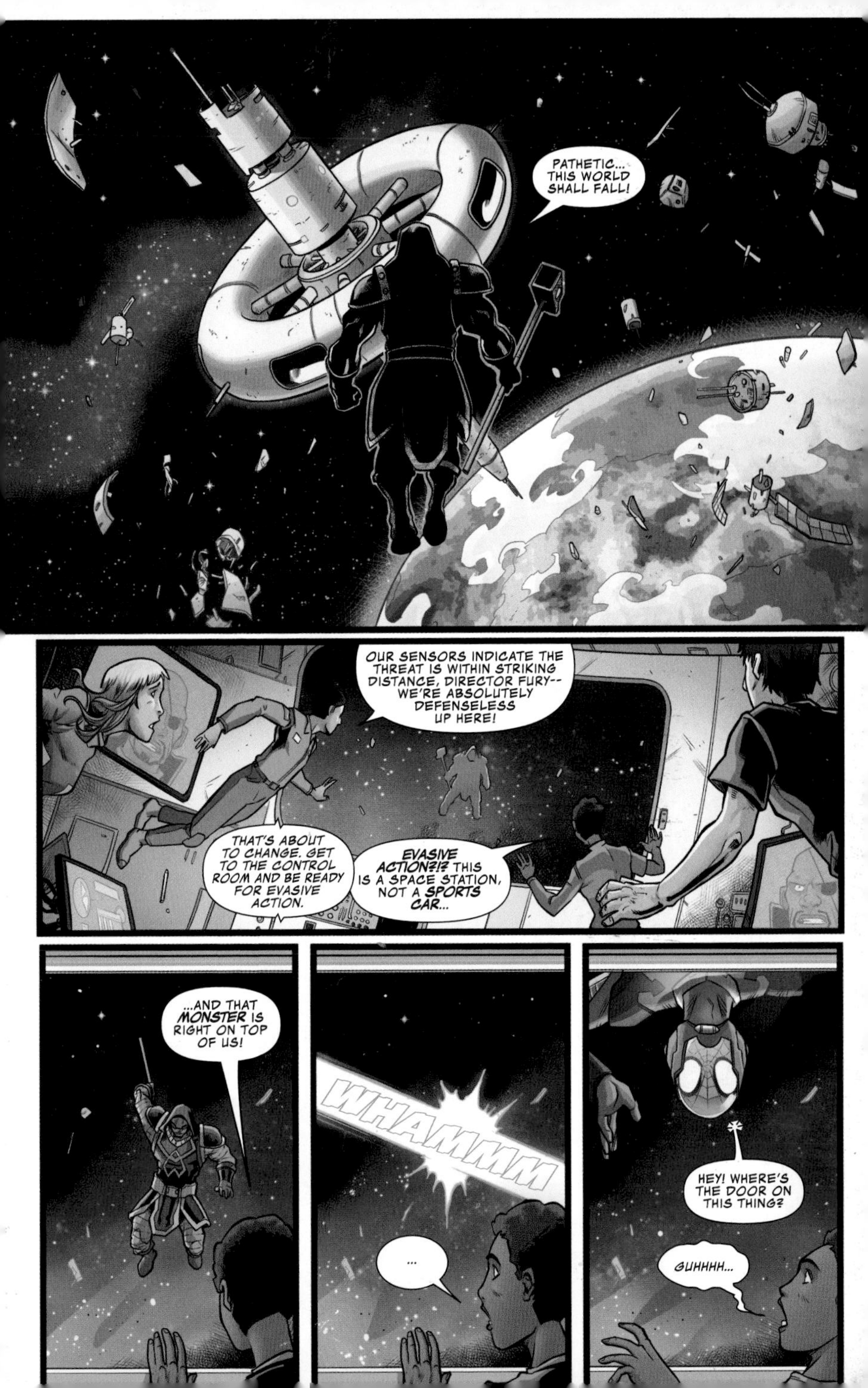
PATHETIC... THIS WORLD SHALL FALL!
OUR SENSORS INDICATE THE THREAT IS WITHIN STRIKING DISTANCE, DIRECTOR FURY-- WE'RE ABSOLUTELY DEFENSELESS UP HERE!
THAT'S ABOUT TO CHANGE. GET TO THE CONTROL ROOM AND BE READY FOR EVASIVE ACTION.
EVASIVE ACTION?!? THIS IS A SPACE STATION, NOT A SPORTS CAR...
...AND THAT MONSTER IS RIGHT ON TOP OF US!
WHAMMMM
...
HEY! WHERE'S THE DOOR ON THIS THING?
GUHHHH...

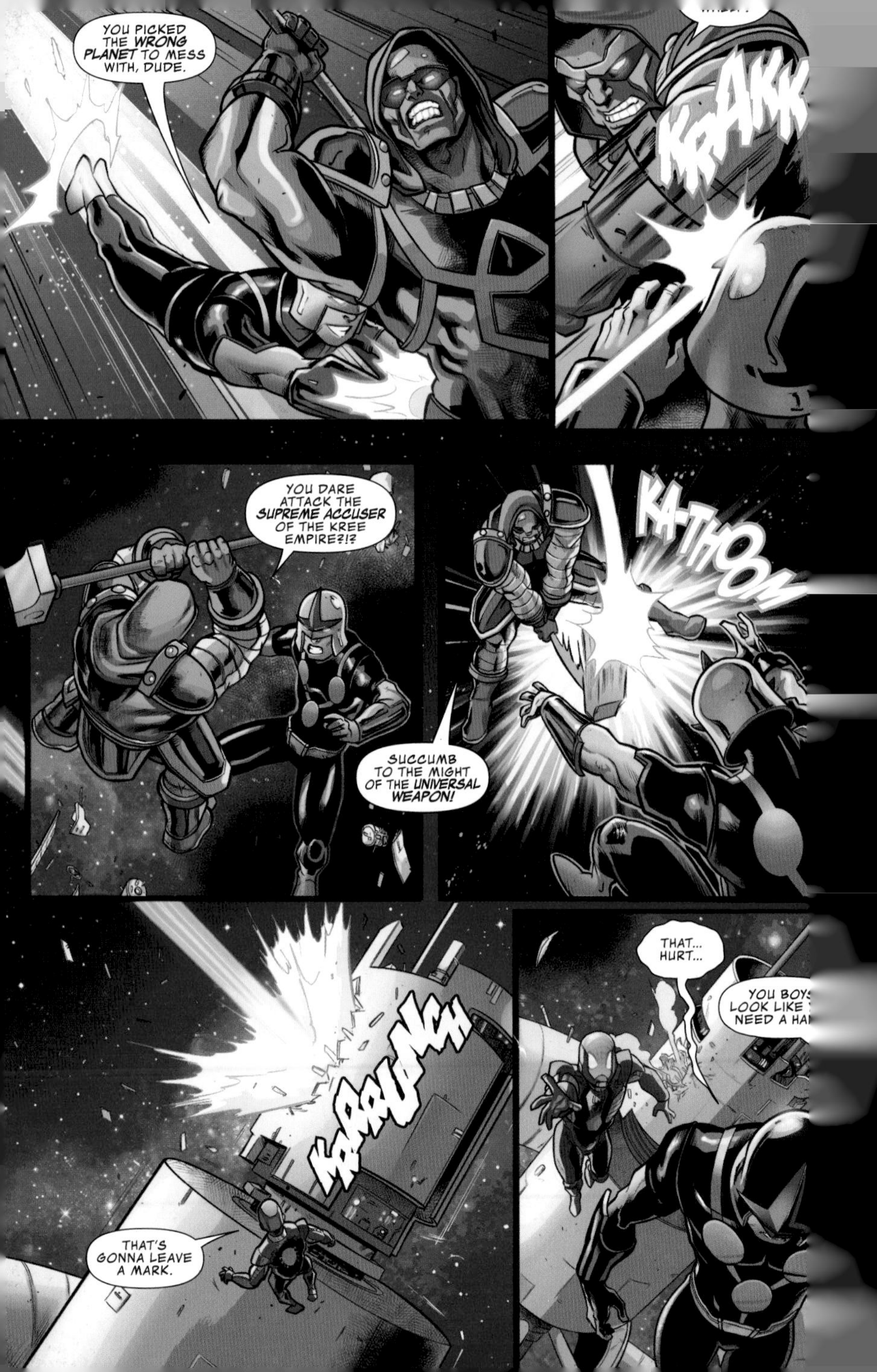
YOU PICKED THE WRONG PLANET TO MESS WITH, DUDE.
KRAKK
YOU DARE ATTACK THE SUPREME ACCUSER OF THE KREE EMPIRE?!?
SUCCUMB TO THE MIGHT OF THE UNIVERSAL WEAPON!
KA-THOOM
KARRUNCH
THAT'S GONNA LEAVE A MARK.
THAT... HURT...
YOU BOYS LOOK LIKE
NEED A HA

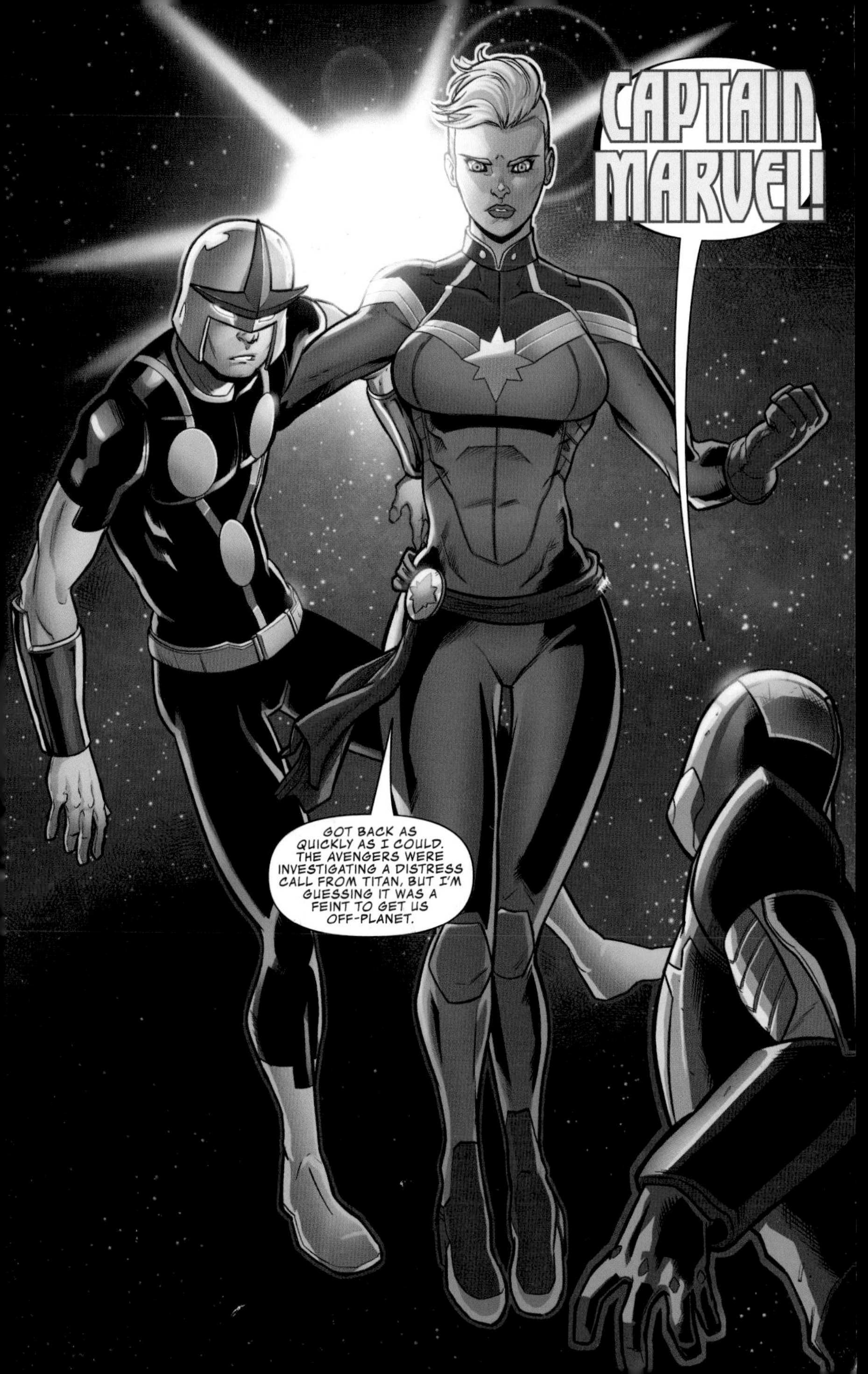
CAPTAIN MARVEL!
GOT BACK AS QUICKLY AS I COULD. THE AVENGERS WERE INVESTIGATING A DISTRESS CALL FROM TITAN, BUT I'M GUESSING IT WAS A FEINT TO GET US OFF-PLANET.

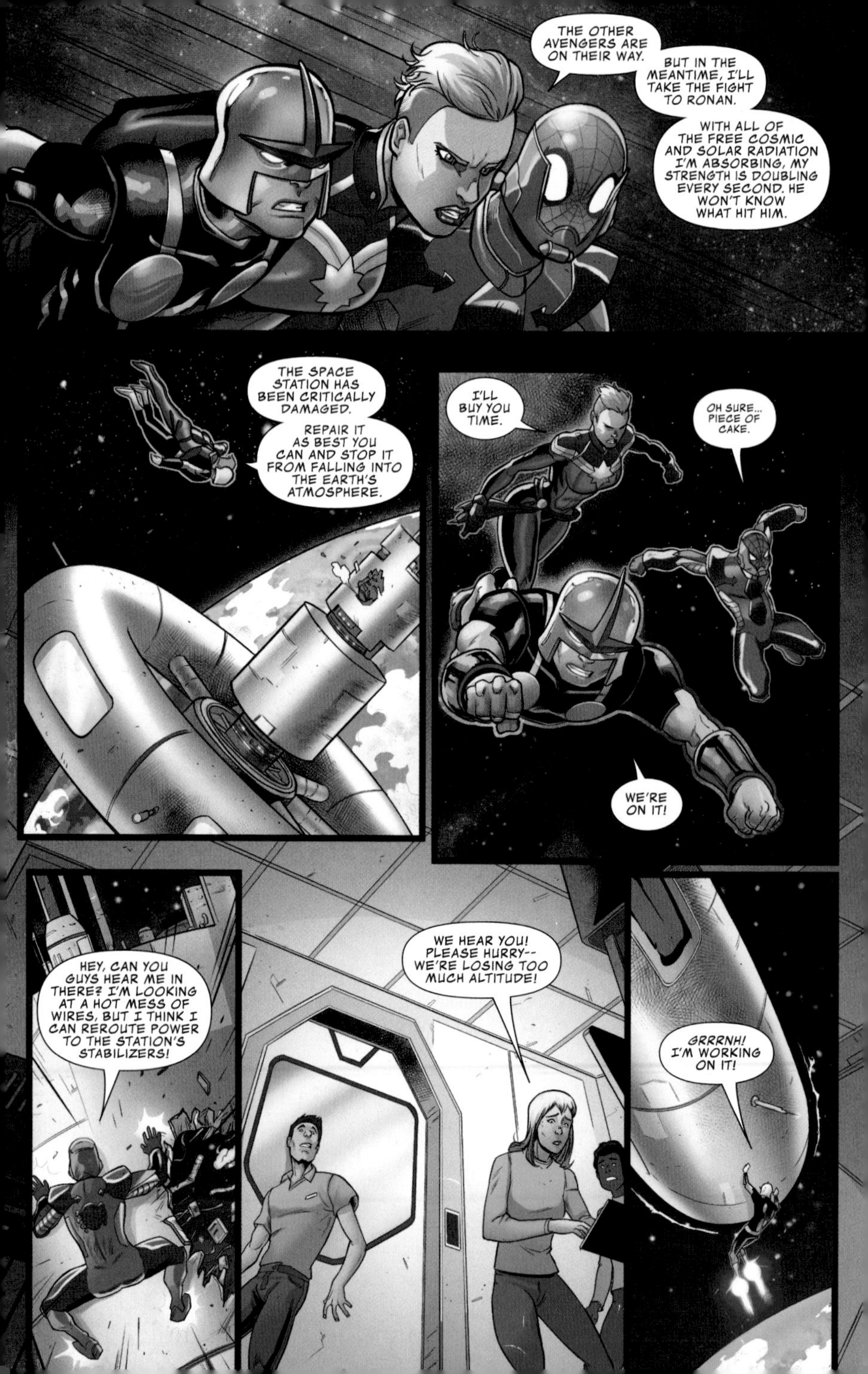
THE OTHER AVENGERS ARE ON THEIR WAY.
BUT IN THE MEANTIME, I'LL TAKE THE FIGHT TO RONAN.
WITH ALL OF THE FREE COSMIC AND SOLAR RADIATION I'M ABSORBING, MY STRENGTH IS DOUBLING EVERY SECOND. HE WON'T KNOW WHAT HIT HIM.
THE SPACE STATION HAS BEEN CRITICALLY DAMAGED.
REPAIR IT AS BEST YOU CAN AND STOP IT FROM FALLING INTO THE EARTH'S ATMOSPHERE.
I'LL BUY YOU TIME.
OH SURE... PIECE OF CAKE.
WE'RE ON IT!
HEY, CAN YOU GUYS HEAR ME IN THERE? I'M LOOKING AT A HOT MESS OF WIRES, BUT I THINK I CAN REROUTE POWER TO THE STATION'S STABILIZERS!
WE HEAR YOU! PLEASE HURRY-- WE'RE LOSING TOO MUCH ALTITUDE!
GRRRNH! I'M WORKING ON IT!

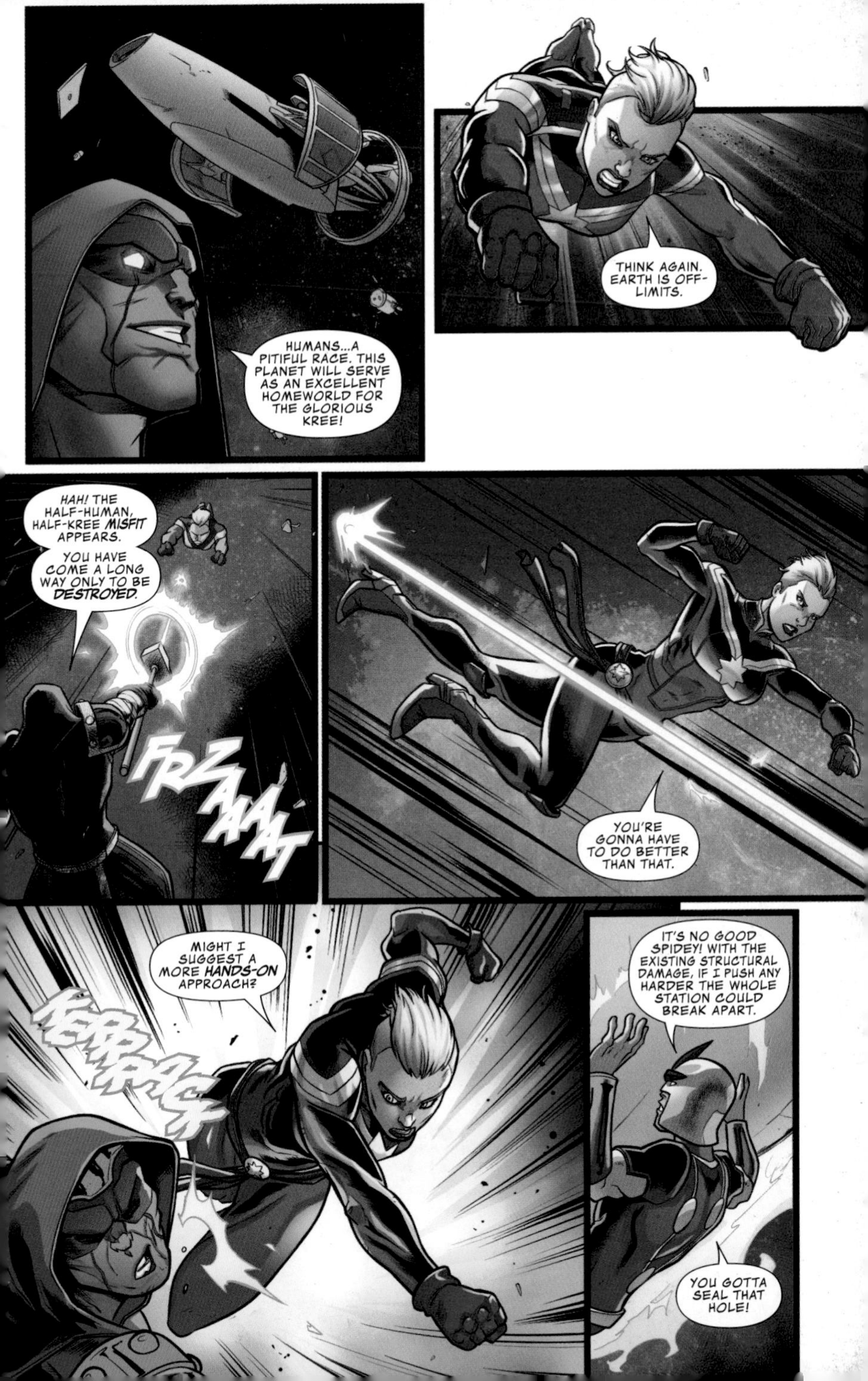
HUMANS...A PITIFUL RACE. THIS PLANET WILL SERVE AS AN EXCELLENT HOMEWORLD FOR THE GLORIOUS KREE!
THINK AGAIN. EARTH IS OFF-LIMITS.
HAH! THE HALF-HUMAN, HALF-KREE MISFIT APPEARS.
YOU HAVE COME A LONG WAY ONLY TO BE DESTROYED.
FRZAAAAT
YOU'RE GONNA HAVE TO DO BETTER THAN THAT.
MIGHT I SUGGEST A MORE HANDS-ON APPROACH?
KERRACK
IT'S NO GOOD SPIDEY! WITH THE EXISTING STRUCTURAL DAMAGE, IF I PUSH ANY HARDER THE WHOLE STATION COULD BREAK APART.
YOU GOTTA SEAL THAT HOLE!

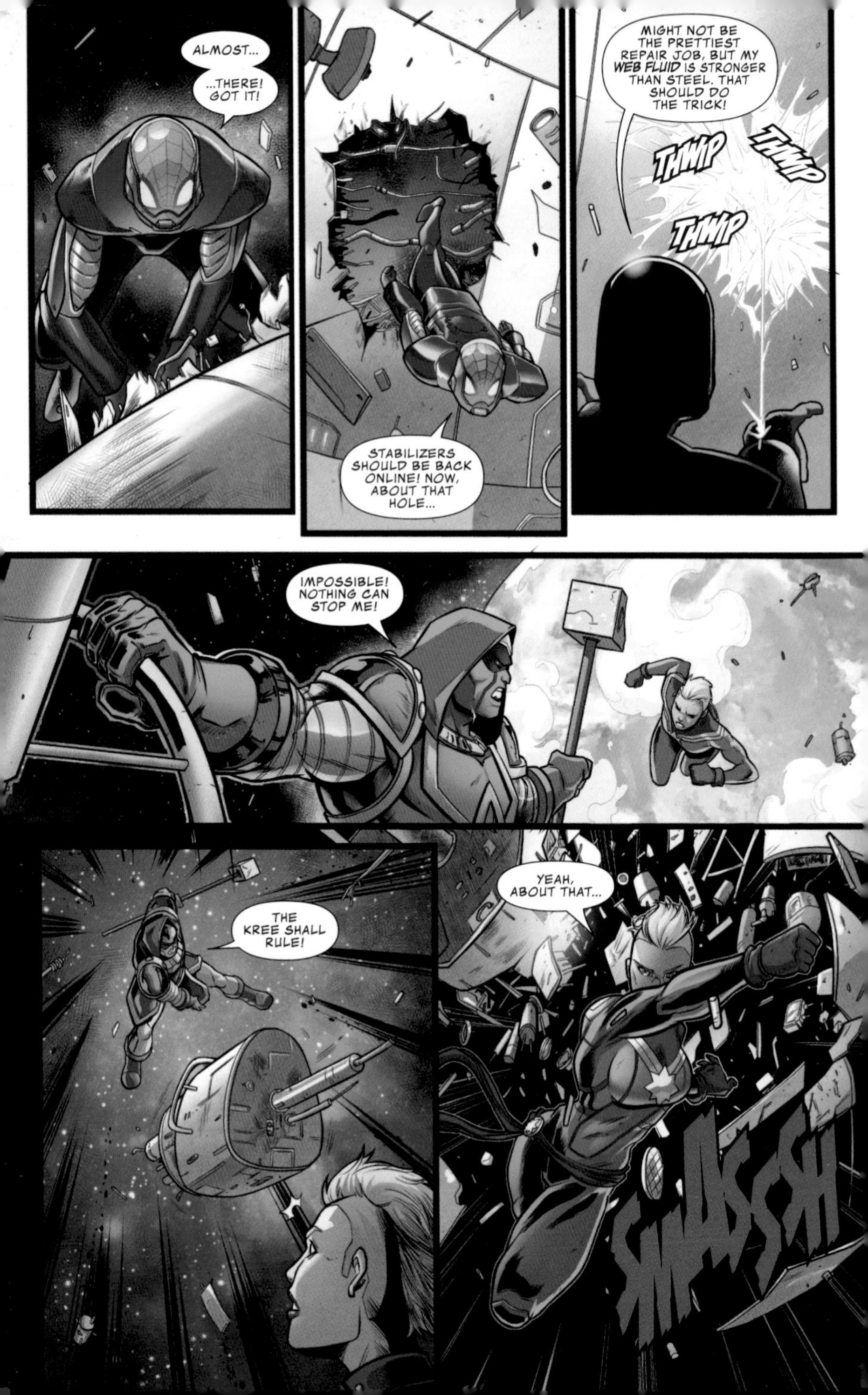
ALMOST...
...THERE! GOT IT!
STABILIZERS SHOULD BE BACK ONLINE! NOW, ABOUT THAT HOLE...
MIGHT NOT BE THE PRETTIEST REPAIR JOB, BUT MY WEB FLUID IS STRONGER THAN STEEL. THAT SHOULD DO THE TRICK!
THWIP
THWIP
THWIP
IMPOSSIBLE! NOTHING CAN STOP ME!
THE KREE SHALL RULE!
YEAH, ABOUT THAT...
SMASSSH

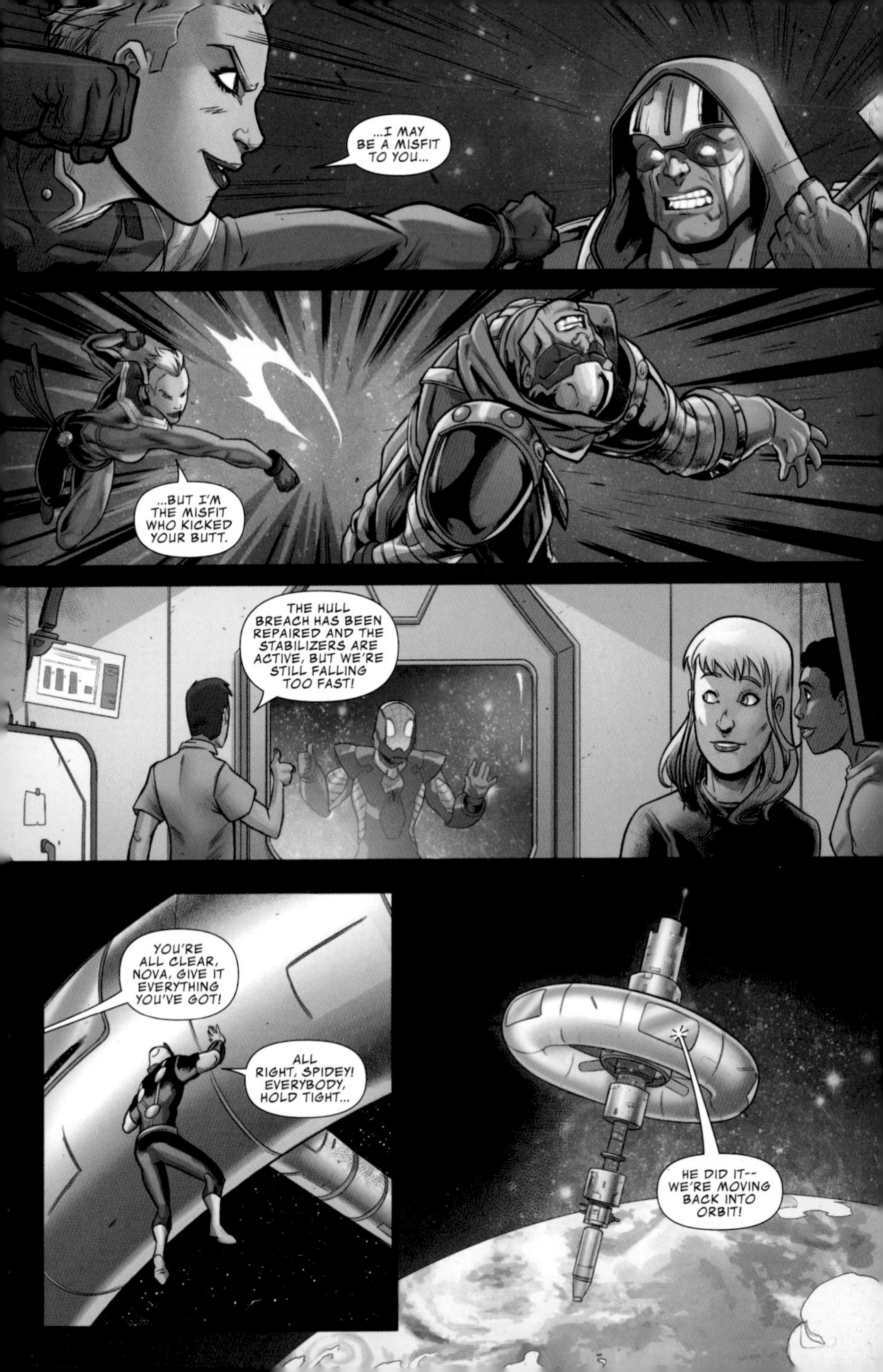
...I MAY BE A MISFIT TO YOU...
...BUT I'M THE MISFIT WHO KICKED YOUR BUTT.
THE HULL BREACH HAS BEEN REPAIRED AND THE STABILIZERS ARE ACTIVE, BUT WE'RE STILL FALLING TOO FAST!
YOU'RE ALL CLEAR, NOVA, GIVE IT EVERYTHING YOU'VE GOT!
ALL RIGHT, SPIDEY! EVERYBODY, HOLD TIGHT...
HE DID IT-- WE'RE MOVING BACK INTO ORBIT!

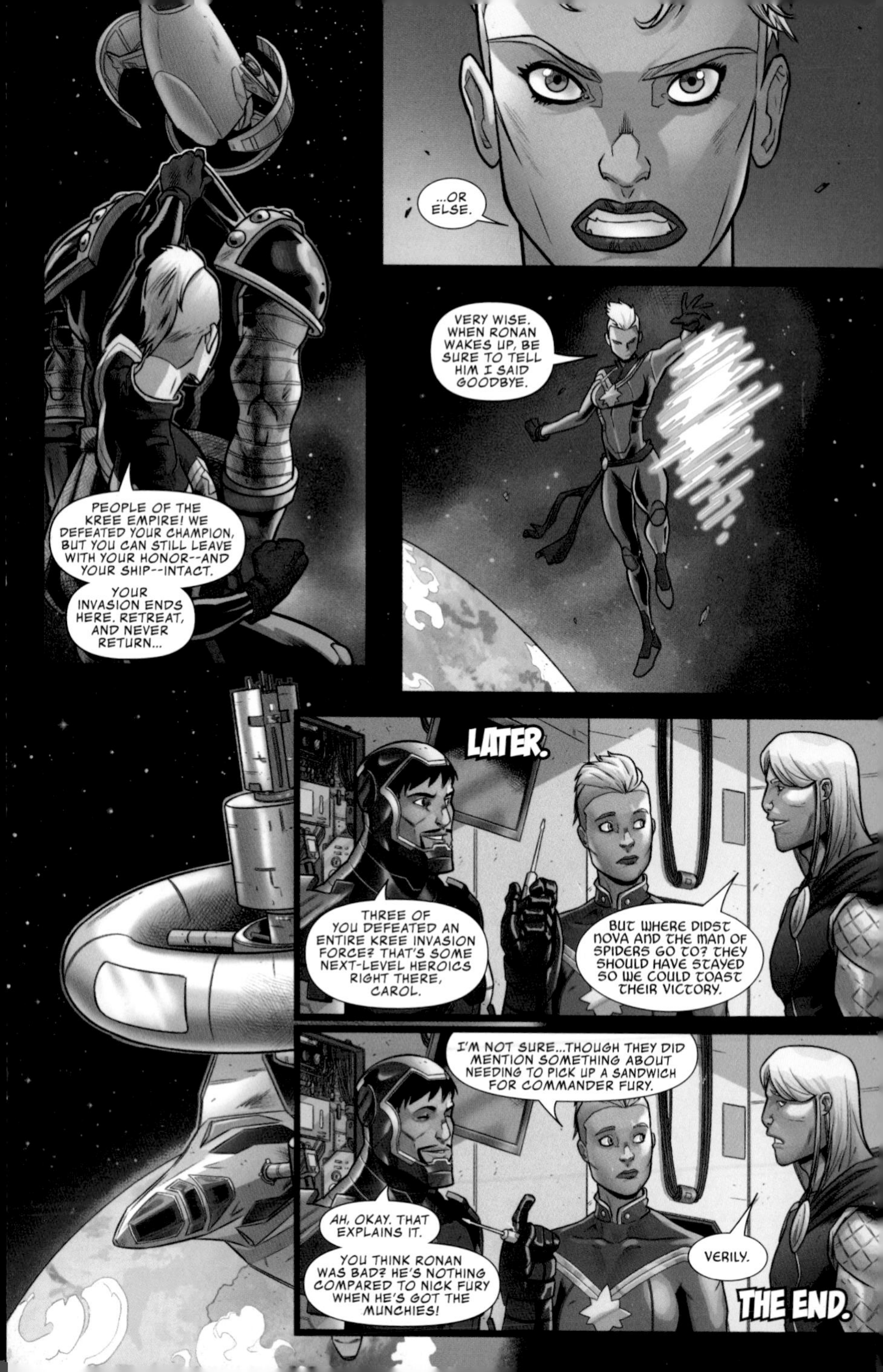

...OR ELSE.
PEOPLE OF THE KREE EMPIRE! WE DEFEATED YOUR CHAMPION, BUT YOU CAN STILL LEAVE WITH YOUR HONOR--AND YOUR SHIP--INTACT.
YOUR INVASION ENDS HERE. RETREAT, AND NEVER RETURN...
VERY WISE. WHEN RONAN WAKES UP, BE SURE TO TELL HIM I SAID GOODBYE.
LATER.
THREE OF YOU DEFEATED AN ENTIRE KREE INVASION FORCE? THAT'S SOME NEXT-LEVEL HEROICS RIGHT THERE, CAROL.
BUT WHERE DIDST NOVA AND THE MAN OF SPIDERS GO TO? THEY SHOULD HAVE STAYED SO WE COULD TOAST THEIR VICTORY.
I'M NOT SURE...THOUGH THEY DID MENTION SOMETHING ABOUT NEEDING TO PICK UP A SANDWICH FOR COMMANDER FURY.
AH, OKAY. THAT EXPLAINS IT.
YOU THINK RONAN WAS BAD? HE'S NOTHING COMPARED TO NICK FURY WHEN HE'S GOT THE MUNCHIES!
VERILY.
THE END.

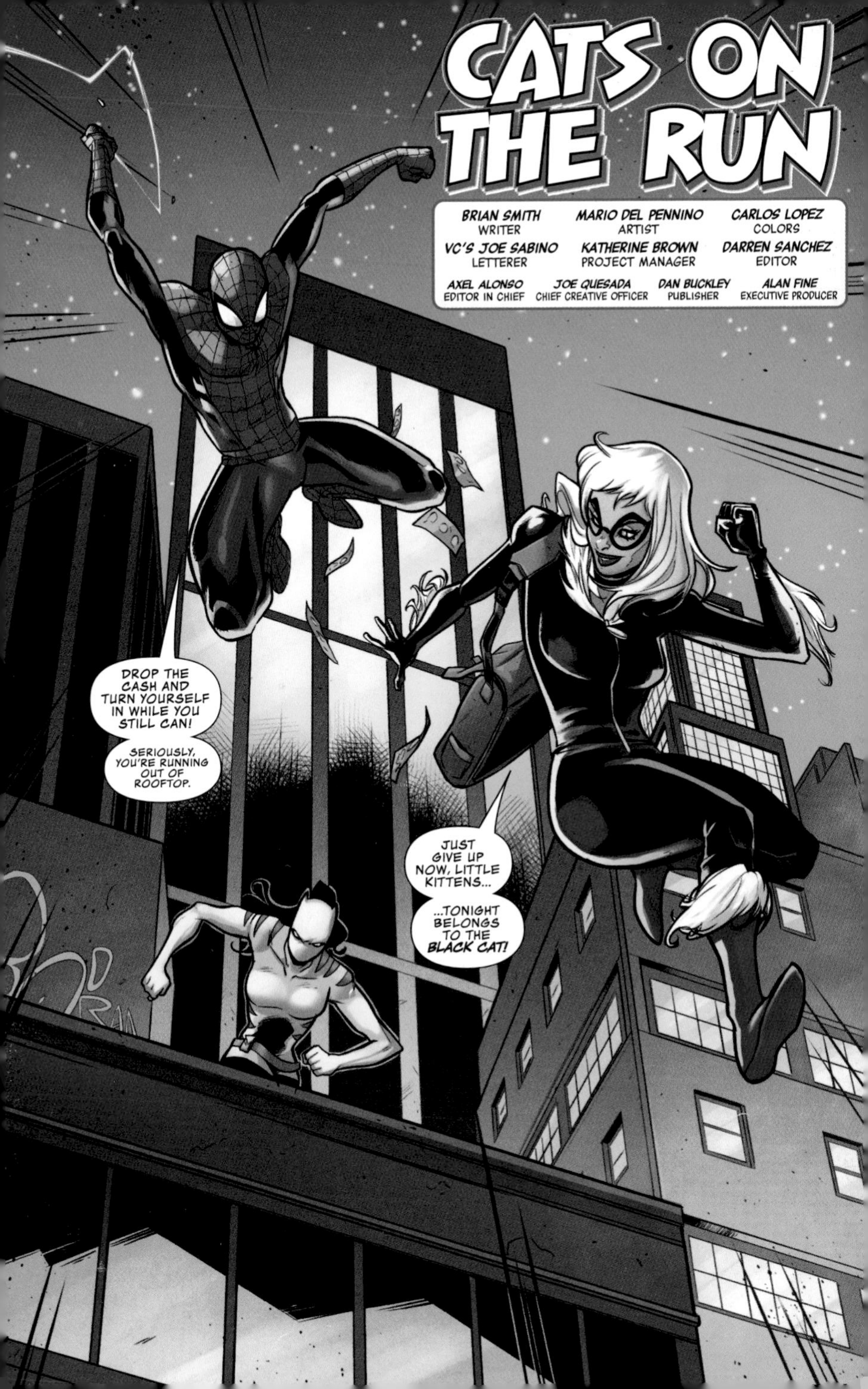
CATS ON THE RUN
BRIAN SMITH WRITER
MARIO DEL PENNINO ARTIST
CARLOS LOPEZ COLORS
VC'S JOE SABINO LETTERER
KATHERINE BROWN PROJECT MANAGER
DARREN SANCHEZ EDITOR
AXEL ALONSO EDITOR IN CHIEF
JOE QUESADA CHIEF CREATIVE OFFICER
DAN BUCKLEY PUBLISHER
ALAN FINE EXECUTIVE PRODUCER
DROP THE CASH AND TURN YOURSELF IN WHILE YOU STILL CAN!
SERIOUSLY, YOU'RE RUNNING OUT OF ROOFTOP.
JUST GIVE UP NOW, LITTLE KITTENS...
...TONIGHT BELONGS TO THE BLACK CAT!

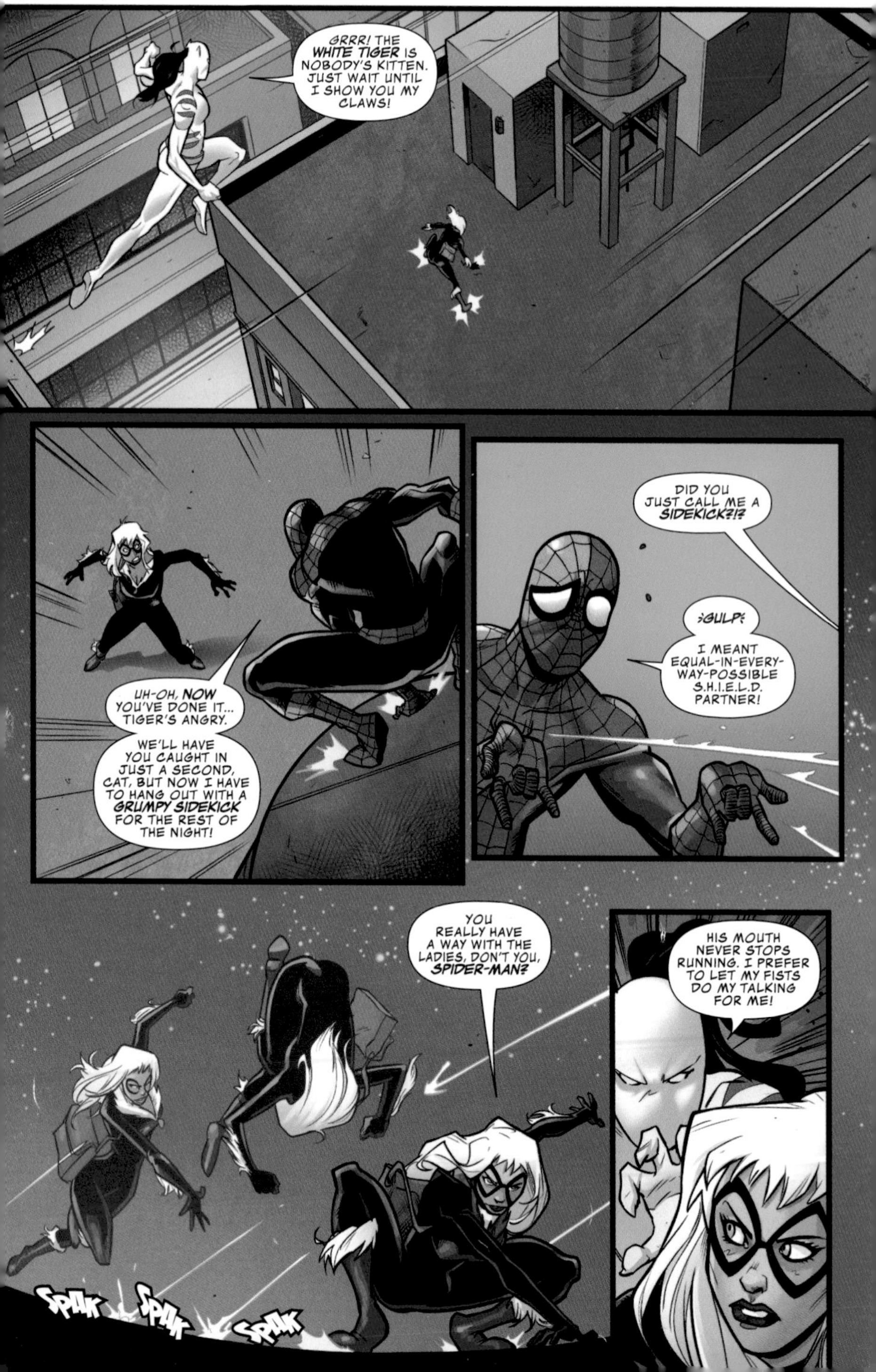
GRRR! THE WHITE TIGER IS NOBODY'S KITTEN. JUST WAIT UNTIL I SHOW YOU MY CLAWS!
UH-OH, NOW YOU'VE DONE IT... TIGER'S ANGRY.
WE'LL HAVE YOU CAUGHT IN JUST A SECOND, CAT, BUT NOW I HAVE TO HANG OUT WITH A GRUMPY SIDEKICK FOR THE REST OF THE NIGHT!
DID YOU JUST CALL ME A SIDEKICK?!?
GULP
I MEANT EQUAL-IN-EVERY-WAY-POSSIBLE S.H.I.E.L.D. PARTNER!
YOU REALLY HAVE A WAY WITH THE LADIES, DON'T YOU, SPIDER-MAN?
SPAK SPAK SPAK
HIS MOUTH NEVER STOPS RUNNING. I PREFER TO LET MY FISTS DO MY TALKING FOR ME!

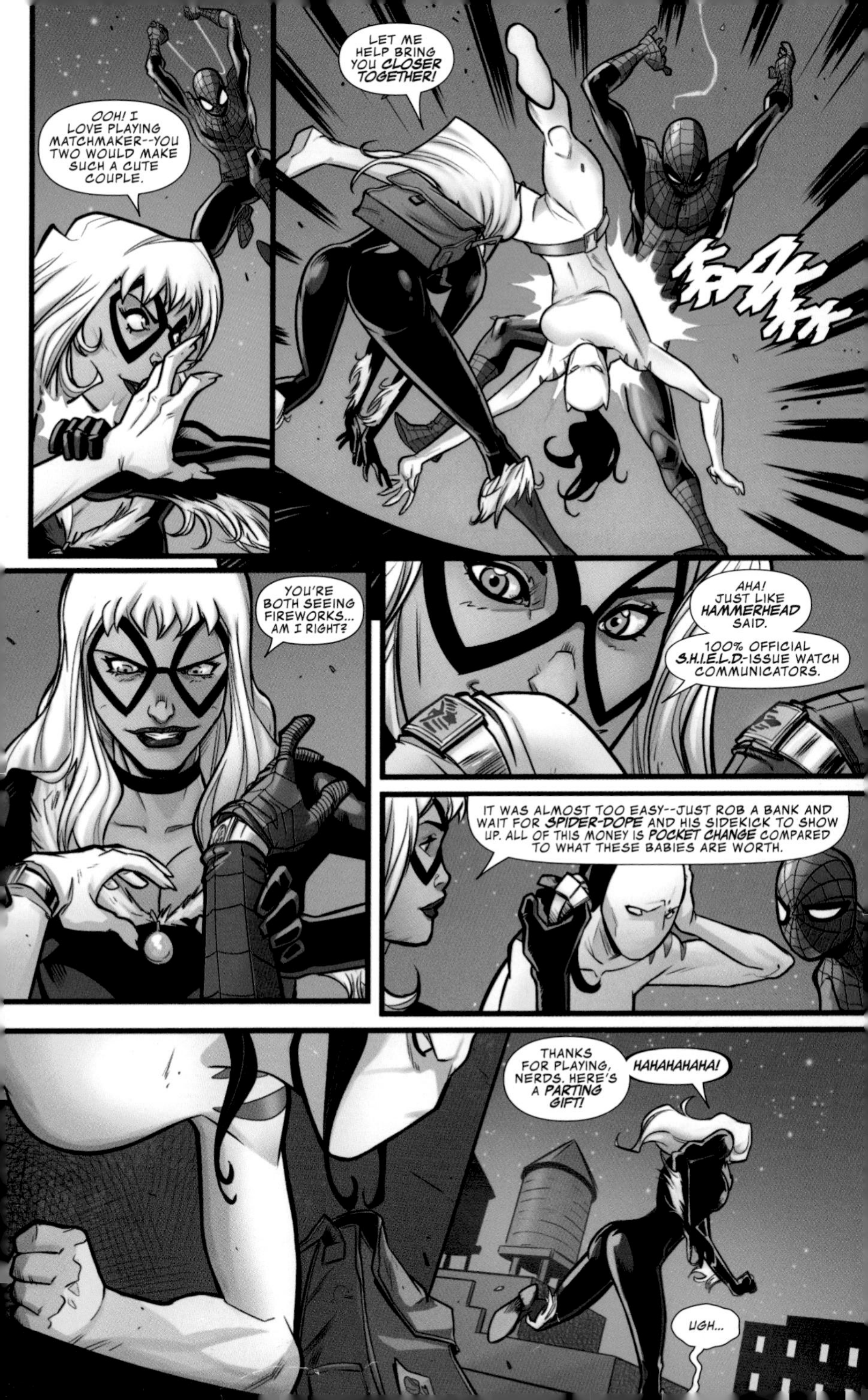
OOH! I LOVE PLAYING MATCHMAKER--YOU TWO WOULD MAKE SUCH A CUTE COUPLE.
LET ME HELP BRING YOU CLOSER TOGETHER!
KRAKK
YOU'RE BOTH SEEING FIREWORKS... AM I RIGHT?
AHA! JUST LIKE HAMMERHEAD SAID.
100% OFFICIAL S.H.I.E.L.D.-ISSUE WATCH COMMUNICATORS.
IT WAS ALMOST TOO EASY--JUST ROB A BANK AND WAIT FOR SPIDER-DOPE AND HIS SIDEKICK TO SHOW UP. ALL OF THIS MONEY IS POCKET CHANGE COMPARED TO WHAT THESE BABIES ARE WORTH.
THANKS FOR PLAYING, NERDS. HERE'S A PARTING GIFT!
HAHAHAHAHA!
UGH...

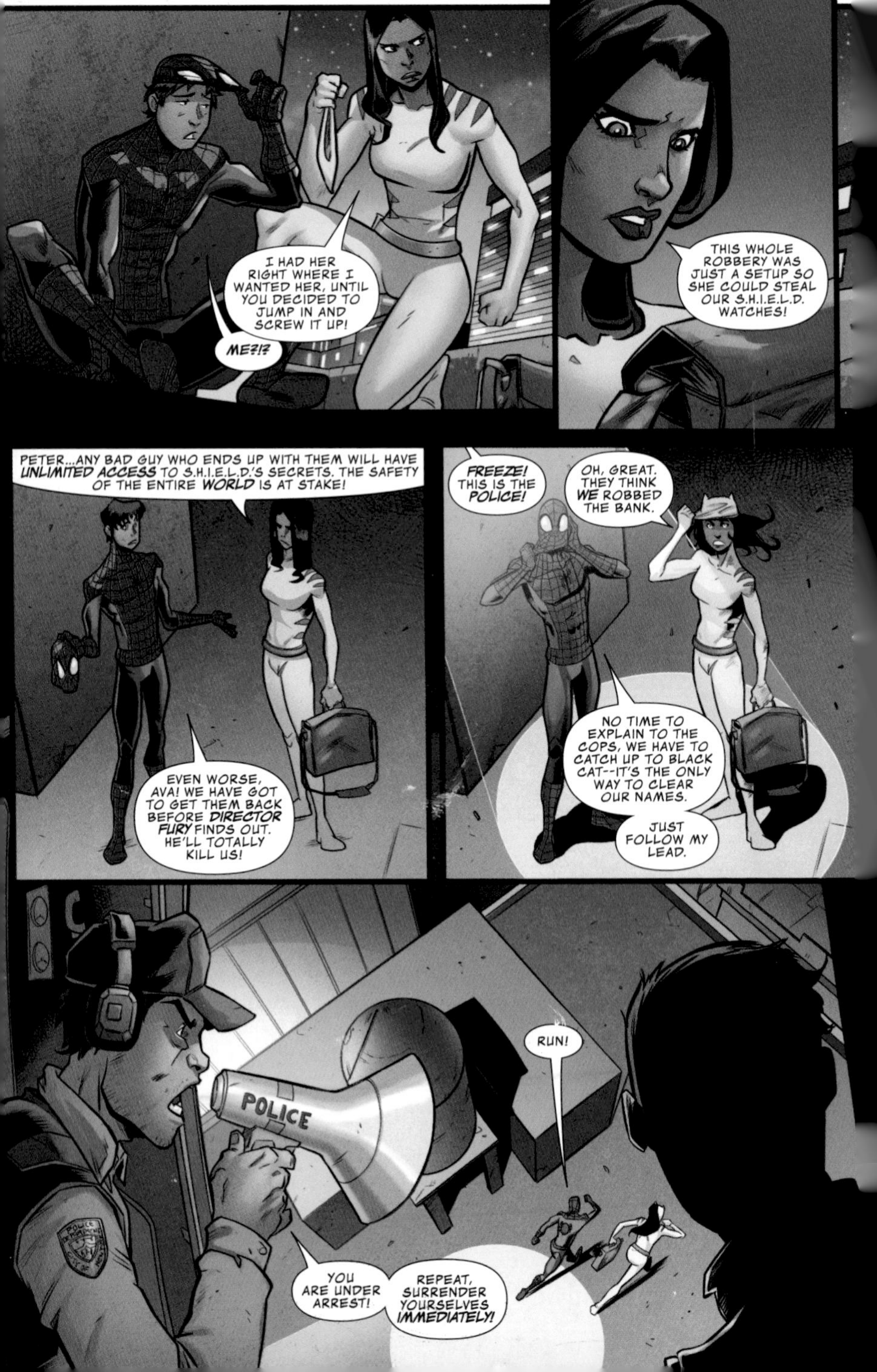

I HAD HER RIGHT WHERE I WANTED HER, UNTIL YOU DECIDED TO JUMP IN AND SCREW IT UP!
ME?!?
THIS WHOLE ROBBERY WAS JUST A SETUP SO SHE COULD STEAL OUR S.H.I.E.L.D. WATCHES!
PETER...ANY BAD GUY WHO ENDS UP WITH THEM WILL HAVE UNLIMITED ACCESS TO S.H.I.E.L.D.'S SECRETS. THE SAFETY OF THE ENTIRE WORLD IS AT STAKE!
EVEN WORSE, AVA! WE HAVE GOT TO GET THEM BACK BEFORE DIRECTOR FURY FINDS OUT. HE'LL TOTALLY KILL US!
FREEZE! THIS IS THE POLICE!
OH, GREAT. THEY THINK WE ROBBED THE BANK.
NO TIME TO EXPLAIN TO THE COPS, WE HAVE TO CATCH UP TO BLACK CAT--IT'S THE ONLY WAY TO CLEAR OUR NAMES.
JUST FOLLOW MY LEAD.
POLICE
RUN!
YOU ARE UNDER ARREST!
REPEAT, SURRENDER YOURSELVES IMMEDIATELY!

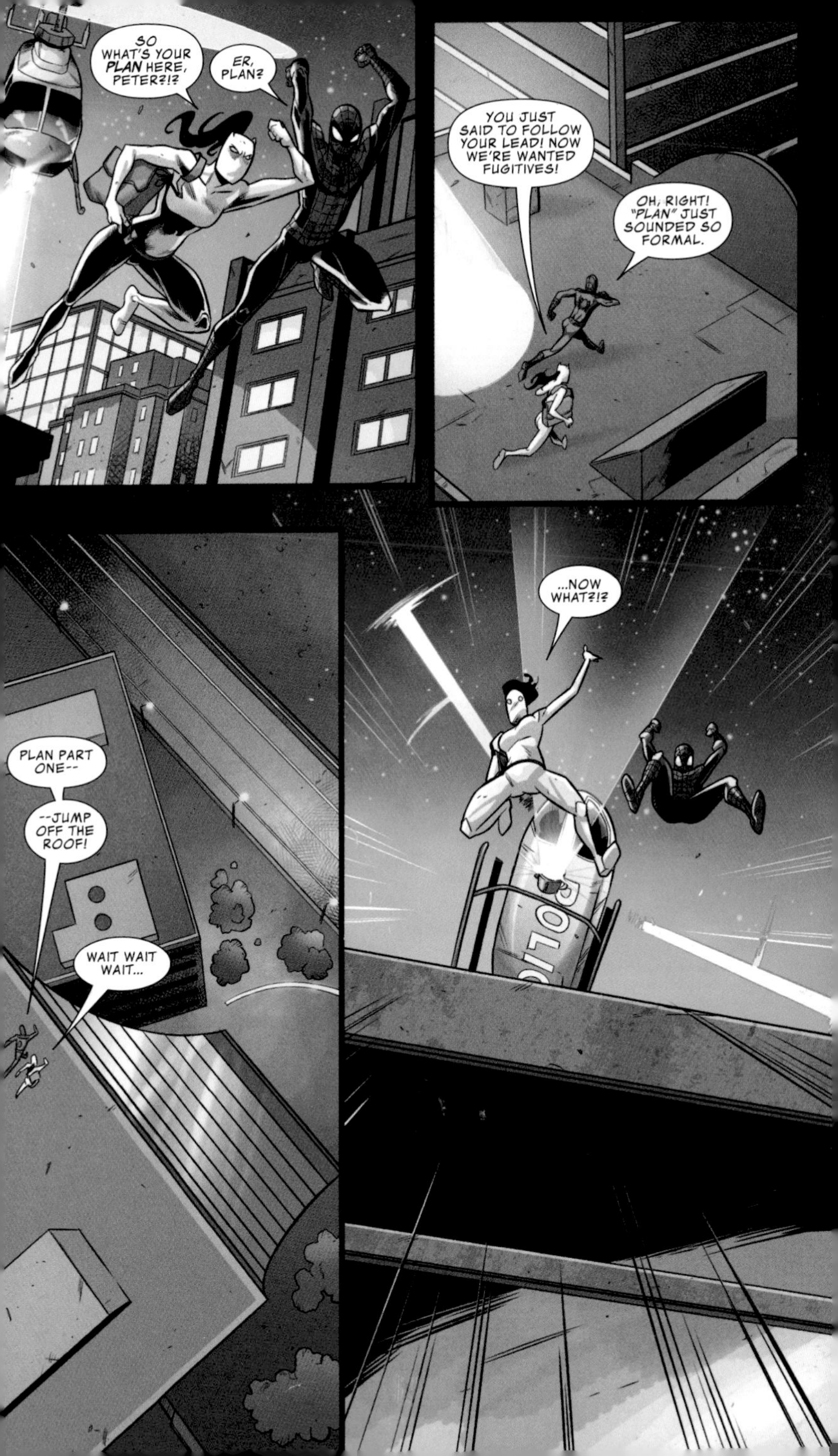
SO WHAT'S YOUR PLAN HERE, PETER?!?
ER, PLAN?
YOU JUST SAID TO FOLLOW YOUR LEAD! NOW WE'RE WANTED FUGITIVES!
OH, RIGHT! "PLAN" JUST SOUNDED SO FORMAL.
PLAN PART ONE--
--JUMP OFF THE ROOF!
WAIT WAIT WAIT...
...NOW WHAT?!?
POLIC

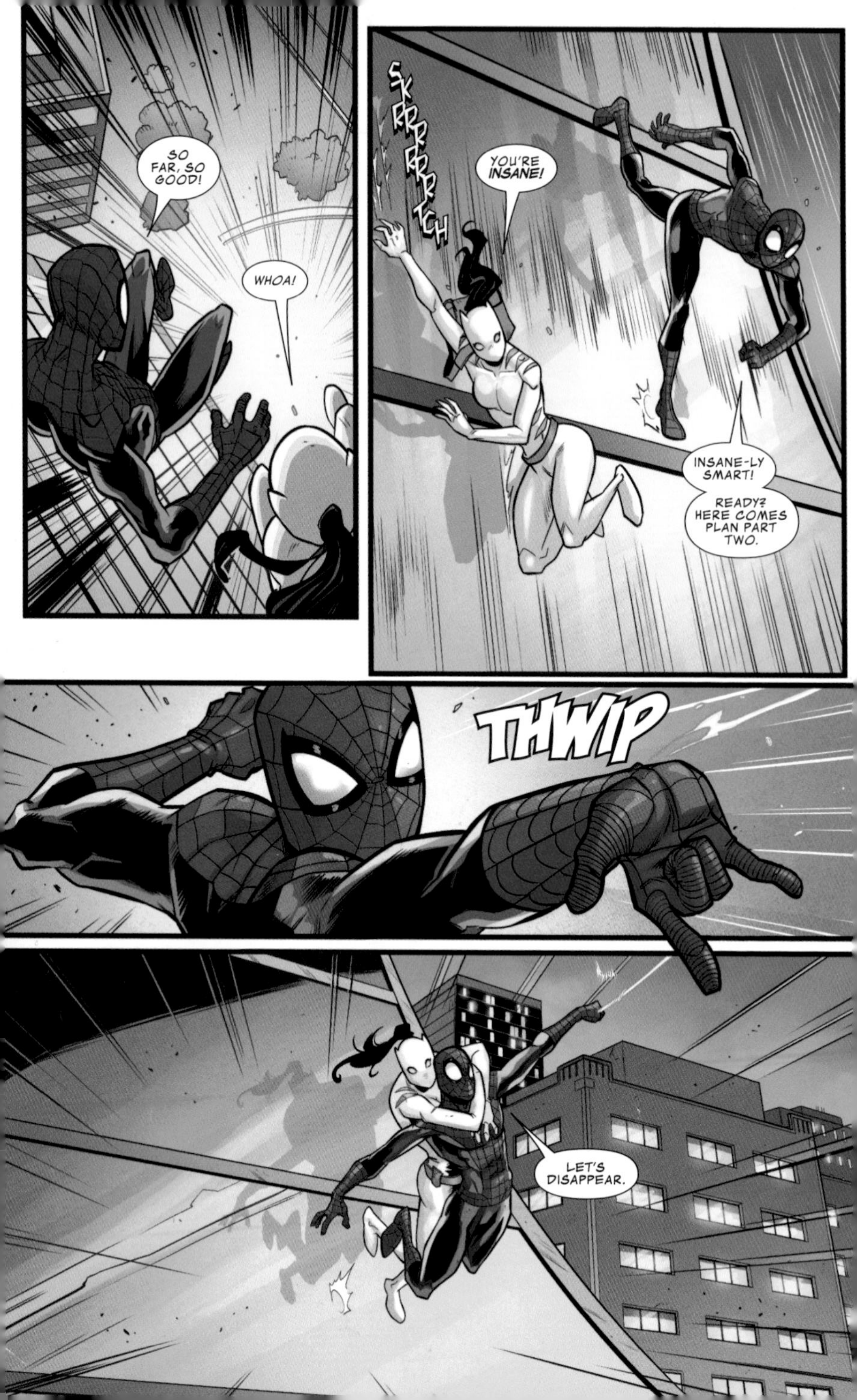

SO FAR, SO GOOD!
WHOA!
SKRRRRRRTCH
YOU'RE INSANE!
INSANE-LY SMART!
READY? HERE COMES PLAN PART TWO.
THWIP
LET'S DISAPPEAR.

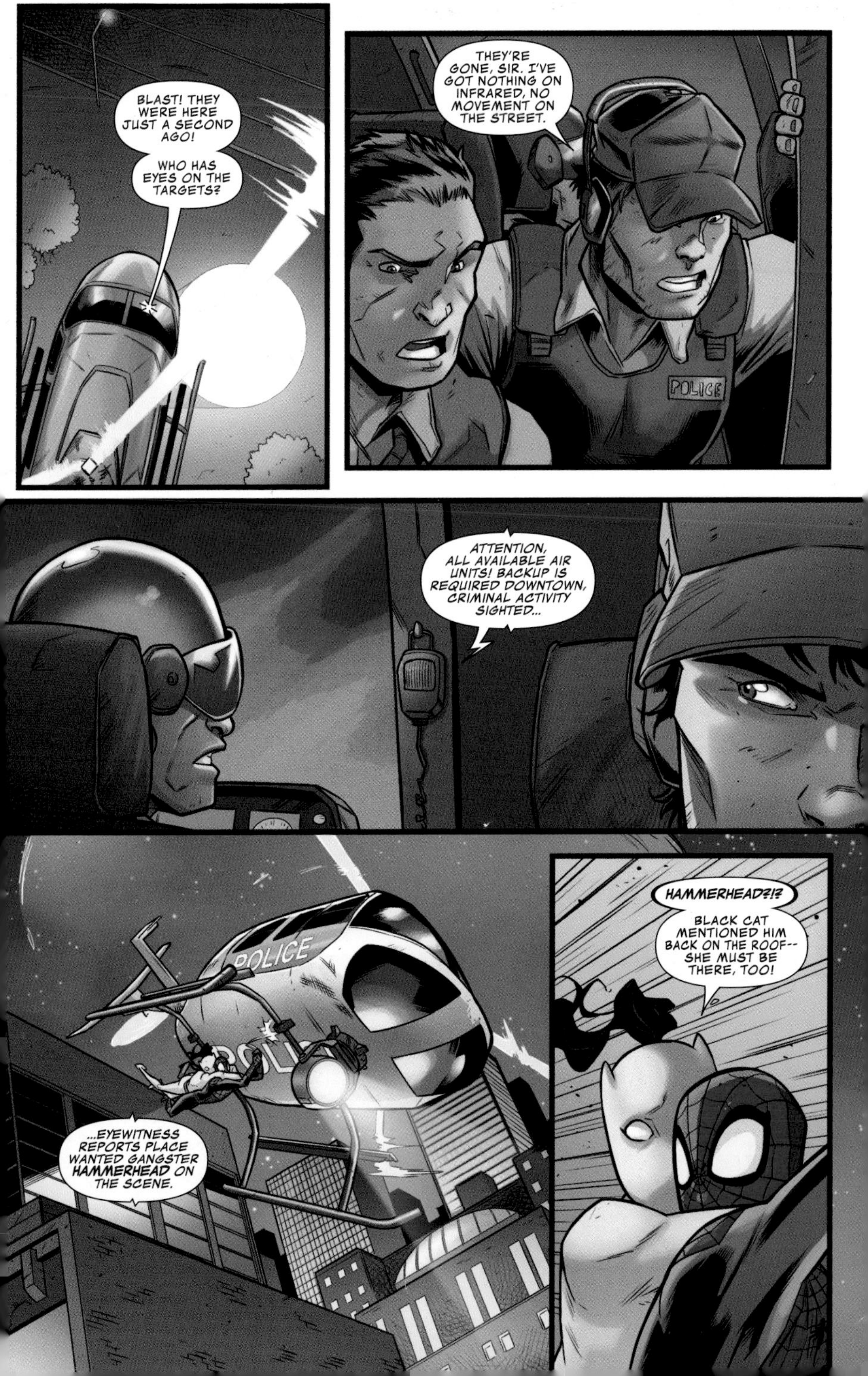
BLAST! THEY WERE HERE JUST A SECOND AGO!
WHO HAS EYES ON THE TARGETS?
THEY'RE GONE, SIR. I'VE GOT NOTHING ON INFRARED, NO MOVEMENT ON THE STREET.
POLICE
ATTENTION, ALL AVAILABLE AIR UNITS! BACKUP IS REQUIRED DOWNTOWN, CRIMINAL ACTIVITY SIGHTED...
POLICE
...EYEWITNESS REPORTS PLACE WANTED GANGSTER HAMMERHEAD ON THE SCENE.
HAMMERHEAD?!?
BLACK CAT MENTIONED HIM BACK ON THE ROOF-- SHE MUST BE THERE, TOO!

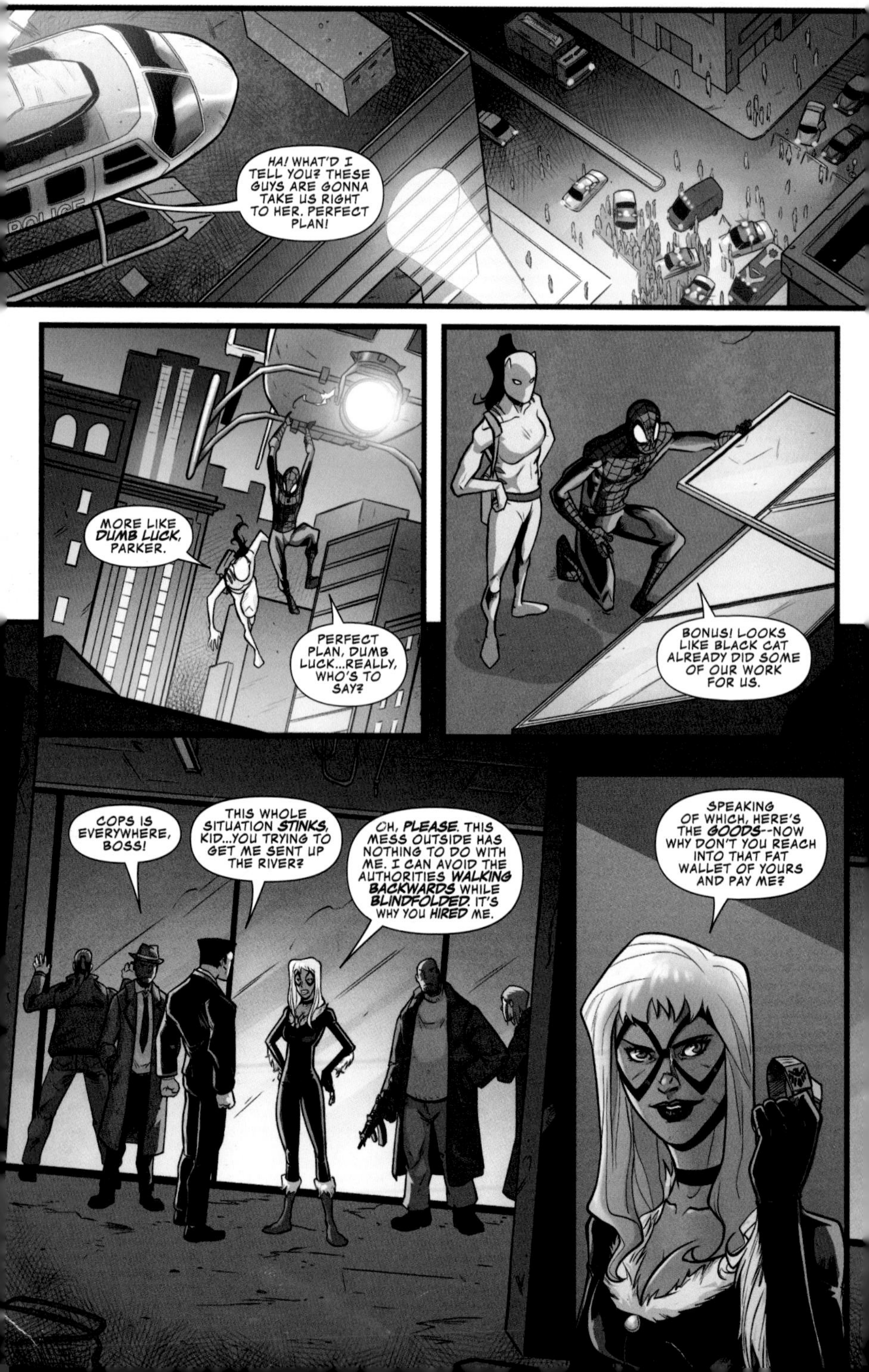
HA! WHAT'D I TELL YOU? THESE GUYS ARE GONNA TAKE US RIGHT TO HER. PERFECT PLAN!
POLICE
MORE LIKE DUMB LUCK, PARKER.
PERFECT PLAN, DUMB LUCK...REALLY, WHO'S TO SAY?
BONUS! LOOKS LIKE BLACK CAT ALREADY DID SOME OF OUR WORK FOR US.
COPS IS EVERYWHERE, BOSS!
THIS WHOLE SITUATION STINKS, KID...YOU TRYING TO GET ME SENT UP THE RIVER?
OH, PLEASE. THIS MESS OUTSIDE HAS NOTHING TO DO WITH ME. I CAN AVOID THE AUTHORITIES WALKING BACKWARDS WHILE BLINDFOLDED. IT'S WHY YOU HIRED ME.
SPEAKING OF WHICH, HERE'S THE GOODS--NOW WHY DON'T YOU REACH INTO THAT FAT WALLET OF YOURS AND PAY ME?

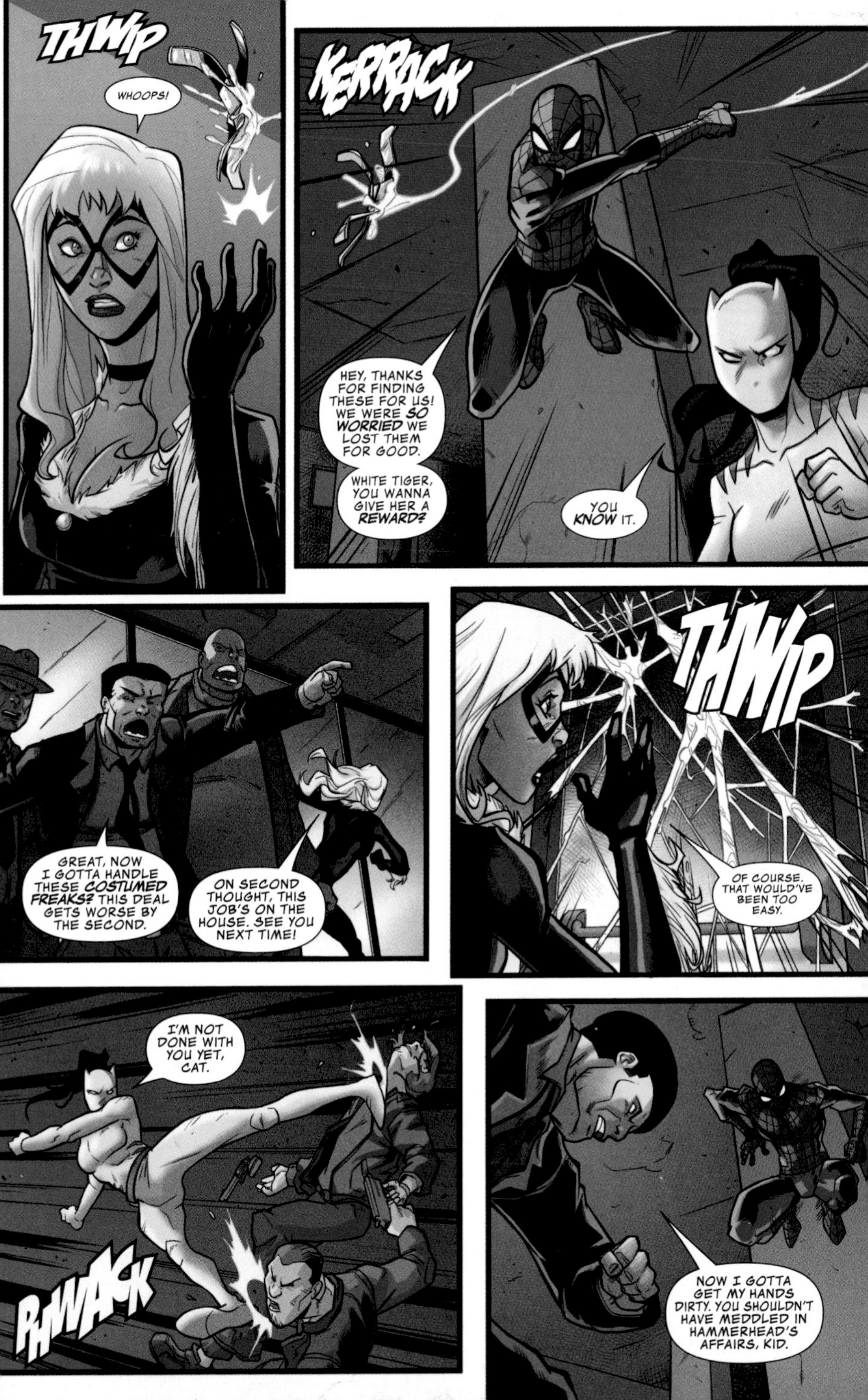
THWIP
WHOOPS!
KERRACK
HEY, THANKS FOR FINDING THESE FOR US! WE WERE SO WORRIED WE LOST THEM FOR GOOD.
WHITE TIGER, YOU WANNA GIVE HER A REWARD?
YOU KNOW IT.
GREAT, NOW I GOTTA HANDLE THESE COSTUMED FREAKS? THIS DEAL GETS WORSE BY THE SECOND.
ON SECOND THOUGHT, THIS JOB'S ON THE HOUSE. SEE YOU NEXT TIME!
THWIP
OF COURSE. THAT WOULD'VE BEEN TOO EASY.
I'M NOT DONE WITH YOU YET, CAT.
RHWACK
NOW I GOTTA GET MY HANDS DIRTY. YOU SHOULDN'T HAVE MEDDLED IN HAMMERHEAD'S AFFAIRS, KID.

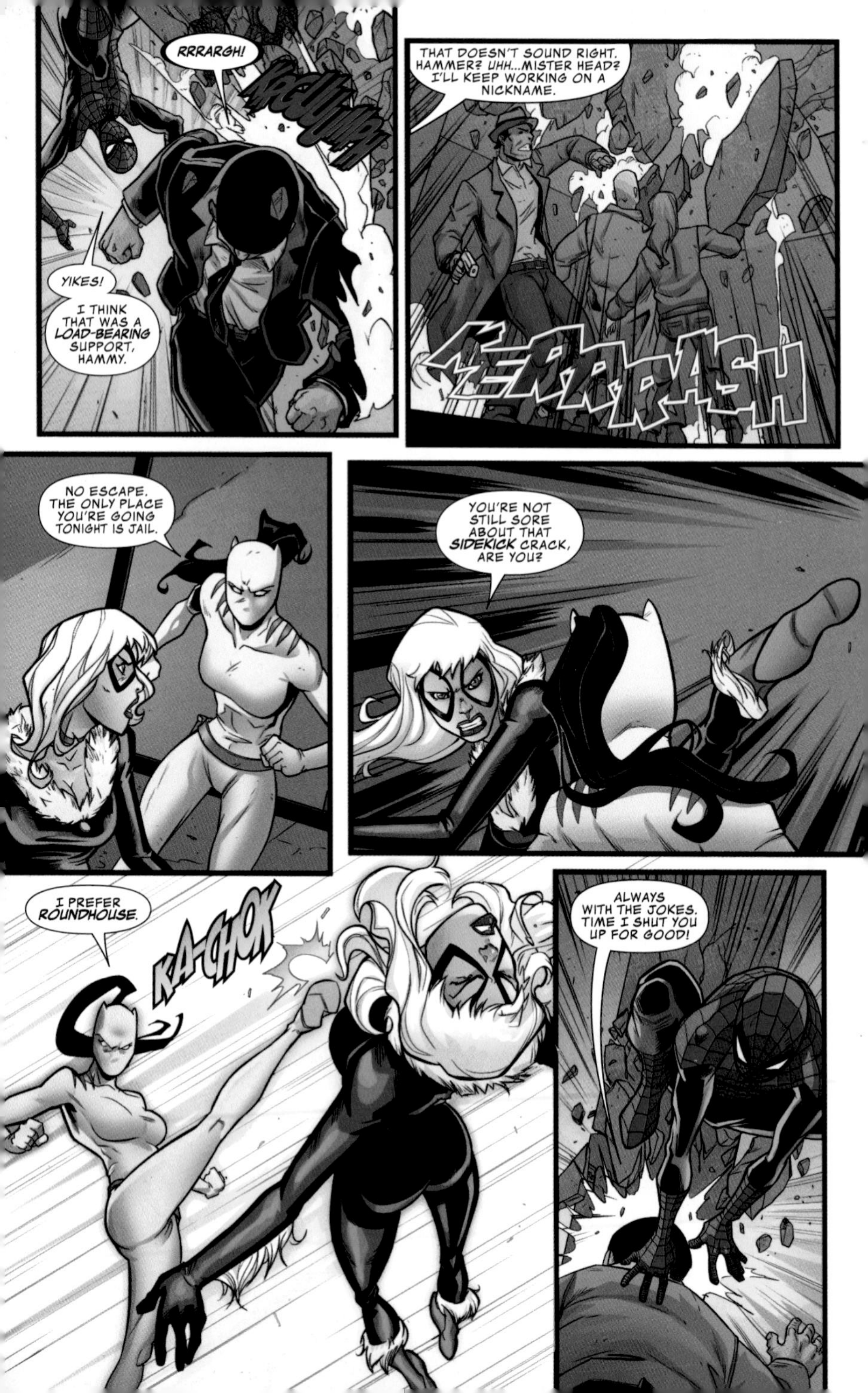
RRRARGH!
KRUNNNCH
YIKES!
I THINK THAT WAS A LOAD-BEARING SUPPORT, HAMMY.
THAT DOESN'T SOUND RIGHT. HAMMER? UHH...MISTER HEAD? I'LL KEEP WORKING ON A NICKNAME.
KERRRASH
NO ESCAPE. THE ONLY PLACE YOU'RE GOING TONIGHT IS JAIL.
YOU'RE NOT STILL SORE ABOUT THAT SIDEKICK CRACK, ARE YOU?
I PREFER ROUNDHOUSE.
KA-CHOK
ALWAYS WITH THE JOKES. TIME I SHUT YOU UP FOR GOOD!

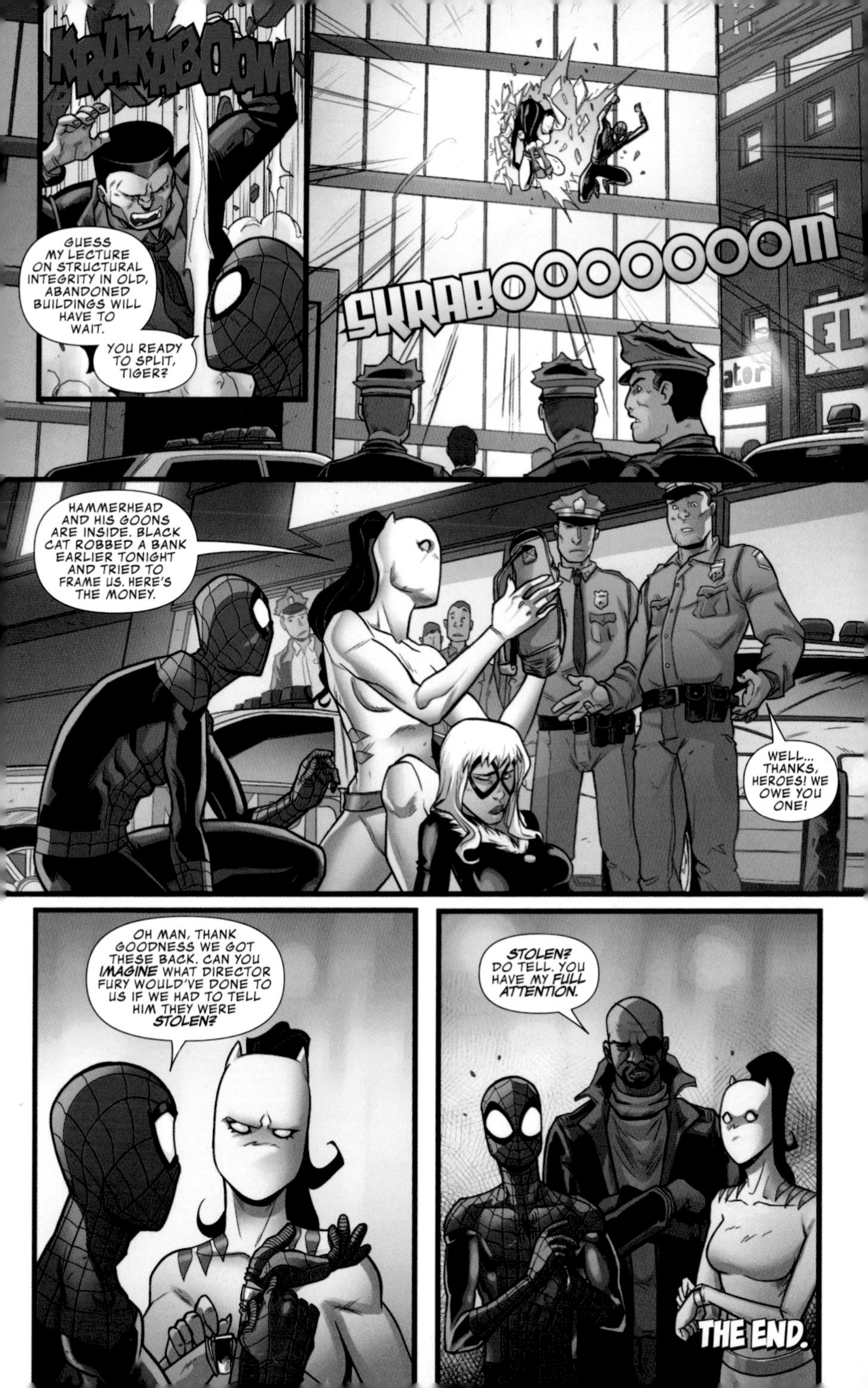
KRAKABOOM
GUESS MY LECTURE ON STRUCTURAL INTEGRITY IN OLD, ABANDONED BUILDINGS WILL HAVE TO WAIT.
YOU READY TO SPLIT, TIGER?
SKRABOOOOOOOOM
HAMMERHEAD AND HIS GOONS ARE INSIDE. BLACK CAT ROBBED A BANK EARLIER TONIGHT AND TRIED TO FRAME US. HERE'S THE MONEY.
WELL... THANKS, HEROES! WE OWE YOU ONE!
OH MAN, THANK GOODNESS WE GOT THESE BACK. CAN YOU IMAGINE WHAT DIRECTOR FURY WOULD'VE DONE TO US IF WE HAD TO TELL HIM THEY WERE STOLEN?
STOLEN? DO TELL. YOU HAVE MY FULL ATTENTION.
THE END.

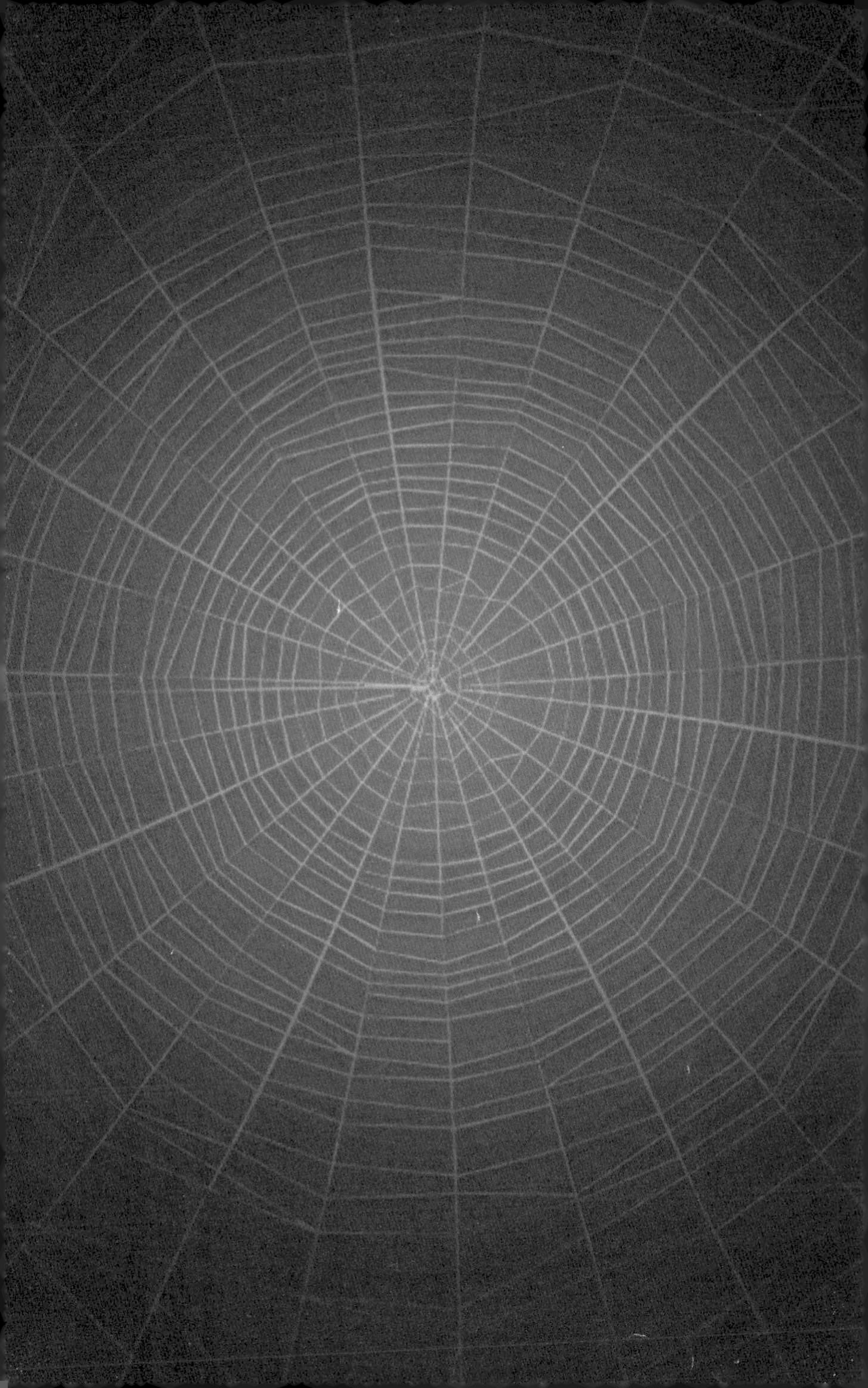

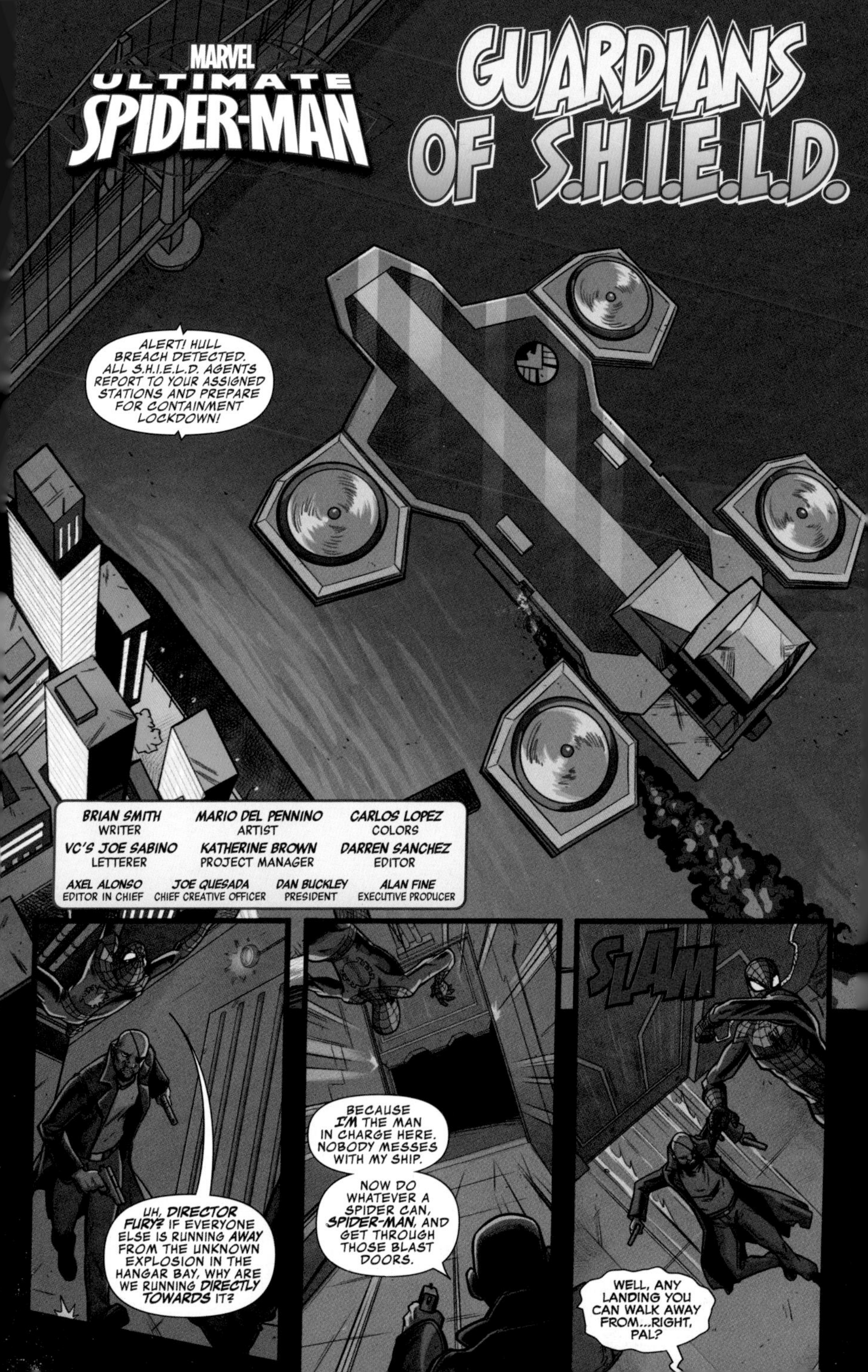

MARVEL
ULTIMATE
SPIDER-MAN
GUARDIANS OF S.H.I.E.L.D.
ALERT! HULL BREACH DETECTED. ALL S.H.I.E.L.D. AGENTS REPORT TO YOUR ASSIGNED STATIONS AND PREPARE FOR CONTAINMENT LOCKDOWN!
BRIAN SMITH WRITER
MARIO DEL PENNINO ARTIST
CARLOS LOPEZ COLORS
VC'S JOE SABINO LETTERER
KATHERINE BROWN PROJECT MANAGER
DARREN SANCHEZ EDITOR
AXEL ALONSO EDITOR IN CHIEF
JOE QUESADA CHIEF CREATIVE OFFICER
DAN BUCKLEY PRESIDENT
ALAN FINE EXECUTIVE PRODUCER
UH, DIRECTOR FURY? IF EVERYONE ELSE IS RUNNING AWAY FROM THE UNKNOWN EXPLOSION IN THE HANGAR BAY, WHY ARE WE RUNNING DIRECTLY TOWARDS IT?
BECAUSE I'M THE MAN IN CHARGE HERE. NOBODY MESSES WITH MY SHIP.
NOW DO WHATEVER A SPIDER CAN, SPIDER-MAN, AND GET THROUGH THOSE BLAST DOORS.
SLAM
WELL, ANY LANDING YOU CAN WALK AWAY FROM...RIGHT, PAL?

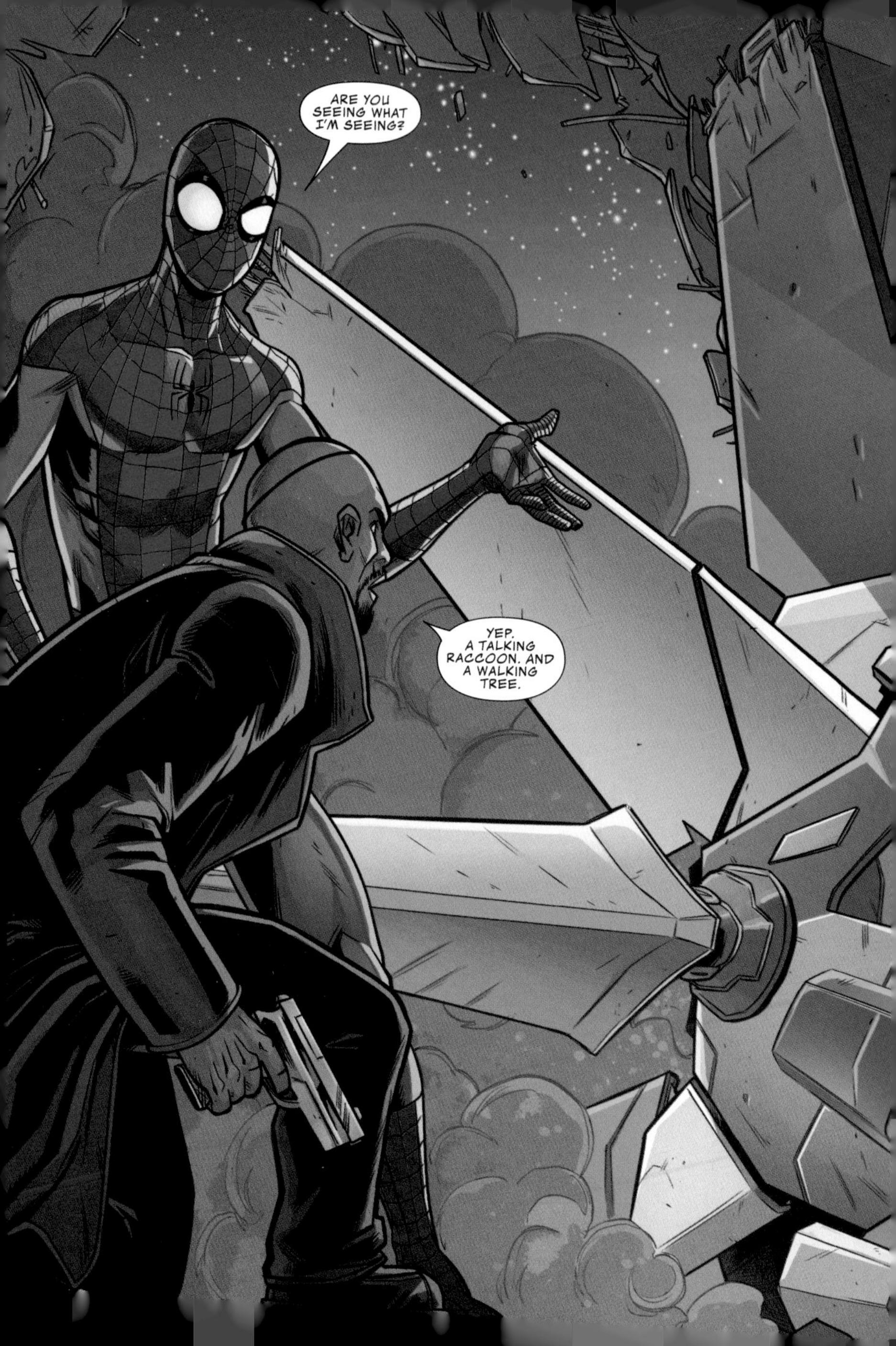
ARE YOU SEEING WHAT I'M SEEING?
YEP. A TALKING RACCOON. AND A WALKING TREE.

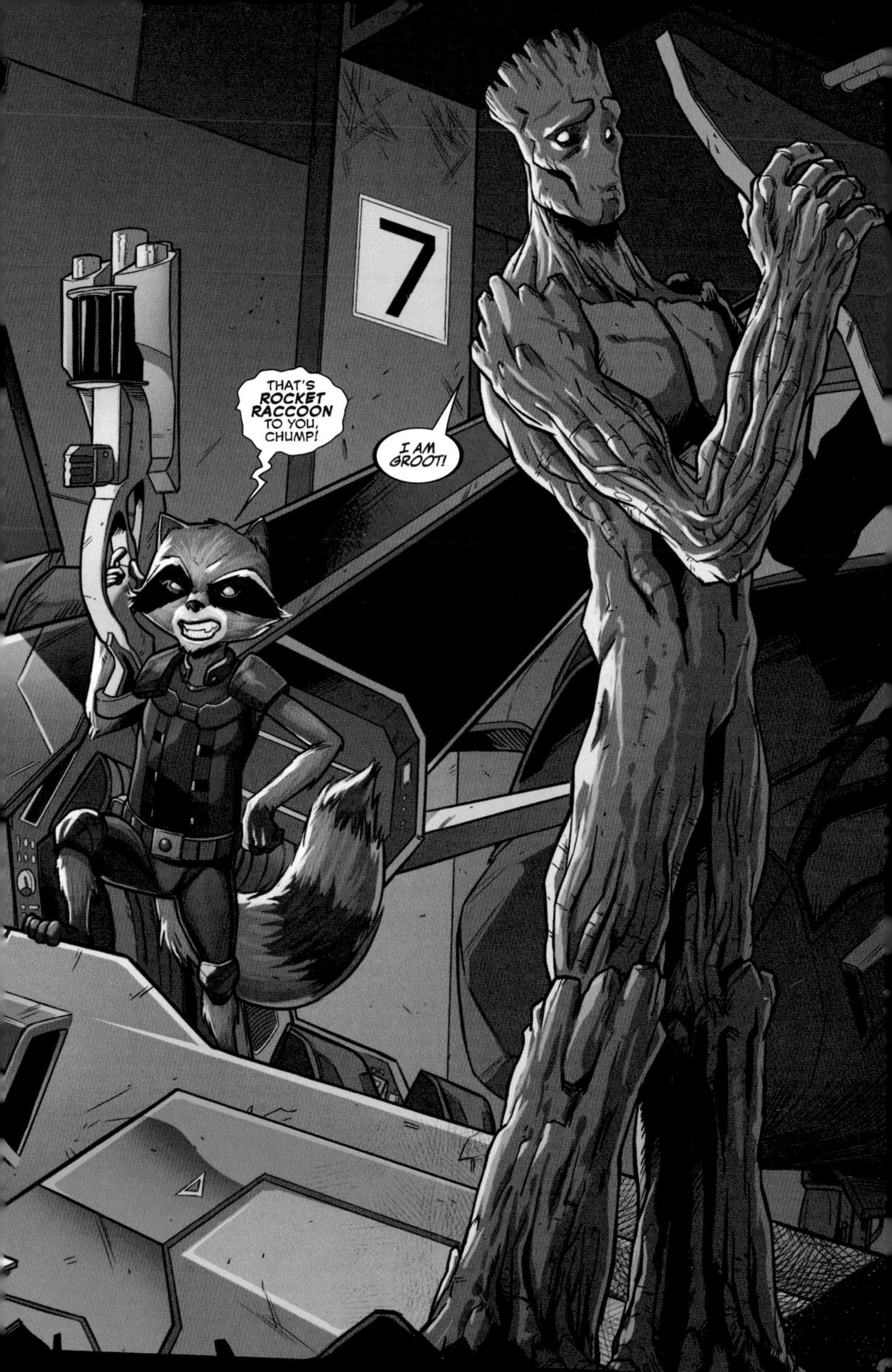
7
THAT'S ROCKET RACCOON TO YOU, CHUMP!
I AM GROOT!

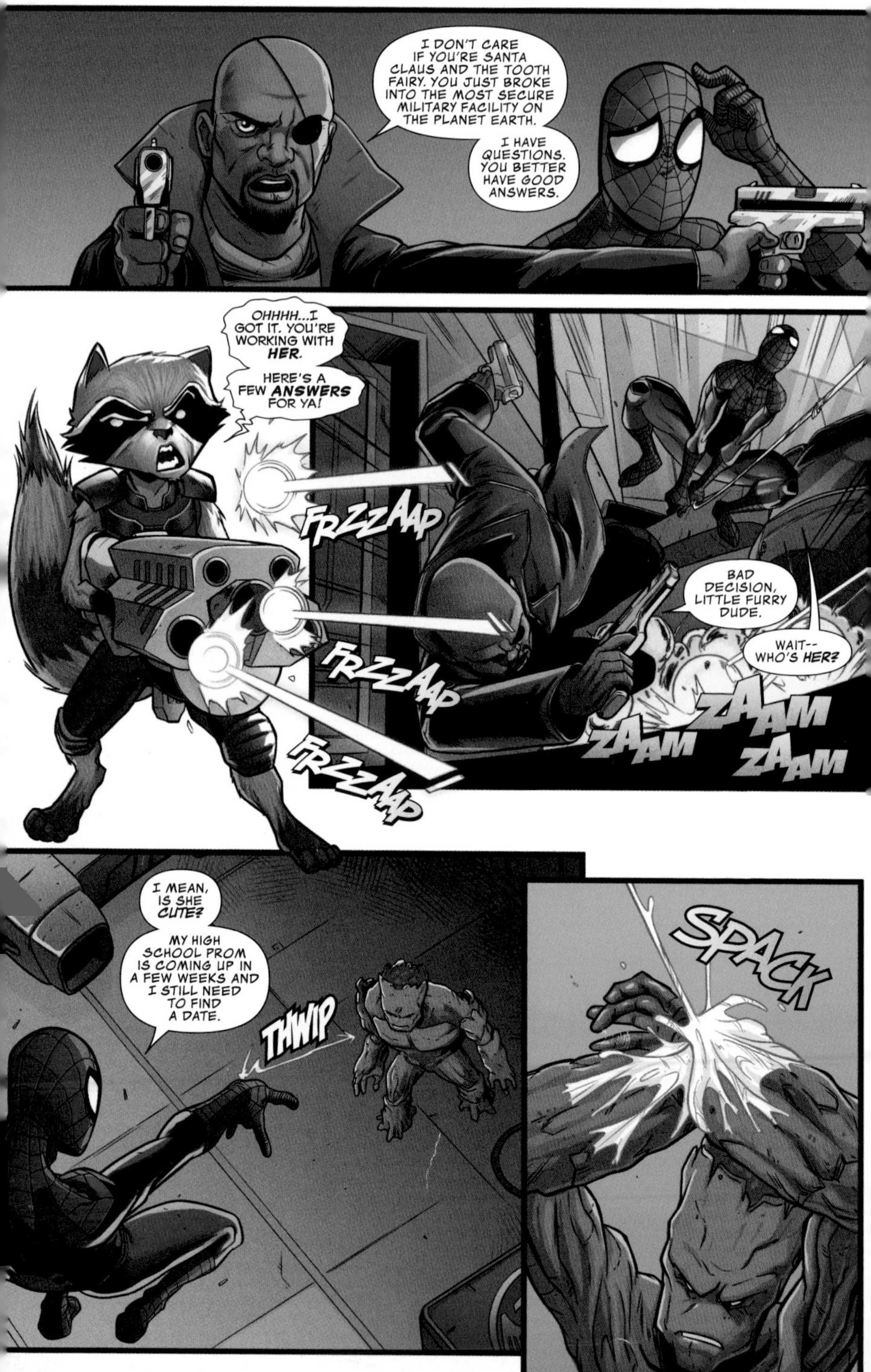
I DON'T CARE IF YOU'RE SANTA CLAUS AND THE TOOTH FAIRY. YOU JUST BROKE INTO THE MOST SECURE MILITARY FACILITY ON THE PLANET EARTH.
I HAVE QUESTIONS. YOU BETTER HAVE GOOD ANSWERS.
OHHHH...I GOT IT. YOU'RE WORKING WITH **HER**.
HERE'S A FEW **ANSWERS** FOR YA!
FRZZAAP
FRZZAAP
FRZZAAP
BAD DECISION, LITTLE FURRY DUDE.
WAIT-- WHO'S **HER?**
ZAAM
ZAAM
ZAAM
I MEAN, IS SHE **CUTE?**
MY HIGH SCHOOL PROM IS COMING UP IN A FEW WEEKS AND I STILL NEED TO FIND A DATE.
THWIP
SPACK

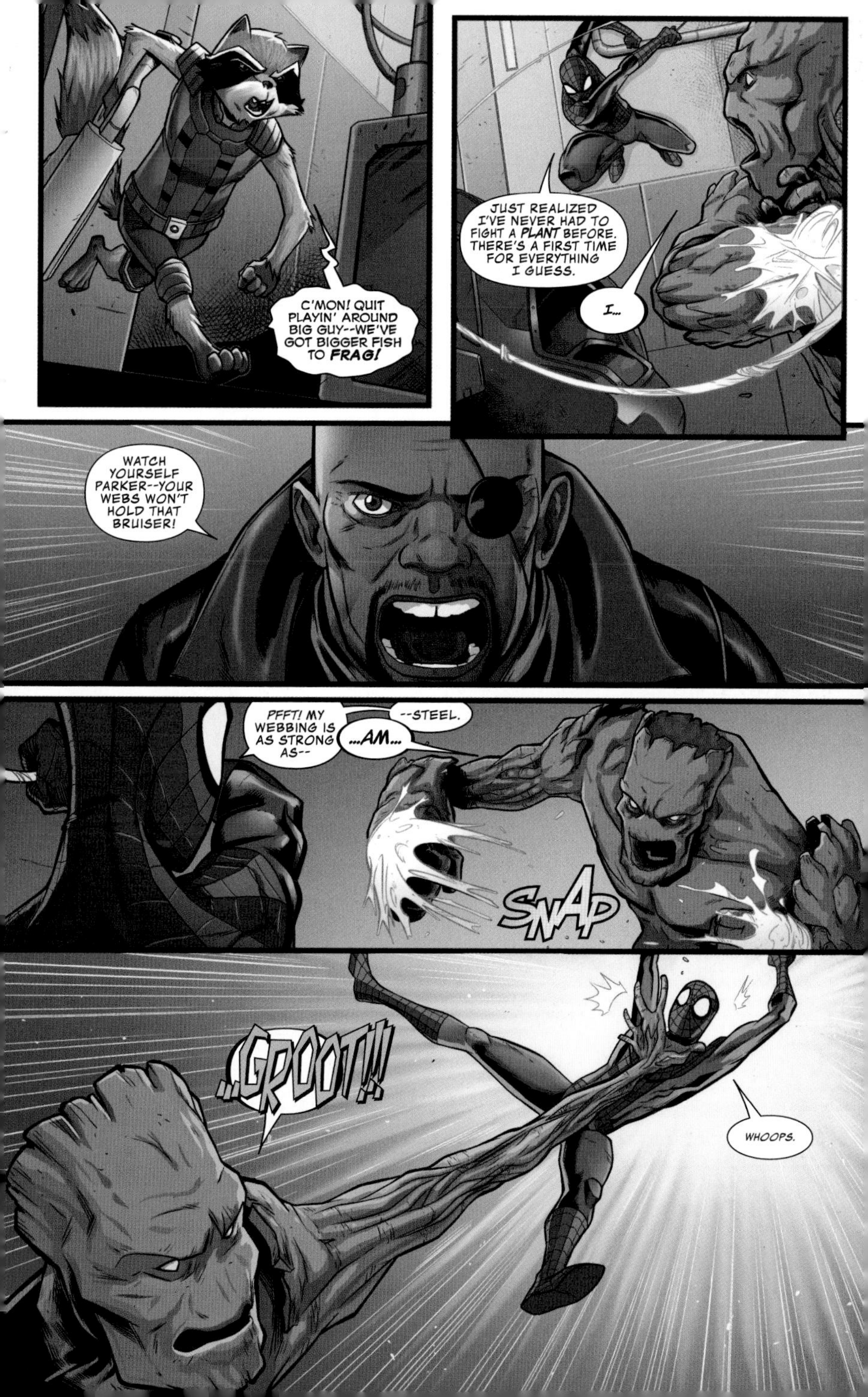
C'MON! QUIT PLAYIN' AROUND BIG GUY--WE'VE GOT BIGGER FISH TO FRAG!
JUST REALIZED I'VE NEVER HAD TO FIGHT A PLANT BEFORE. THERE'S A FIRST TIME FOR EVERYTHING I GUESS.
I...
WATCH YOURSELF PARKER--YOUR WEBS WON'T HOLD THAT BRUISER!
PFFT! MY WEBBING IS AS STRONG AS--
...AM...
--STEEL.
SNAP
...GROOT!!!
WHOOPS.

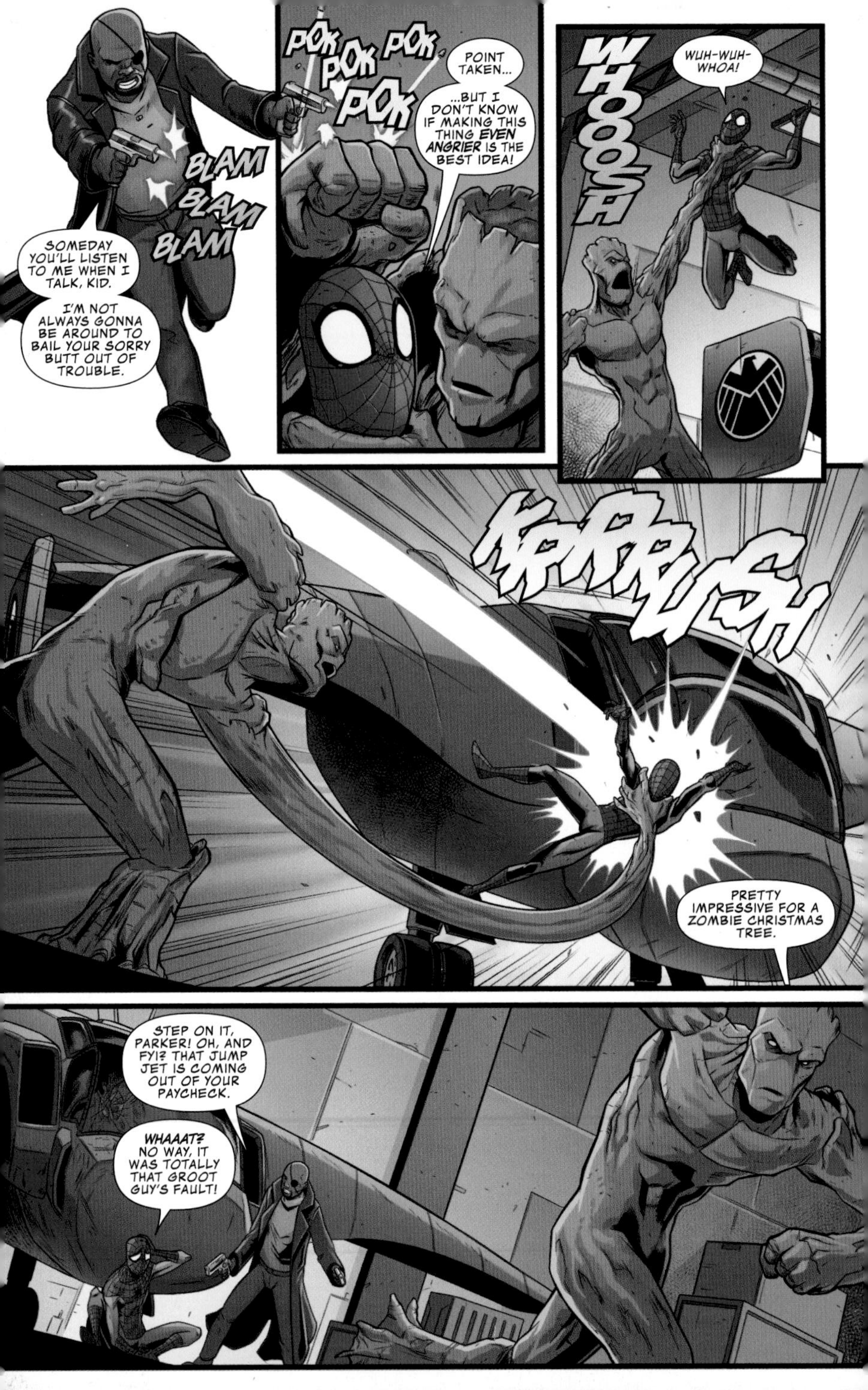
BLAM
BLAM
BLAM
SOMEDAY YOU'LL LISTEN TO ME WHEN I TALK, KID.
I'M NOT ALWAYS GONNA BE AROUND TO BAIL YOUR SORRY BUTT OUT OF TROUBLE.
POK POK POK POK POK
POINT TAKEN...
...BUT I DON'T KNOW IF MAKING THIS THING EVEN ANGRIER IS THE BEST IDEA!
WHOOOOSH
WUH-WUH-WHOA!
KRRRUSH
PRETTY IMPRESSIVE FOR A ZOMBIE CHRISTMAS TREE.
STEP ON IT, PARKER! OH, AND FYI? THAT JUMP JET IS COMING OUT OF YOUR PAYCHECK.
WHAAAT? NO WAY, IT WAS TOTALLY THAT GROOT GUY'S FAULT!

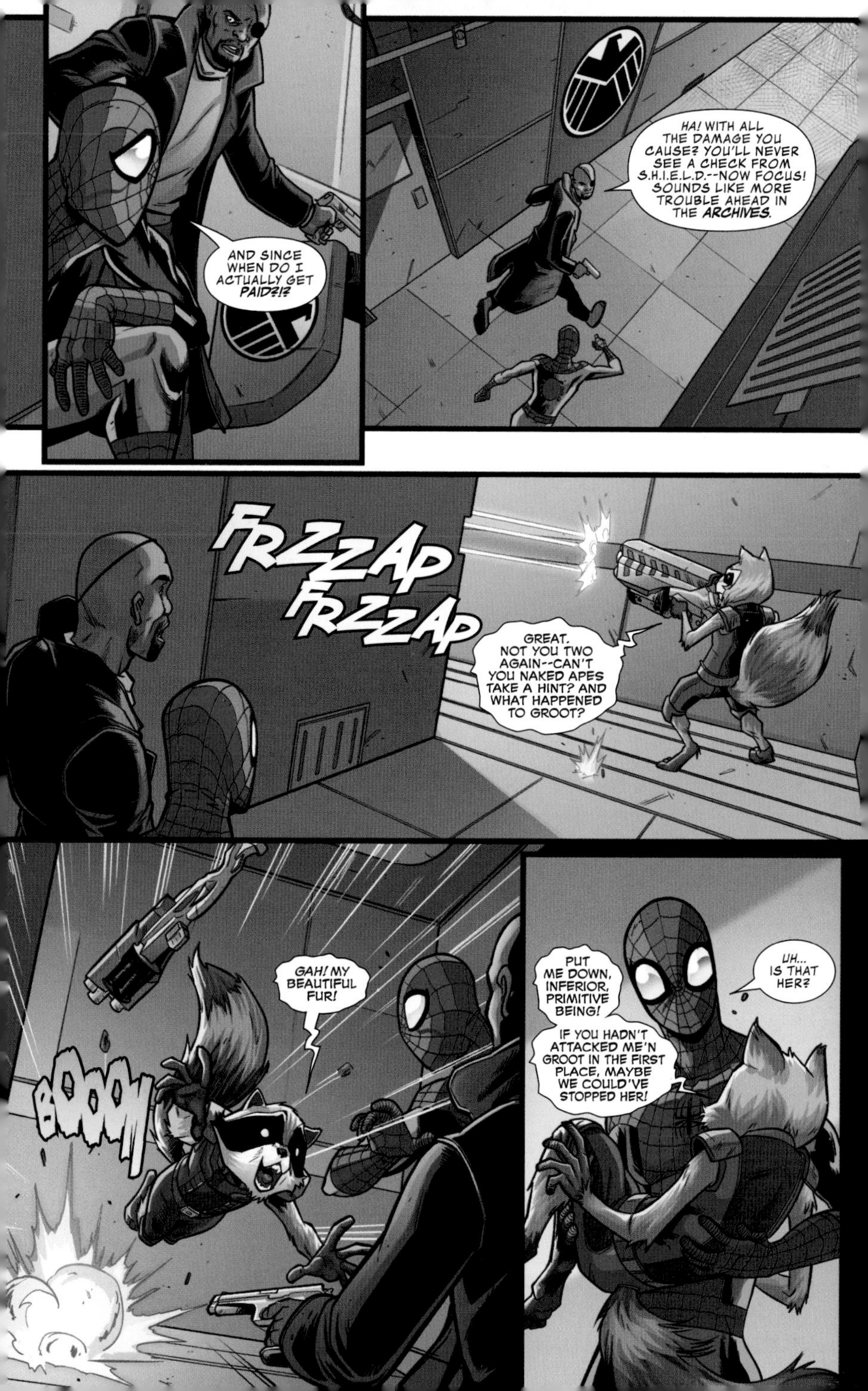
AND SINCE WHEN DO I ACTUALLY GET PAID?!?
HA! WITH ALL THE DAMAGE YOU CAUSE? YOU'LL NEVER SEE A CHECK FROM S.H.I.E.L.D.--NOW FOCUS! SOUNDS LIKE MORE TROUBLE AHEAD IN THE ARCHIVES.
FRZZZAP
FRZZZAP
GREAT. NOT YOU TWO AGAIN--CAN'T YOU NAKED APES TAKE A HINT? AND WHAT HAPPENED TO GROOT?
GAH! MY BEAUTIFUL FUR!
BOOOM
UH... IS THAT HER?
PUT ME DOWN, INFERIOR, PRIMITIVE BEING!
IF YOU HADN'T ATTACKED ME'N GROOT IN THE FIRST PLACE, MAYBE WE COULD'VE STOPPED HER!

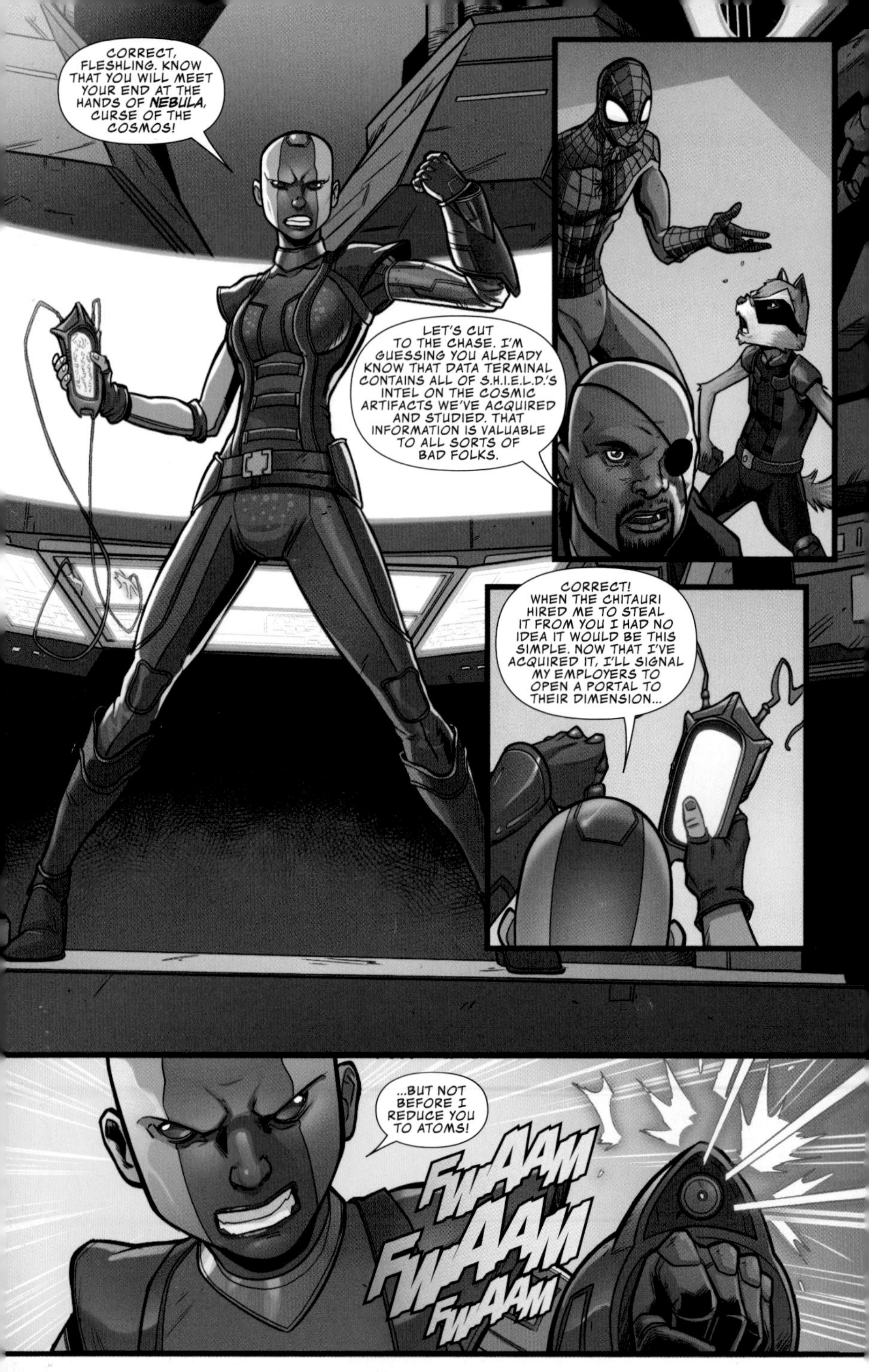

CORRECT, FLESHLING. KNOW THAT YOU WILL MEET YOUR END AT THE HANDS OF **NEBULA**, CURSE OF THE COSMOS!
LET'S CUT TO THE CHASE. I'M GUESSING YOU ALREADY KNOW THAT DATA TERMINAL CONTAINS ALL OF S.H.I.E.L.D.'S INTEL ON THE COSMIC ARTIFACTS WE'VE ACQUIRED AND STUDIED. THAT INFORMATION IS VALUABLE TO ALL SORTS OF BAD FOLKS.
CORRECT! WHEN THE CHITAURI HIRED ME TO STEAL IT FROM YOU I HAD NO IDEA IT WOULD BE THIS SIMPLE. NOW THAT I'VE ACQUIRED IT, I'LL SIGNAL MY EMPLOYERS TO OPEN A PORTAL TO THEIR DIMENSION...
...BUT NOT BEFORE I REDUCE YOU TO ATOMS!
FWAAM
FWAAM
FWAAM

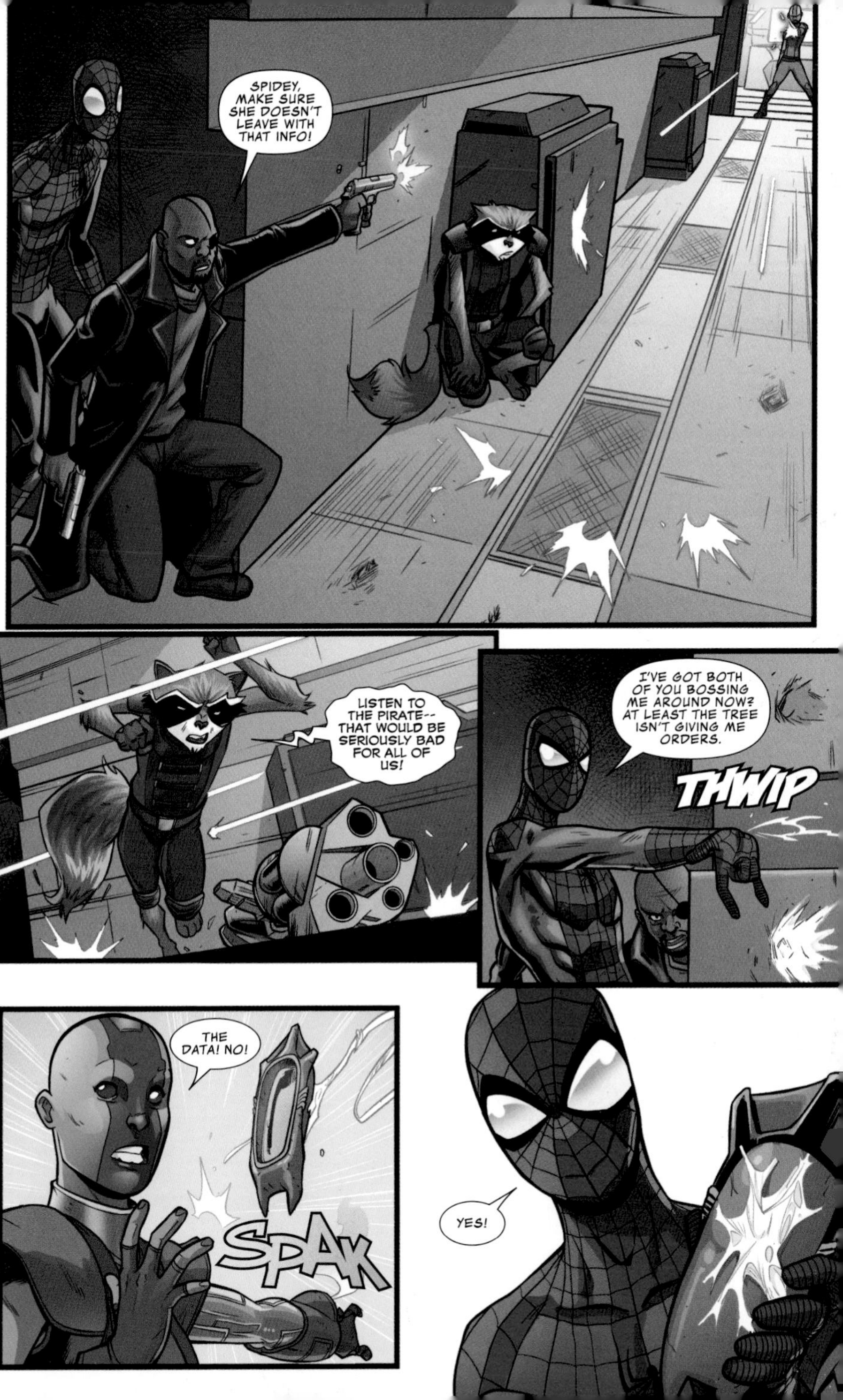
SPIDEY, MAKE SURE SHE DOESN'T LEAVE WITH THAT INFO!
LISTEN TO THE PIRATE-- THAT WOULD BE SERIOUSLY BAD FOR ALL OF US!
I'VE GOT BOTH OF YOU BOSSING ME AROUND NOW? AT LEAST THE TREE ISN'T GIVING ME ORDERS.
THWIP
THE DATA! NO!
SPAK
YES!

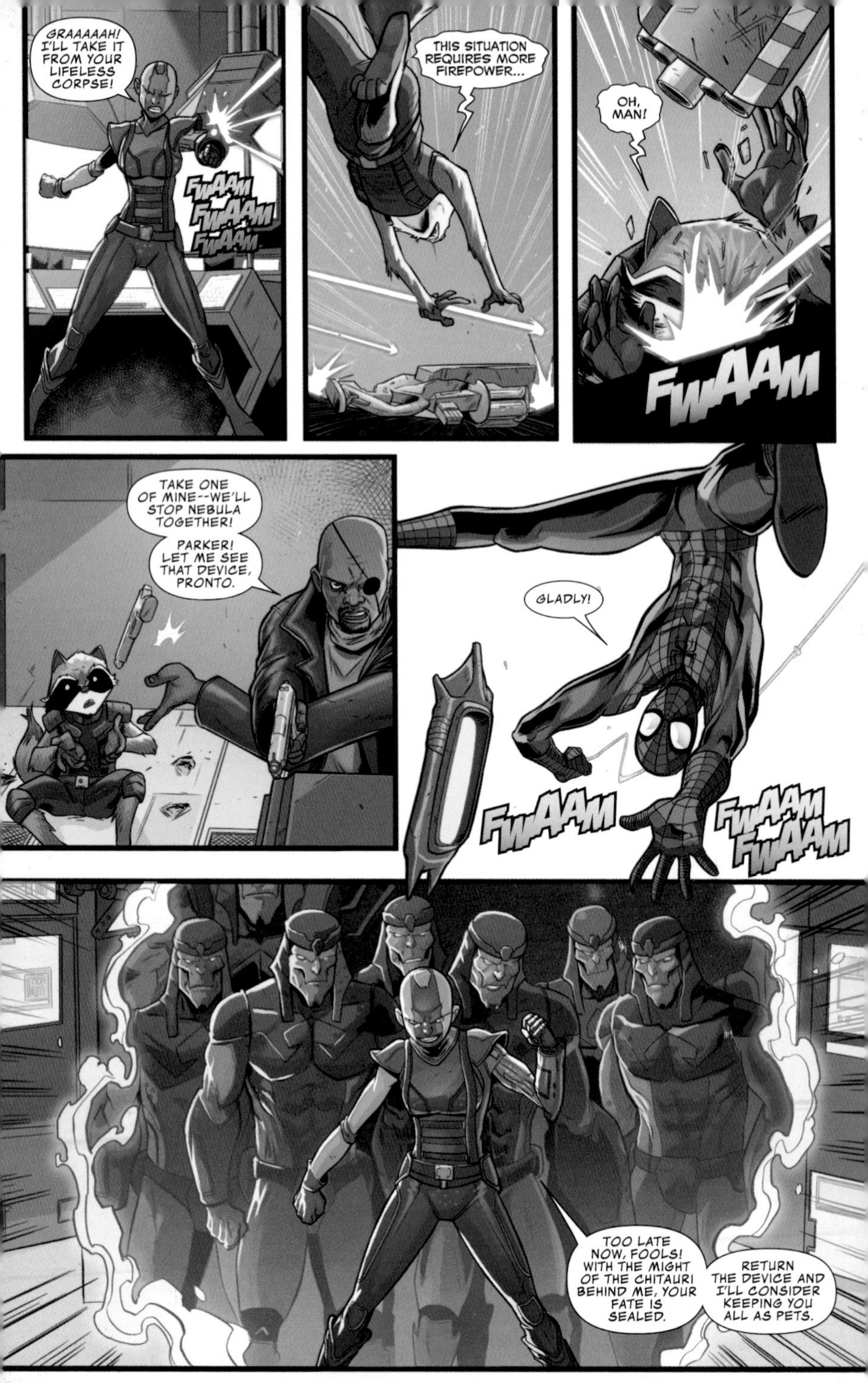
GRAAAAAH! I'LL TAKE IT FROM YOUR LIFELESS CORPSE!
FWAAM FWAAM FWAAM
THIS SITUATION REQUIRES MORE FIREPOWER...
OH, MAN!
FWAAM
TAKE ONE OF MINE--WE'LL STOP NEBULA TOGETHER!
PARKER! LET ME SEE THAT DEVICE, PRONTO.
GLADLY!
FWAAM
FWAAM FWAAM
TOO LATE NOW, FOOLS! WITH THE MIGHT OF THE CHITAURI BEHIND ME, YOUR FATE IS SEALED.
RETURN THE DEVICE AND I'LL CONSIDER KEEPING YOU ALL AS PETS.

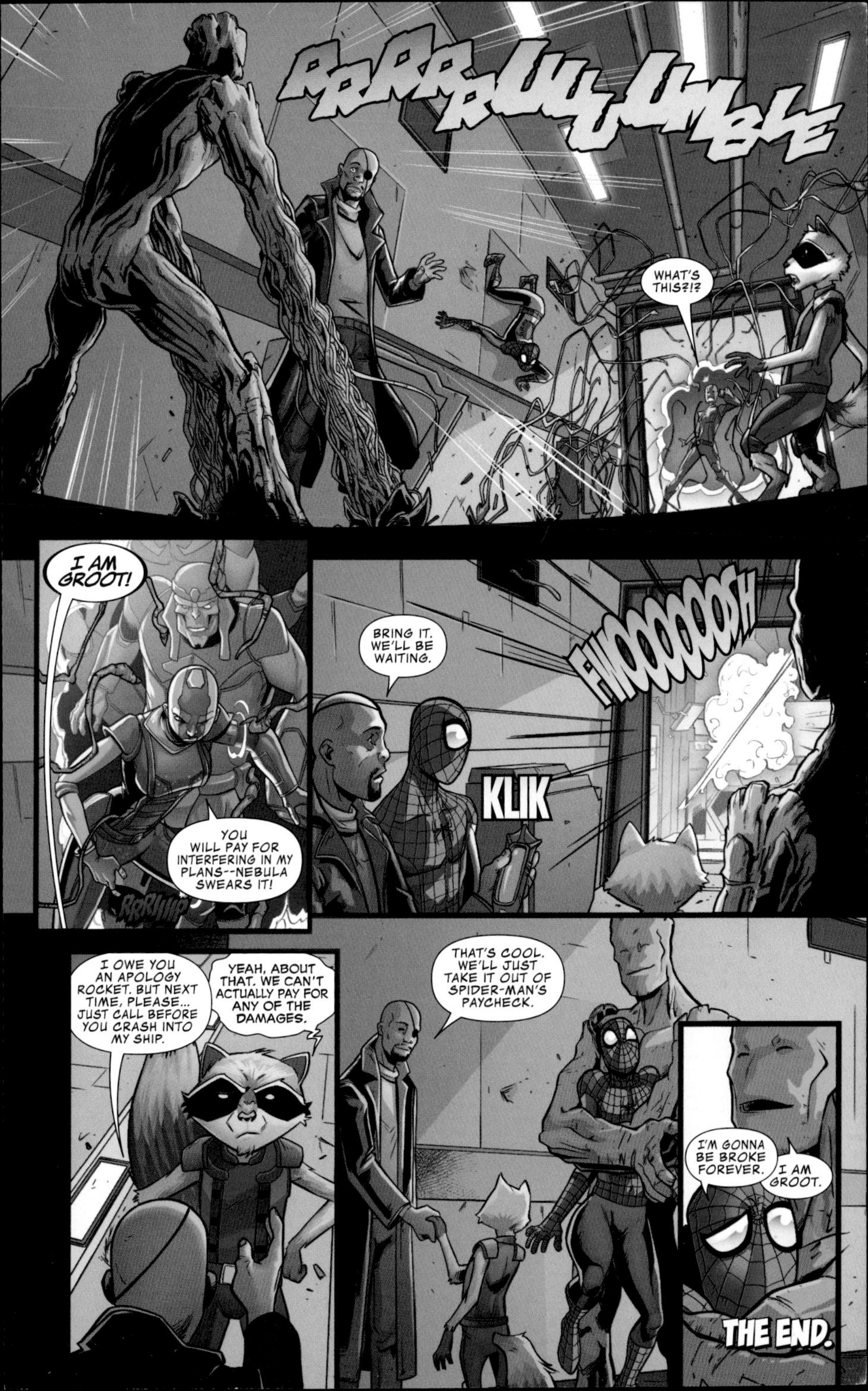
RRRRRRUUUUMBLE
WHAT'S THIS?!?
I AM GROOT!
YOU WILL PAY FOR INTERFERING IN MY PLANS--NEBULA SWEARS IT!
RRRHHHP
BRING IT. WE'LL BE WAITING.
FWOOOOOOSH
KLIK
I OWE YOU AN APOLOGY ROCKET. BUT NEXT TIME, PLEASE... JUST CALL BEFORE YOU CRASH INTO MY SHIP.
YEAH, ABOUT THAT. WE CAN'T ACTUALLY PAY FOR ANY OF THE DAMAGES.
THAT'S COOL. WE'LL JUST TAKE IT OUT OF SPIDER-MAN'S PAYCHECK.
I'M GONNA BE BROKE FOREVER.
I AM GROOT.
THE END.

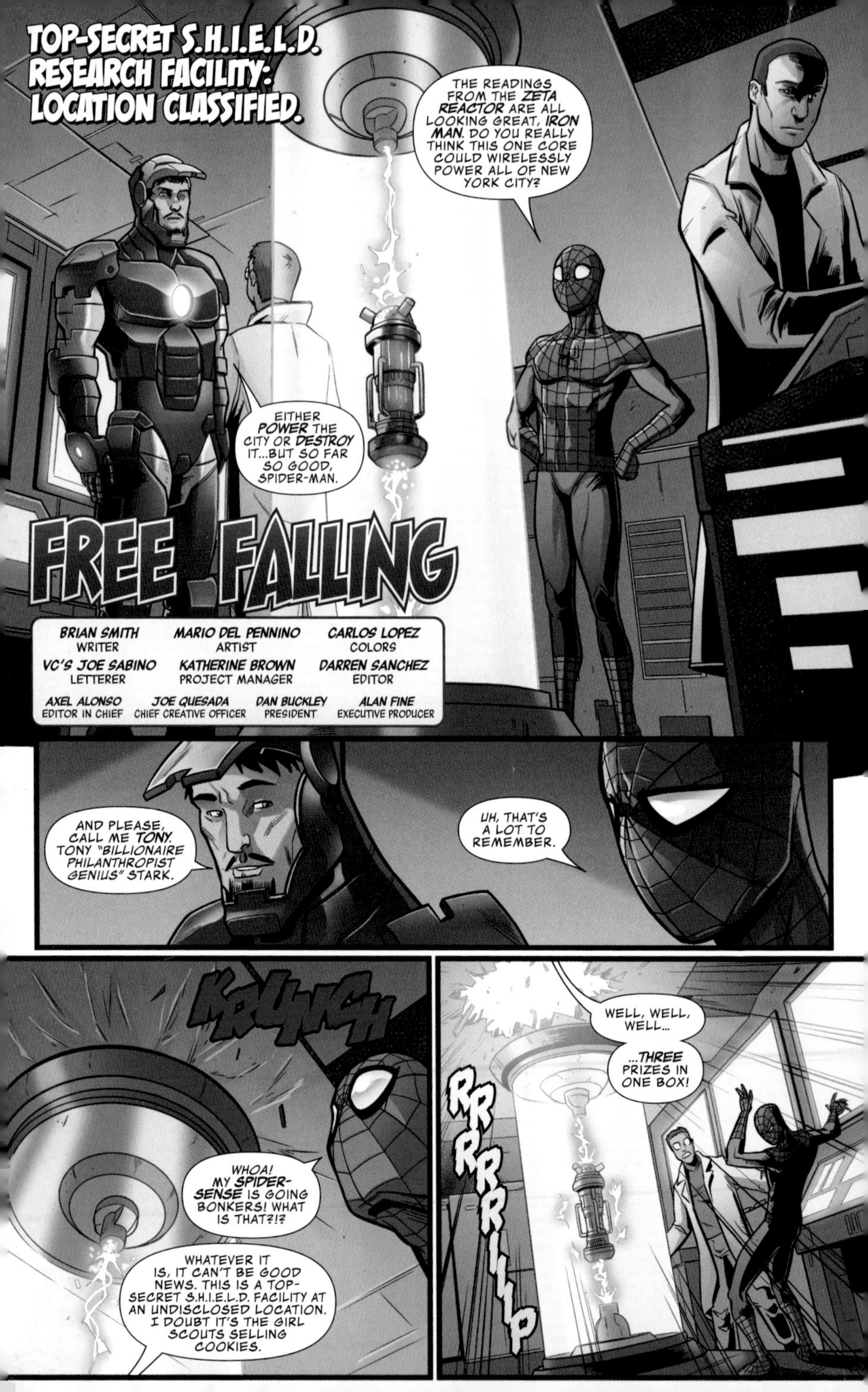
TOP-SECRET S.H.I.E.L.D. RESEARCH FACILITY: LOCATION CLASSIFIED.
THE READINGS FROM THE ZETA REACTOR ARE ALL LOOKING GREAT, IRON MAN. DO YOU REALLY THINK THIS ONE CORE COULD WIRELESSLY POWER ALL OF NEW YORK CITY?
EITHER POWER THE CITY OR DESTROY IT...BUT SO FAR SO GOOD, SPIDER-MAN.
FREE FALLING
BRIAN SMITH WRITER
MARIO DEL PENNINO ARTIST
CARLOS LOPEZ COLORS
VC'S JOE SABINO LETTERER
KATHERINE BROWN PROJECT MANAGER
DARREN SANCHEZ EDITOR
AXEL ALONSO EDITOR IN CHIEF
JOE QUESADA CHIEF CREATIVE OFFICER
DAN BUCKLEY PRESIDENT
ALAN FINE EXECUTIVE PRODUCER
AND PLEASE, CALL ME TONY. TONY "BILLIONAIRE PHILANTHROPIST GENIUS" STARK.
UH, THAT'S A LOT TO REMEMBER.
KRUNCH
WHOA! MY SPIDER-SENSE IS GOING BONKERS! WHAT IS THAT?!?
WHATEVER IT IS, IT CAN'T BE GOOD NEWS. THIS IS A TOP-SECRET S.H.I.E.L.D. FACILITY AT AN UNDISCLOSED LOCATION. I DOUBT IT'S THE GIRL SCOUTS SELLING COOKIES.
RRRRRRIIIP
WELL, WELL, WELL...
...THREE PRIZES IN ONE BOX!

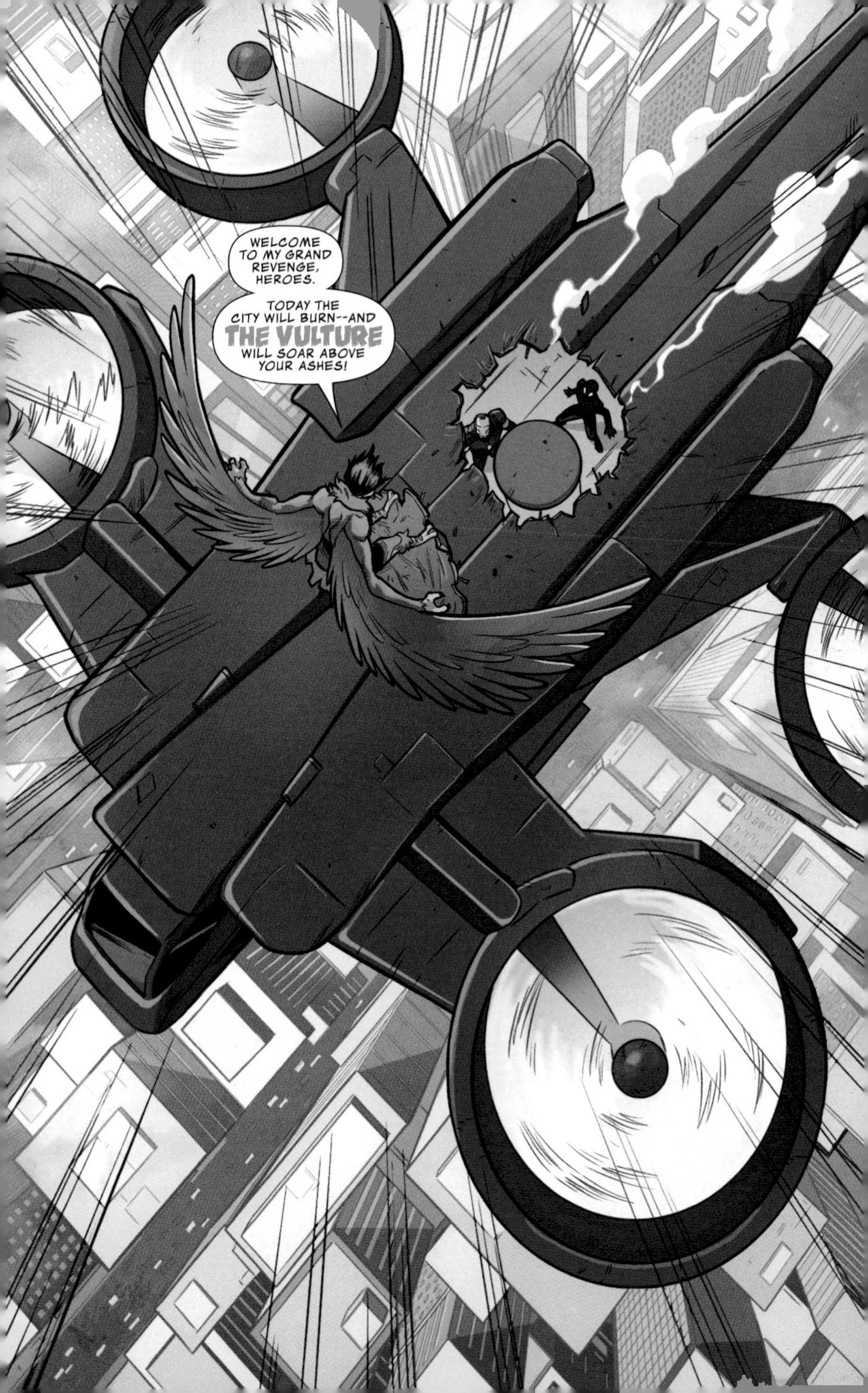
WELCOME TO MY GRAND REVENGE, HEROES.
TODAY THE CITY WILL BURN--AND THE VULTURE WILL SOAR ABOVE YOUR ASHES!

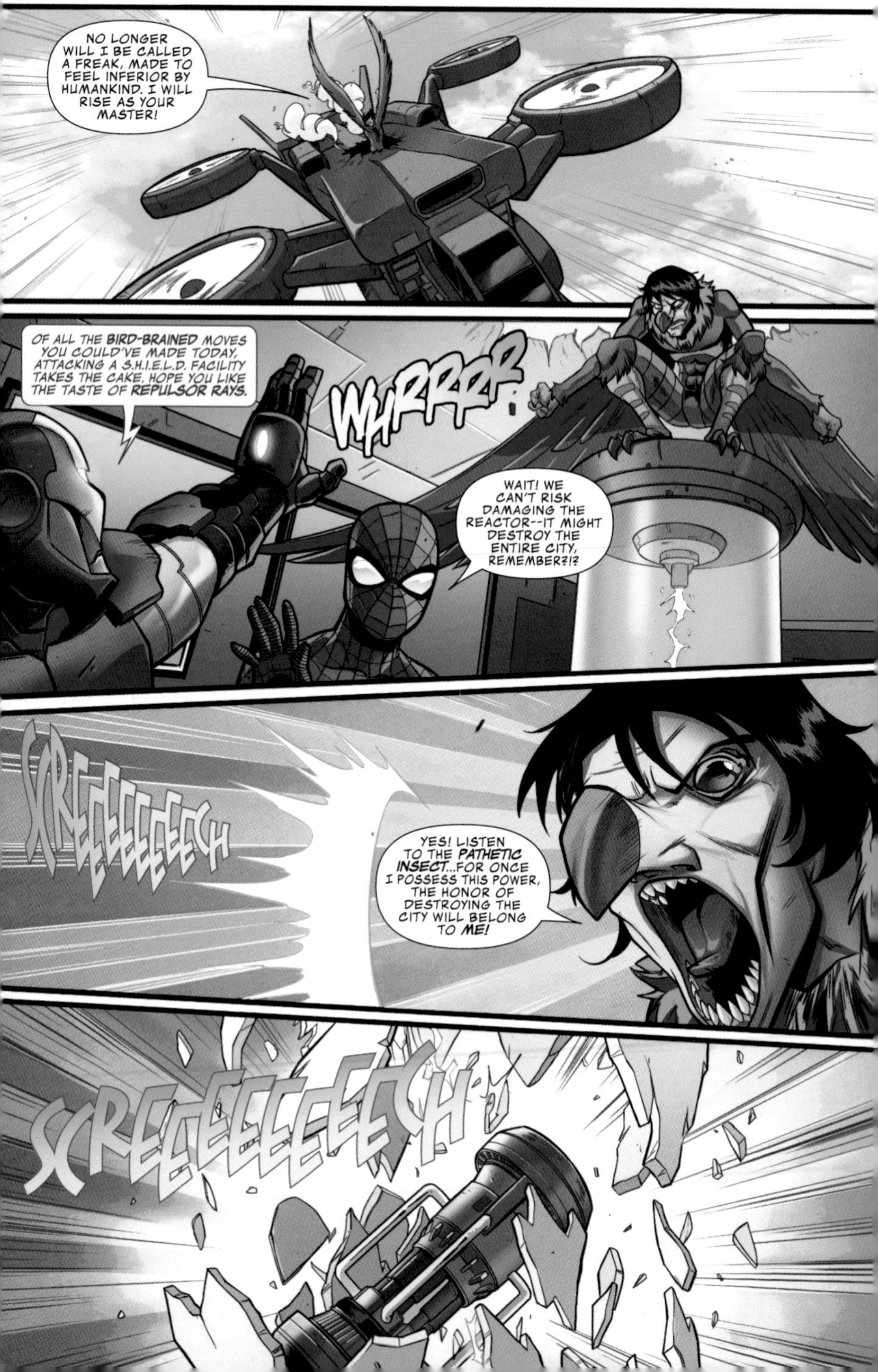
NO LONGER WILL I BE CALLED A FREAK, MADE TO FEEL INFERIOR BY HUMANKIND. I WILL RISE AS YOUR MASTER!
OF ALL THE BIRD-BRAINED MOVES YOU COULD'VE MADE TODAY, ATTACKING A S.H.I.E.L.D. FACILITY TAKES THE CAKE. HOPE YOU LIKE THE TASTE OF REPULSOR RAYS.
WHRRRR
WAIT! WE CAN'T RISK DAMAGING THE REACTOR--IT MIGHT DESTROY THE ENTIRE CITY, REMEMBER?!?
SCREEEEEEEECH
YES! LISTEN TO THE PATHETIC INSECT...FOR ONCE I POSSESS THIS POWER, THE HONOR OF DESTROYING THE CITY WILL BELONG TO ME!
SCREEEEEEEEECH

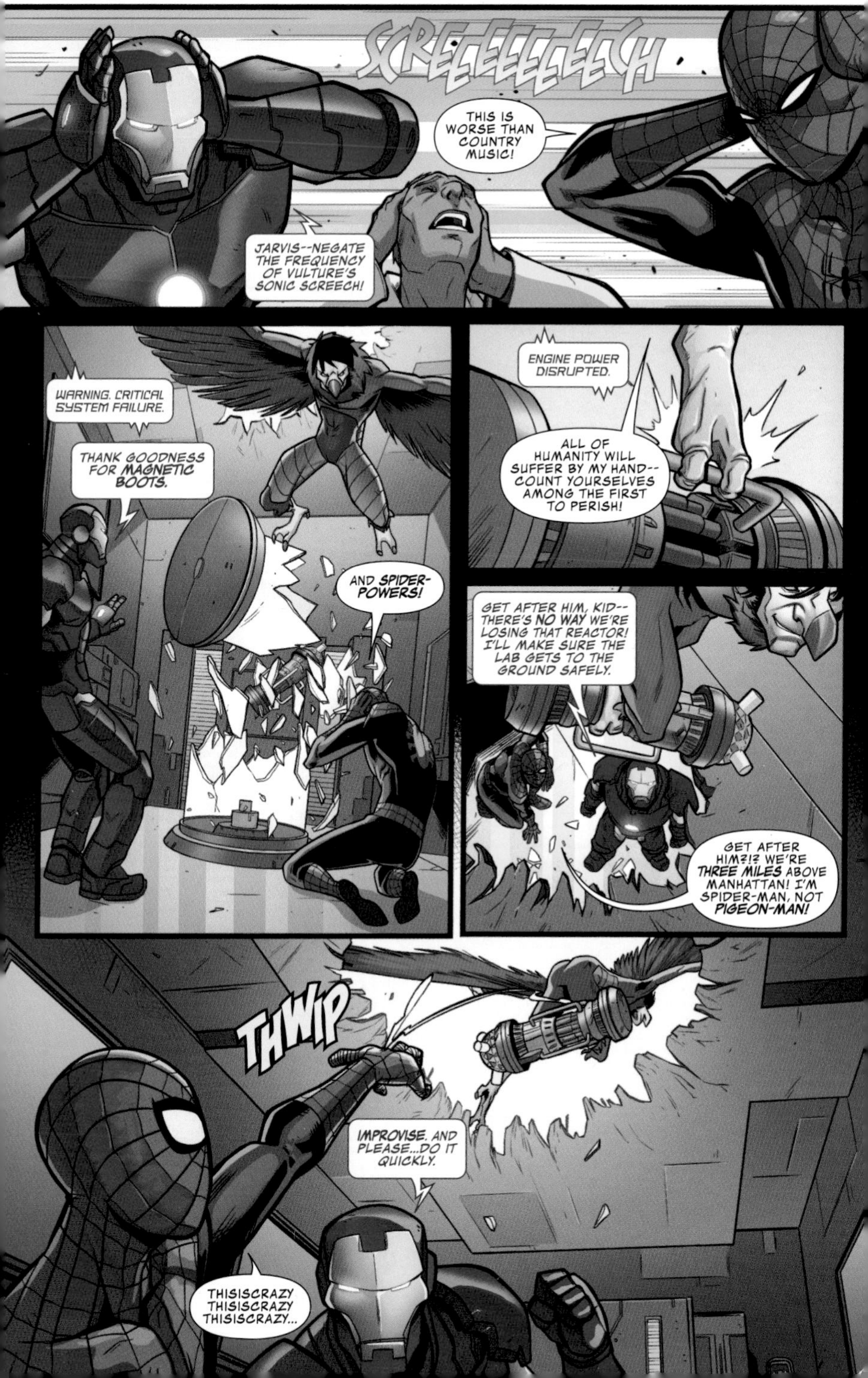
SCREEEEEEEECH
THIS IS WORSE THAN COUNTRY MUSIC!
JARVIS--NEGATE THE FREQUENCY OF VULTURE'S SONIC SCREECH!
WARNING. CRITICAL SYSTEM FAILURE.
THANK GOODNESS FOR MAGNETIC BOOTS.
AND SPIDER-POWERS!
ENGINE POWER DISRUPTED.
ALL OF HUMANITY WILL SUFFER BY MY HAND--COUNT YOURSELVES AMONG THE FIRST TO PERISH!
GET AFTER HIM, KID--THERE'S NO WAY WE'RE LOSING THAT REACTOR! I'LL MAKE SURE THE LAB GETS TO THE GROUND SAFELY.
GET AFTER HIM?!? WE'RE THREE MILES ABOVE MANHATTAN! I'M SPIDER-MAN, NOT PIGEON-MAN!
THWIP
IMPROVISE. AND PLEASE...DO IT QUICKLY.
THISISCRAZY THISISCRAZY THISISCRAZY...

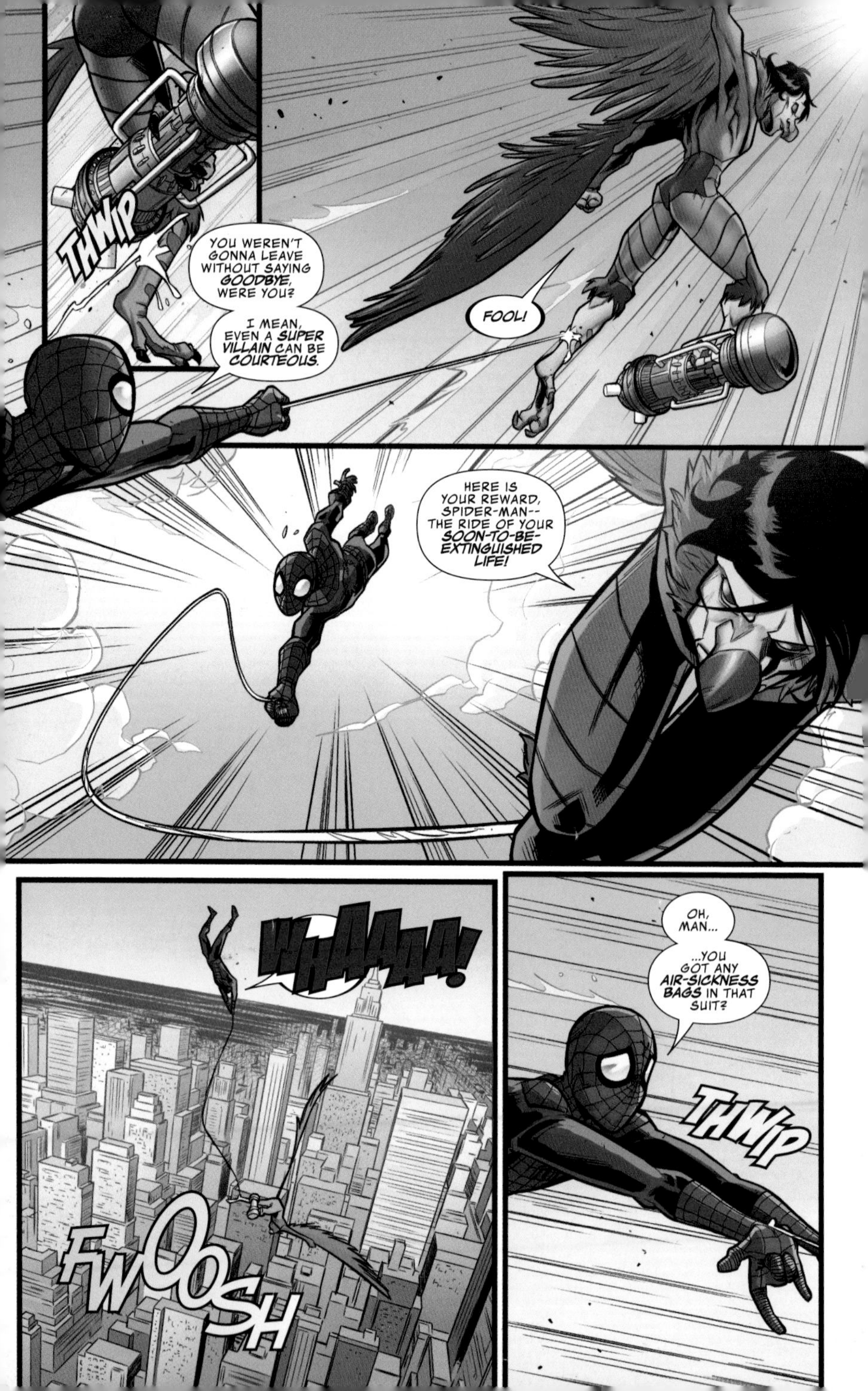
THWIP
YOU WEREN'T GONNA LEAVE WITHOUT SAYING GOODBYE, WERE YOU?
I MEAN, EVEN A SUPER VILLAIN CAN BE COURTEOUS.
FOOL!
HERE IS YOUR REWARD, SPIDER-MAN-- THE RIDE OF YOUR SOON-TO-BE-EXTINGUISHED LIFE!
WHAAAAA!
FWOOSH
OH, MAN...
...YOU GOT ANY AIR-SICKNESS BAGS IN THAT SUIT?
THWIP

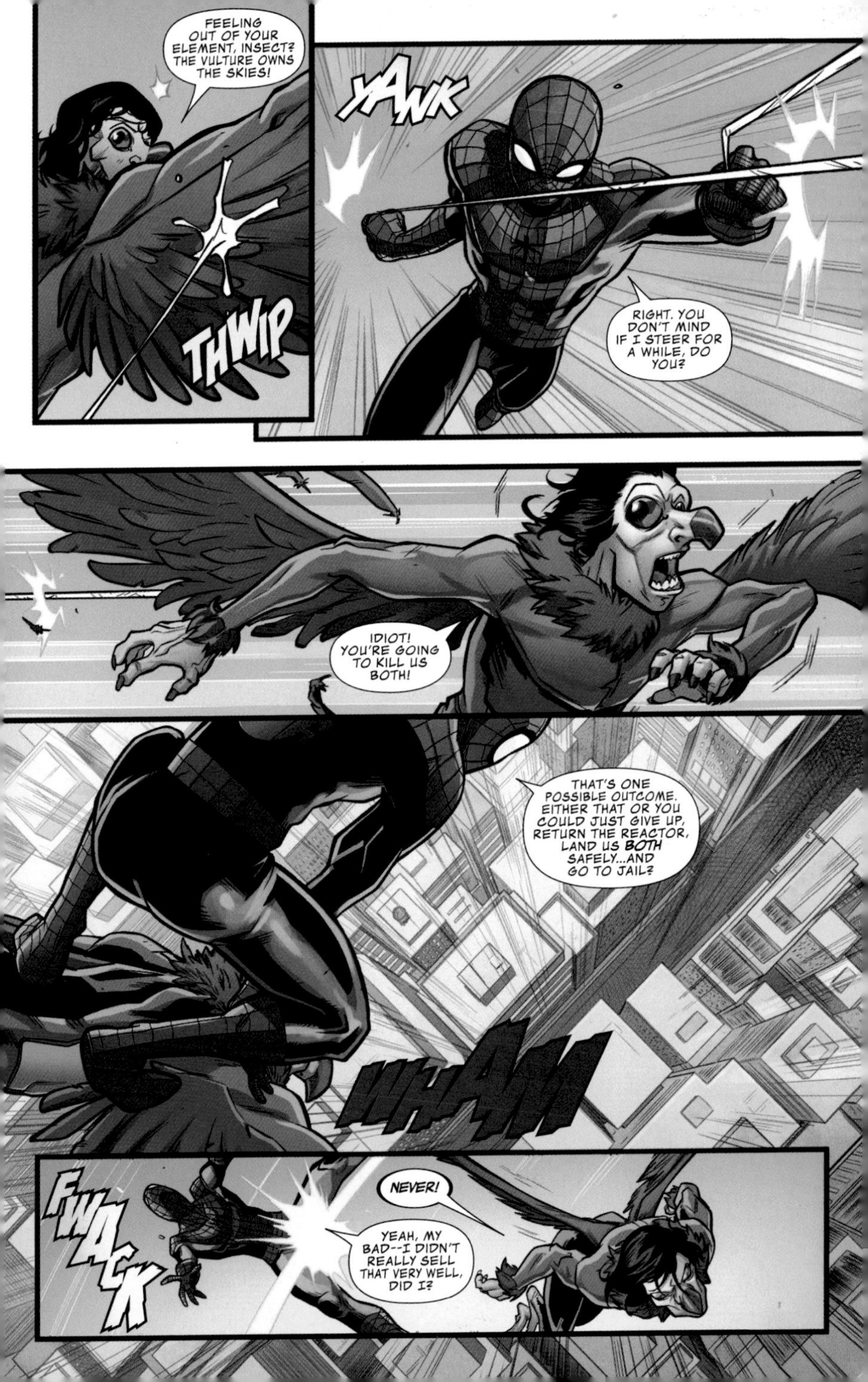
FEELING OUT OF YOUR ELEMENT, INSECT? THE VULTURE OWNS THE SKIES!
THWIP
YANK
RIGHT. YOU DON'T MIND IF I STEER FOR A WHILE, DO YOU?
IDIOT! YOU'RE GOING TO KILL US BOTH!
THAT'S ONE POSSIBLE OUTCOME. EITHER THAT OR YOU COULD JUST GIVE UP, RETURN THE REACTOR, LAND US BOTH SAFELY...AND GO TO JAIL?
WHAM
FWACK
NEVER!
YEAH, MY BAD--I DIDN'T REALLY SELL THAT VERY WELL, DID I?

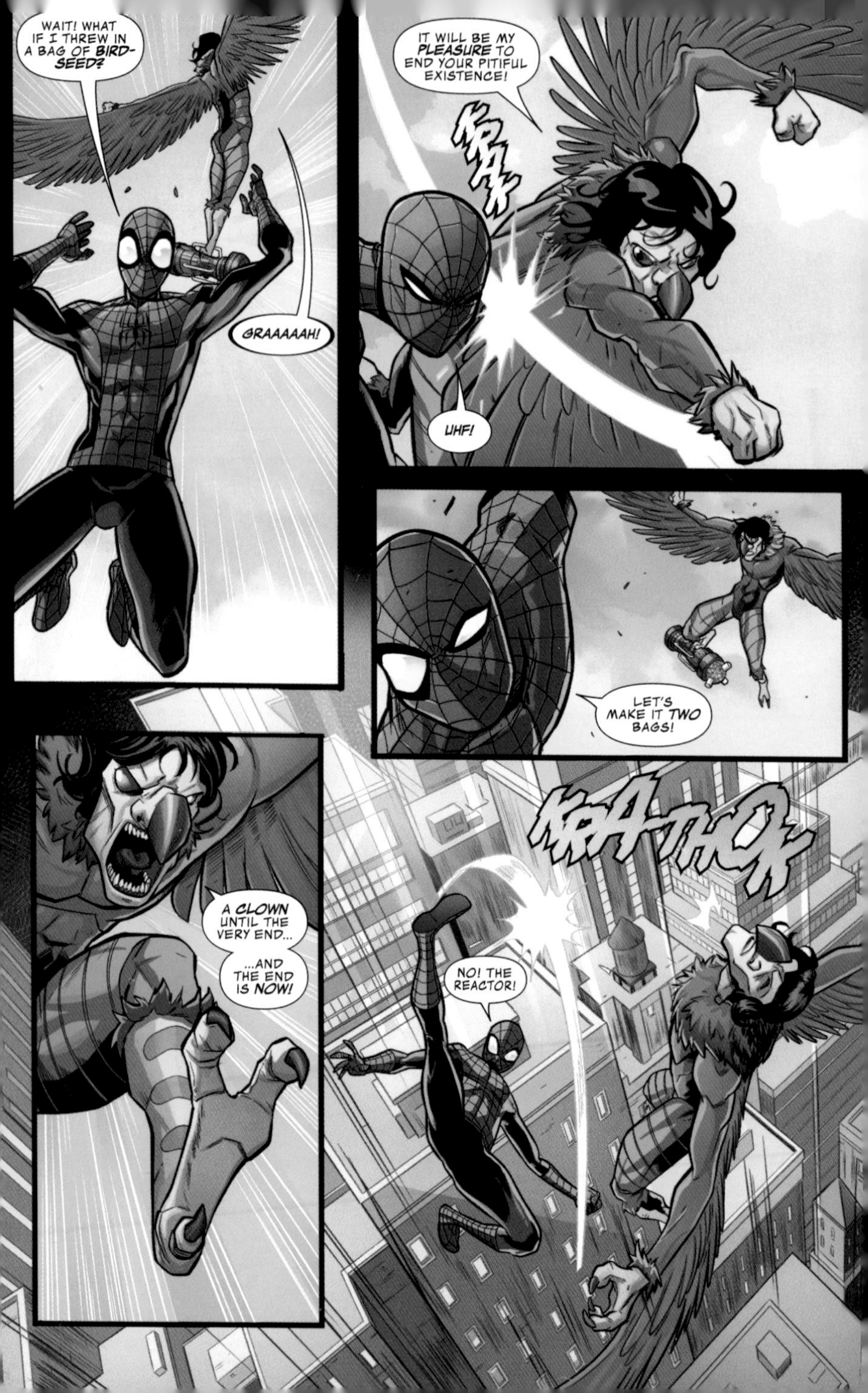
WAIT! WHAT IF I THREW IN A BAG OF BIRD-SEED?
GRAAAAAH!
IT WILL BE MY PLEASURE TO END YOUR PITIFUL EXISTENCE!
UHF!
LET'S MAKE IT TWO BAGS!
A CLOWN UNTIL THE VERY END...
...AND THE END IS NOW!
NO! THE REACTOR!

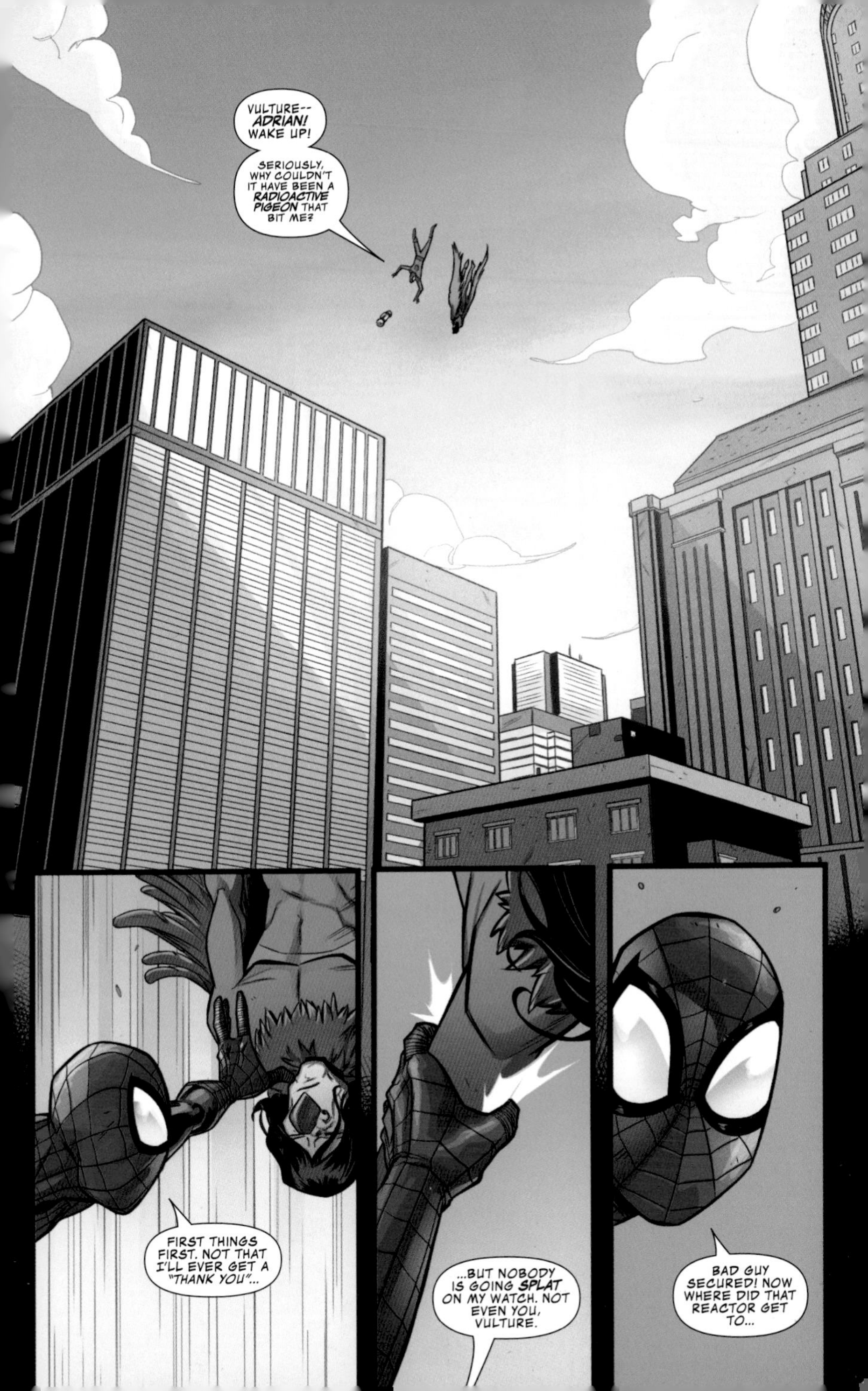
VULTURE-- ADRIAN! WAKE UP!
SERIOUSLY, WHY COULDN'T IT HAVE BEEN A RADIOACTIVE PIGEON THAT BIT ME?
FIRST THINGS FIRST. NOT THAT I'LL EVER GET A "THANK YOU"...
...BUT NOBODY IS GOING SPLAT ON MY WATCH. NOT EVEN YOU, VULTURE.
BAD GUY SECURED! NOW WHERE DID THAT REACTOR GET TO...

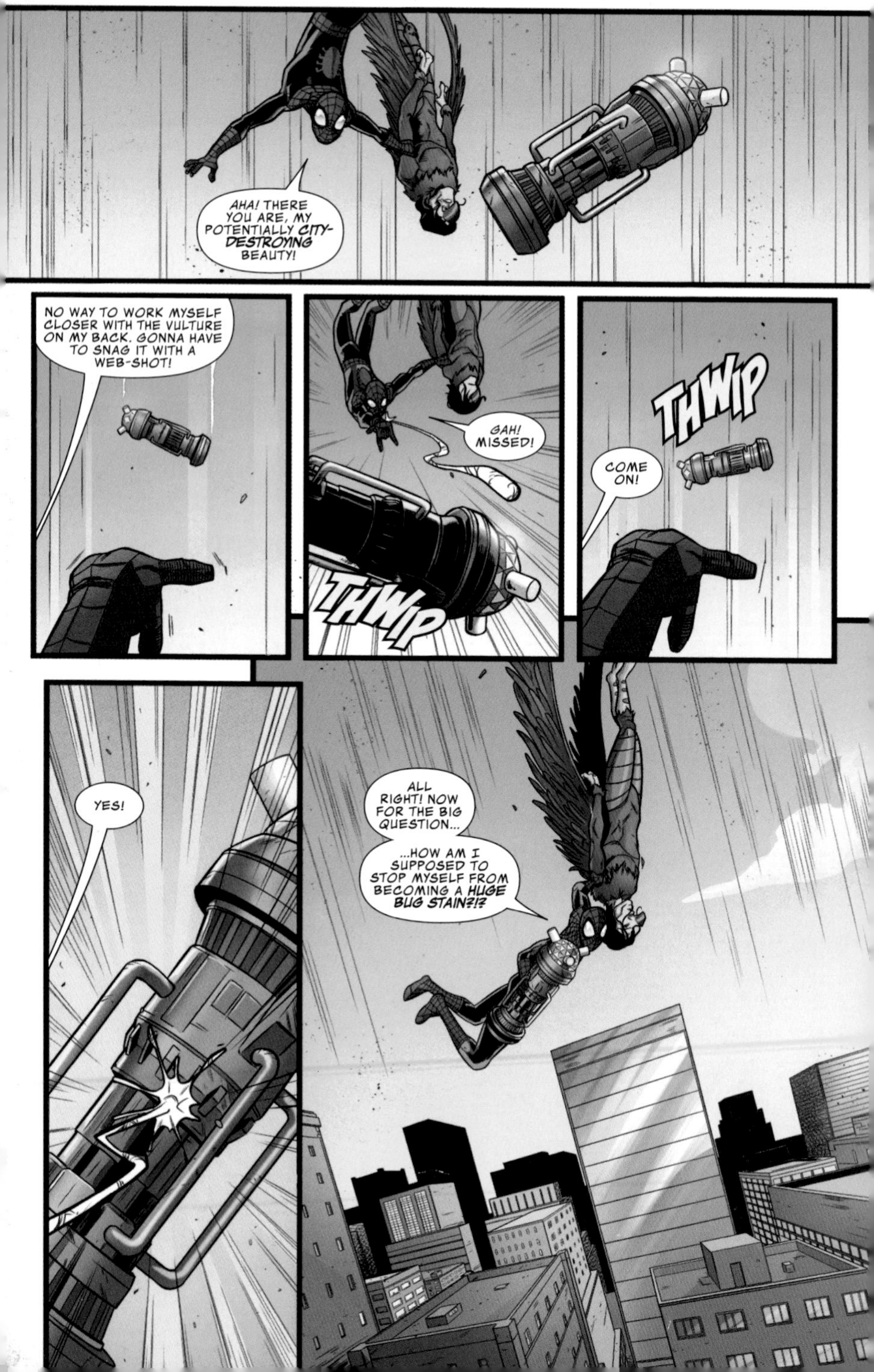
AHA! THERE YOU ARE, MY POTENTIALLY CITY-DESTROYING BEAUTY!
NO WAY TO WORK MYSELF CLOSER WITH THE VULTURE ON MY BACK. GONNA HAVE TO SNAG IT WITH A WEB-SHOT!
THWIP
GAH! MISSED!
THWIP
COME ON!
YES!
ALL RIGHT! NOW FOR THE BIG QUESTION...
...HOW AM I SUPPOSED TO STOP MYSELF FROM BECOMING A HUGE BUG STAIN?!?

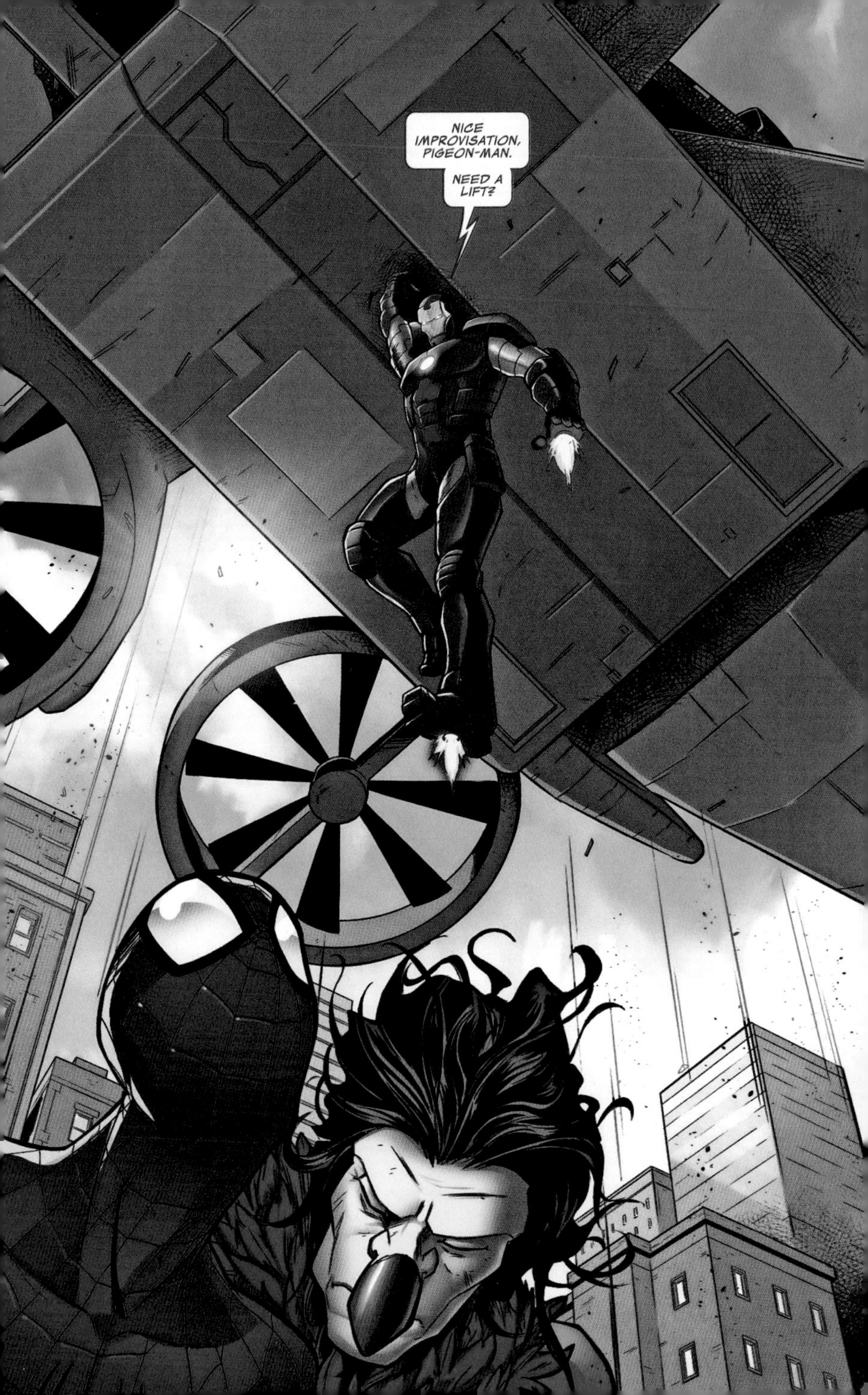
NICE IMPROVISATION, PIGEON-MAN.
NEED A LIFT?

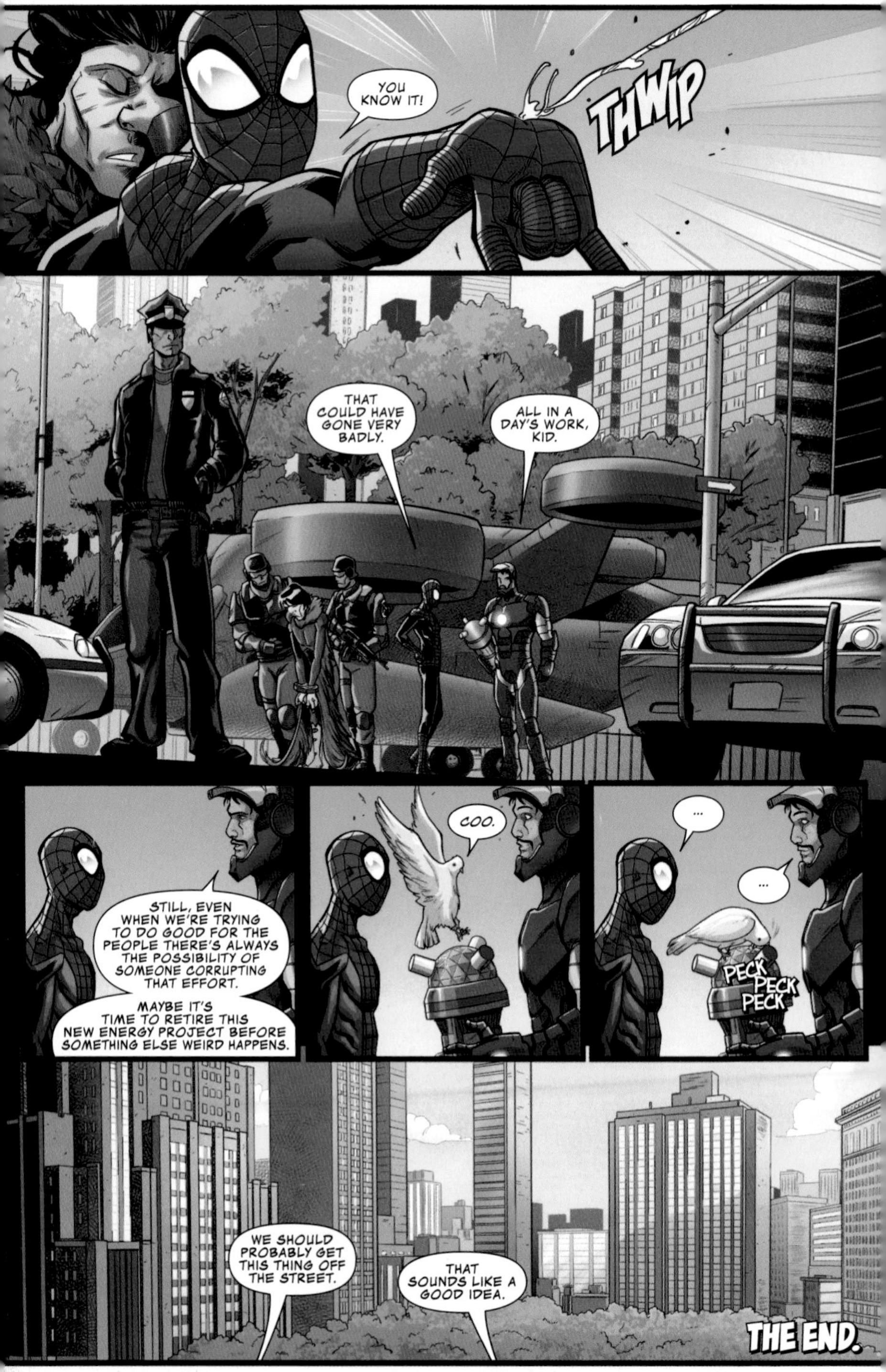
YOU KNOW IT!
THWIP
THAT COULD HAVE GONE VERY BADLY.
ALL IN A DAY'S WORK, KID.
STILL, EVEN WHEN WE'RE TRYING TO DO GOOD FOR THE PEOPLE THERE'S ALWAYS THE POSSIBILITY OF SOMEONE CORRUPTING THAT EFFORT.
MAYBE IT'S TIME TO RETIRE THIS NEW ENERGY PROJECT BEFORE SOMETHING ELSE WEIRD HAPPENS.
COO.
...
...
PECK PECK PECK
WE SHOULD PROBABLY GET THIS THING OFF THE STREET.
THAT SOUNDS LIKE A GOOD IDEA.
THE END.

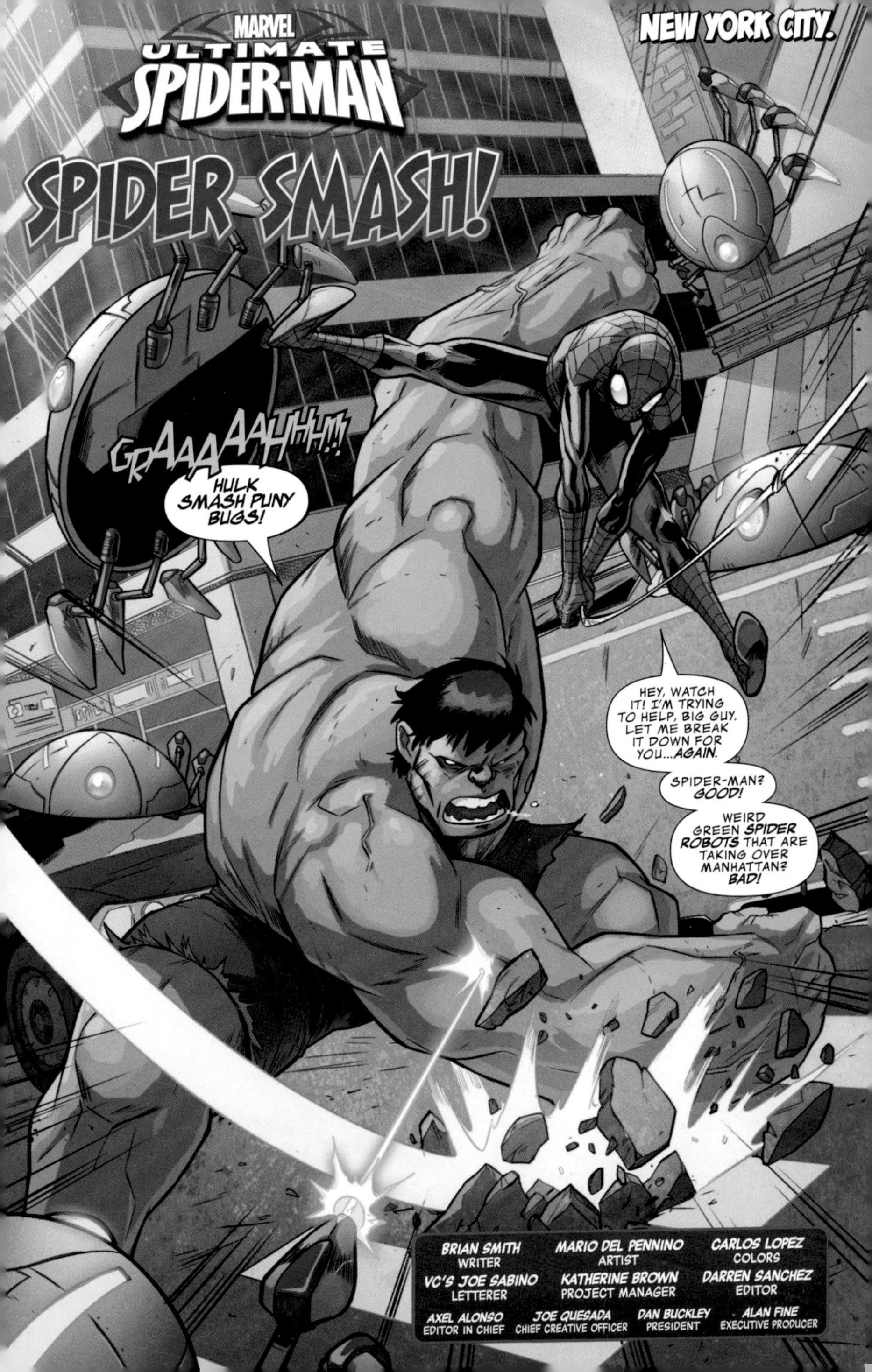
MARVEL
ULTIMATE
SPIDER-MAN
NEW YORK CITY.
SPIDER SMASH!
GRAAAAAHHH!!!
HULK SMASH PUNY BUGS!
HEY, WATCH IT! I'M TRYING TO HELP, BIG GUY. LET ME BREAK IT DOWN FOR YOU...AGAIN.
SPIDER-MAN? GOOD!
WEIRD GREEN SPIDER ROBOTS THAT ARE TAKING OVER MANHATTAN? BAD!
BRIAN SMITH WRITER
MARIO DEL PENNINO ARTIST
CARLOS LOPEZ COLORS
VC'S JOE SABINO LETTERER
KATHERINE BROWN PROJECT MANAGER
DARREN SANCHEZ EDITOR
AXEL ALONSO EDITOR IN CHIEF
JOE QUESADA CHIEF CREATIVE OFFICER
DAN BUCKLEY PRESIDENT
ALAN FINE EXECUTIVE PRODUCER

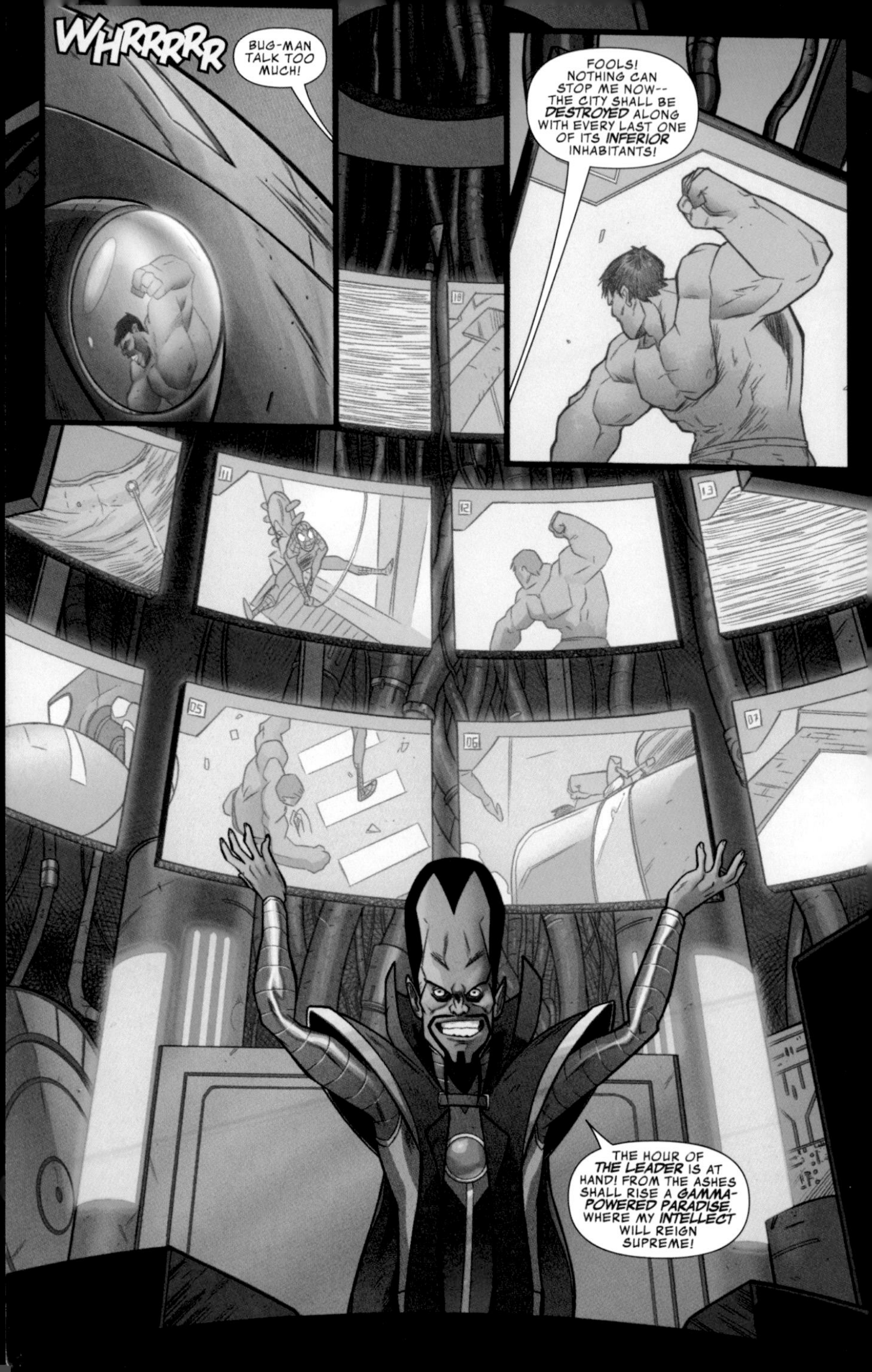
WHRRRRR
BUG-MAN TALK TOO MUCH!
FOOLS! NOTHING CAN STOP ME NOW-- THE CITY SHALL BE DESTROYED ALONG WITH EVERY LAST ONE OF ITS INFERIOR INHABITANTS!
THE HOUR OF THE LEADER IS AT HAND! FROM THE ASHES SHALL RISE A GAMMA-POWERED PARADISE, WHERE MY INTELLECT WILL REIGN SUPREME!

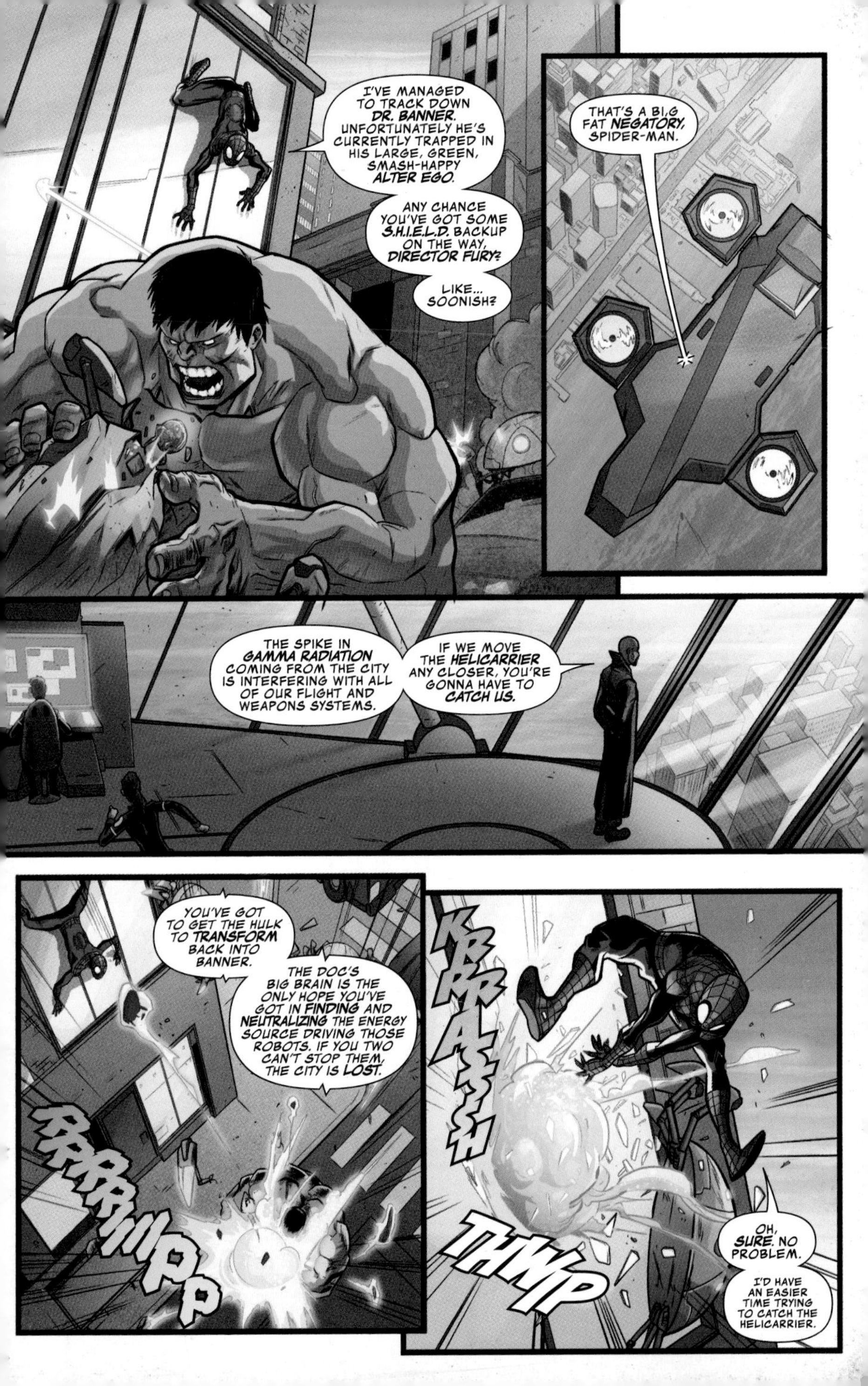
I'VE MANAGED TO TRACK DOWN DR. BANNER. UNFORTUNATELY HE'S CURRENTLY TRAPPED IN HIS LARGE, GREEN, SMASH-HAPPY ALTER EGO.
ANY CHANCE YOU'VE GOT SOME S.H.I.E.L.D. BACKUP ON THE WAY, DIRECTOR FURY?
LIKE... SOONISH?
THAT'S A BIG FAT NEGATORY, SPIDER-MAN.
THE SPIKE IN GAMMA RADIATION COMING FROM THE CITY IS INTERFERING WITH ALL OF OUR FLIGHT AND WEAPONS SYSTEMS.
IF WE MOVE THE HELICARRIER ANY CLOSER, YOU'RE GONNA HAVE TO CATCH US.
YOU'VE GOT TO GET THE HULK TO TRANSFORM BACK INTO BANNER.
THE DOC'S BIG BRAIN IS THE ONLY HOPE YOU'VE GOT IN FINDING AND NEUTRALIZING THE ENERGY SOURCE DRIVING THOSE ROBOTS. IF YOU TWO CAN'T STOP THEM, THE CITY IS LOST.
RRRRIIIPP
KRRAASSH
THWIP
OH, SURE. NO PROBLEM.
I'D HAVE AN EASIER TIME TRYING TO CATCH THE HELICARRIER.

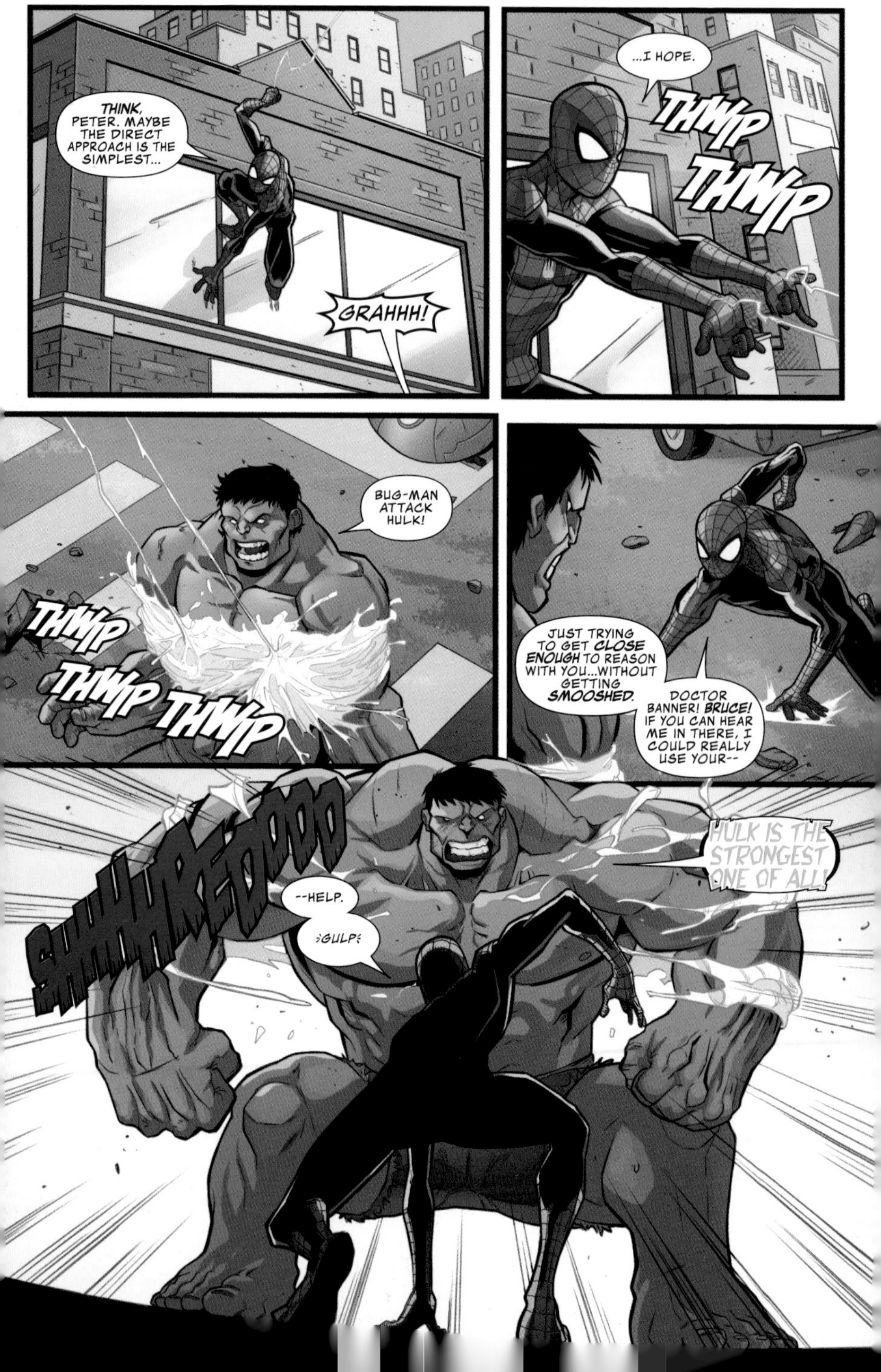
THINK, PETER. MAYBE THE DIRECT APPROACH IS THE SIMPLEST...
GRAHHH!
...I HOPE.
THWIP
THWIP
BUG-MAN ATTACK HULK!
THWIP
THWIP
THWIP
JUST TRYING TO GET CLOSE ENOUGH TO REASON WITH YOU...WITHOUT GETTING SMOOSHED.
DOCTOR BANNER! BRUCE! IF YOU CAN HEAR ME IN THERE, I COULD REALLY USE YOUR--
SHHHRRRED
HULK IS THE STRONGEST ONE OF ALL!
--HELP.
GULP

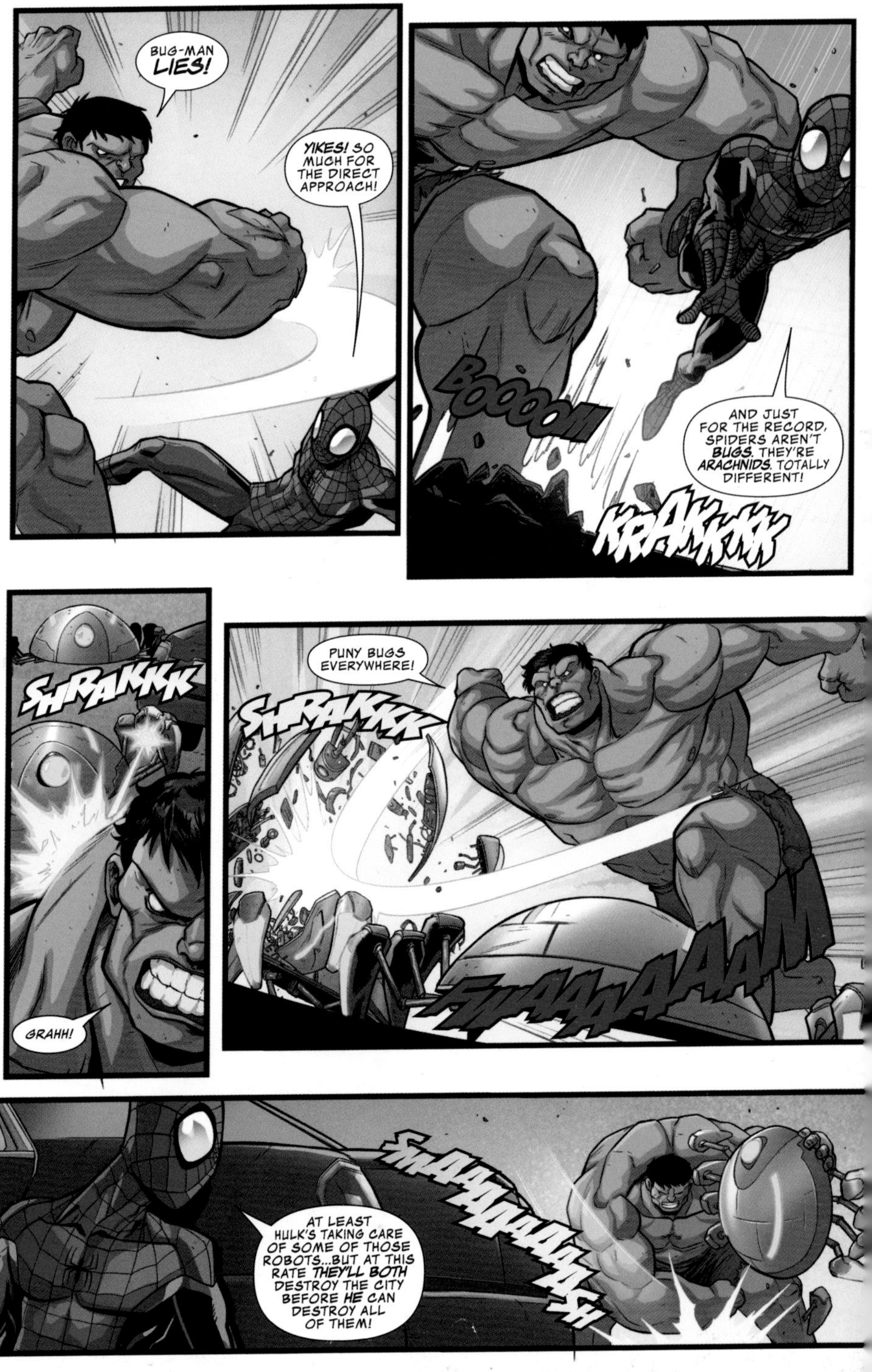
BUG-MAN LIES!
YIKES! SO MUCH FOR THE DIRECT APPROACH!
BOOOOOM
AND JUST FOR THE RECORD, SPIDERS AREN'T BUGS. THEY'RE ARACHNIDS. TOTALLY DIFFERENT!
KRAKKKK
SHRAKKK
GRAHH!
PUNY BUGS EVERYWHERE!
SHRAKKK
FWAAAAAAAAM
SHAAAAAAAASH
AT LEAST HULK'S TAKING CARE OF SOME OF THOSE ROBOTS...BUT AT THIS RATE THEY'LL BOTH DESTROY THE CITY BEFORE HE CAN DESTROY ALL OF THEM!

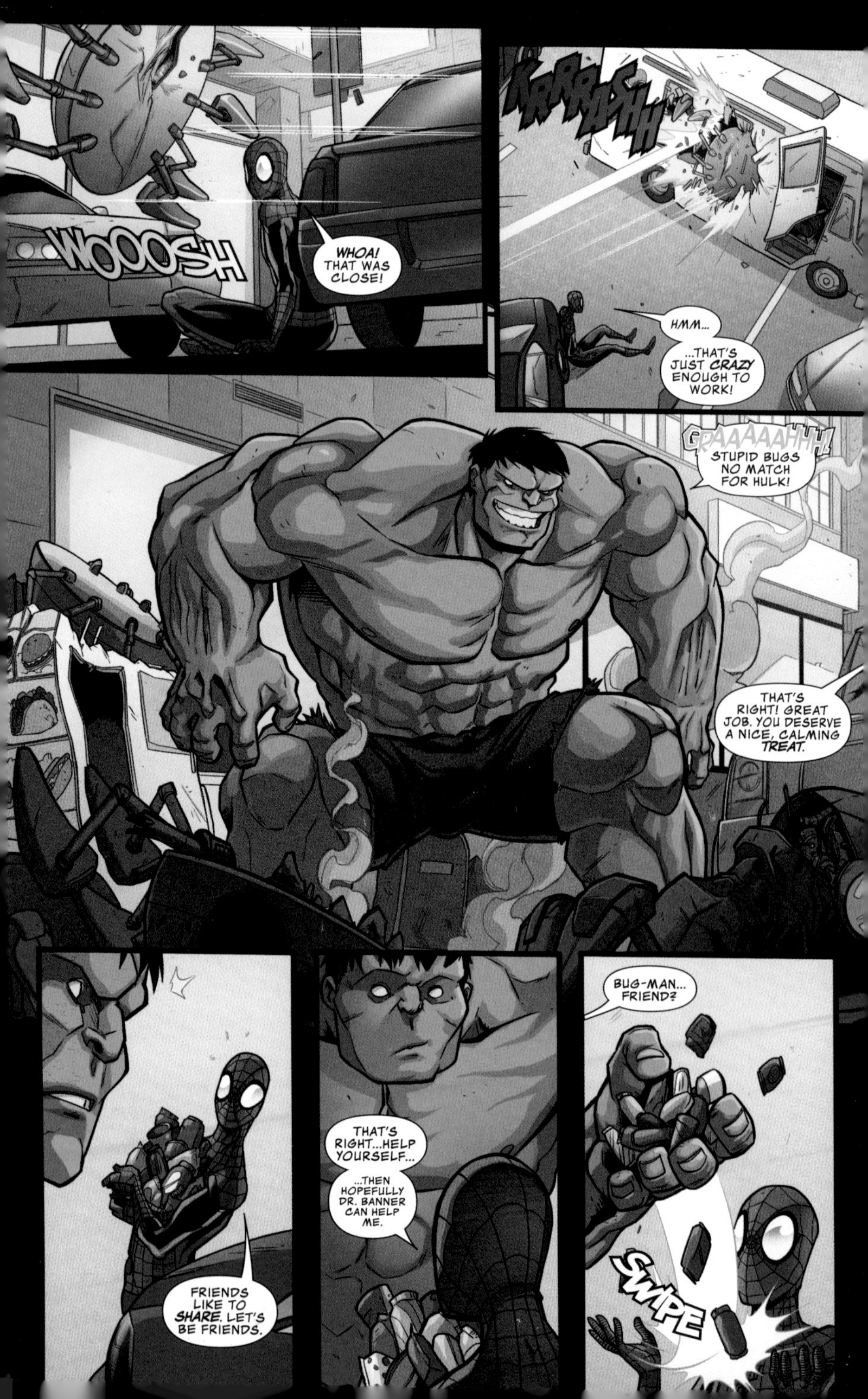
WOOOSH
WHOA! THAT WAS CLOSE!
KRRRASHHH
HMM...
...THAT'S JUST CRAZY ENOUGH TO WORK!
GRAAAAAHHH!
STUPID BUGS NO MATCH FOR HULK!
THAT'S RIGHT! GREAT JOB. YOU DESERVE A NICE, CALMING TREAT.
FRIENDS LIKE TO SHARE. LET'S BE FRIENDS.
THAT'S RIGHT...HELP YOURSELF...
...THEN HOPEFULLY DR. BANNER CAN HELP ME.
BUG-MAN... FRIEND?
SWIPE

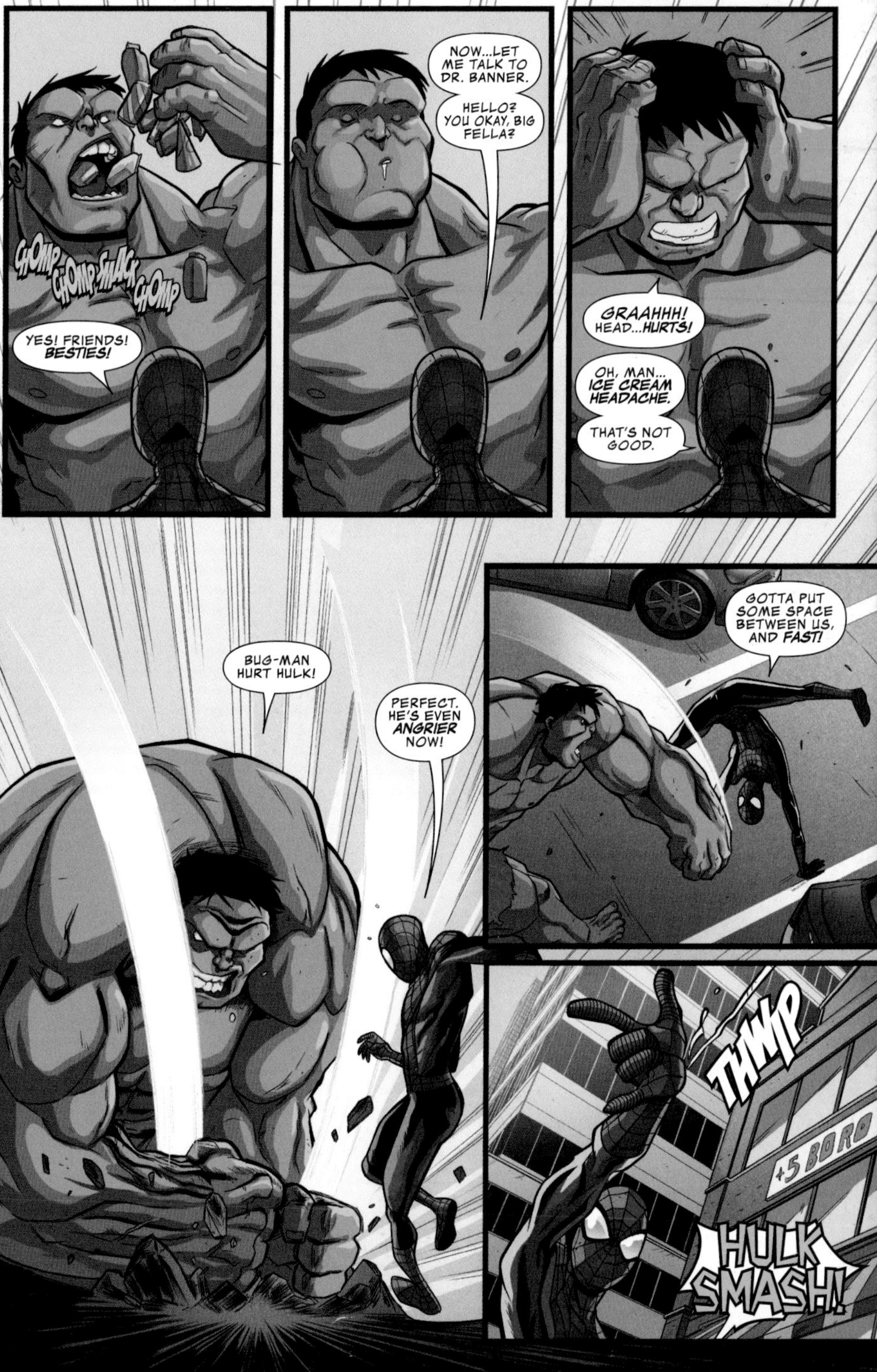
CHOMP CHOMP SMACK CHOMP
YES! FRIENDS! BESTIES!
NOW...LET ME TALK TO DR. BANNER.
HELLO? YOU OKAY, BIG FELLA?
GRAAHHH! HEAD...HURTS!
OH, MAN... ICE CREAM HEADACHE.
THAT'S NOT GOOD.
BUG-MAN HURT HULK!
PERFECT. HE'S EVEN ANGRIER NOW!
GOTTA PUT SOME SPACE BETWEEN US, AND FAST!
THWIP
HULK SMASH!

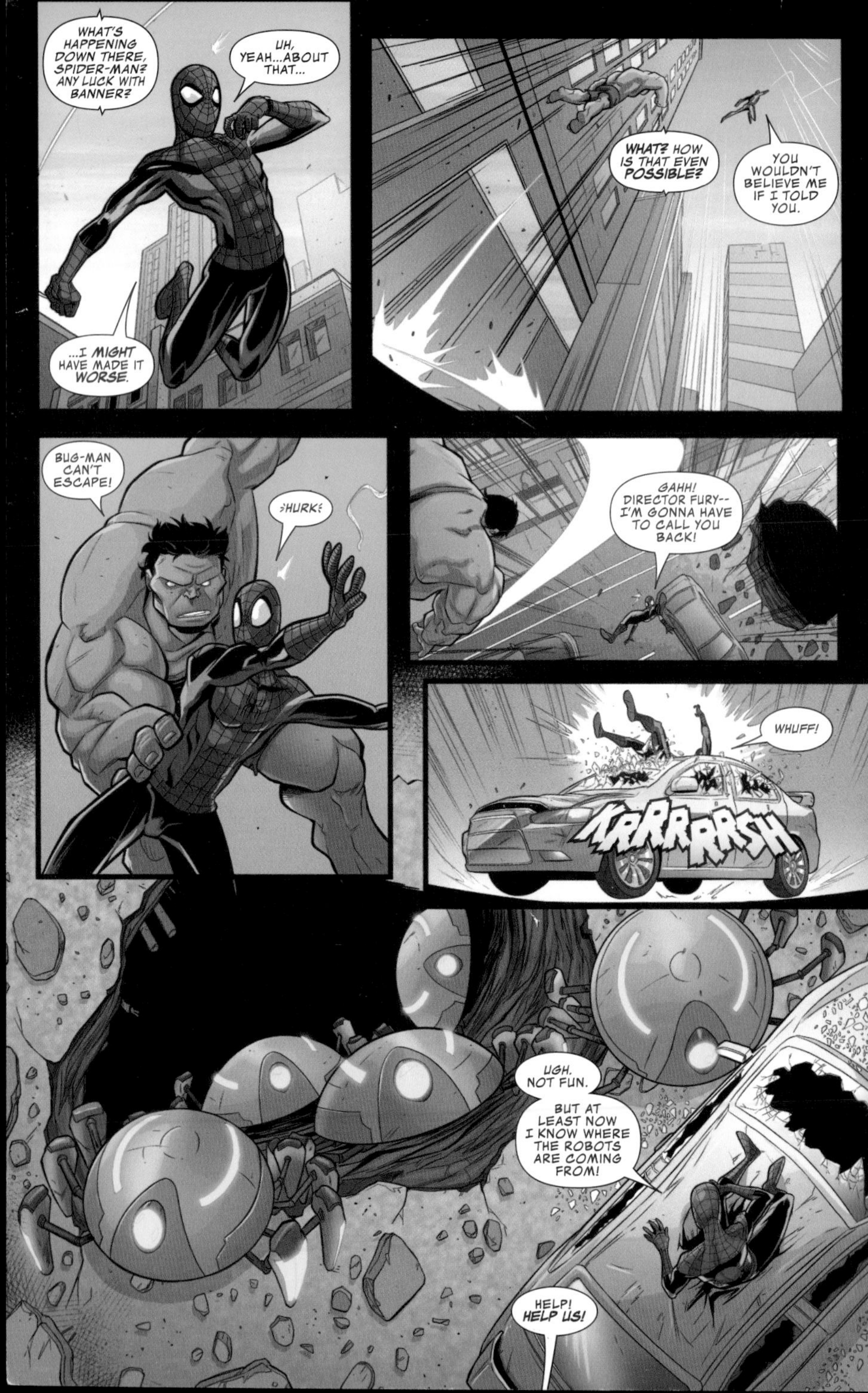
WHAT'S HAPPENING DOWN THERE, SPIDER-MAN? ANY LUCK WITH BANNER?
UH, YEAH...ABOUT THAT...
...I MIGHT HAVE MADE IT WORSE.
WHAT? HOW IS THAT EVEN POSSIBLE?
YOU WOULDN'T BELIEVE ME IF I TOLD YOU.
BUG-MAN CAN'T ESCAPE!
HURK
GAHH! DIRECTOR FURY-- I'M GONNA HAVE TO CALL YOU BACK!
WHUFF!
KRRRRRSH
UGH. NOT FUN.
BUT AT LEAST NOW I KNOW WHERE THE ROBOTS ARE COMING FROM!
HELP! HELP US!

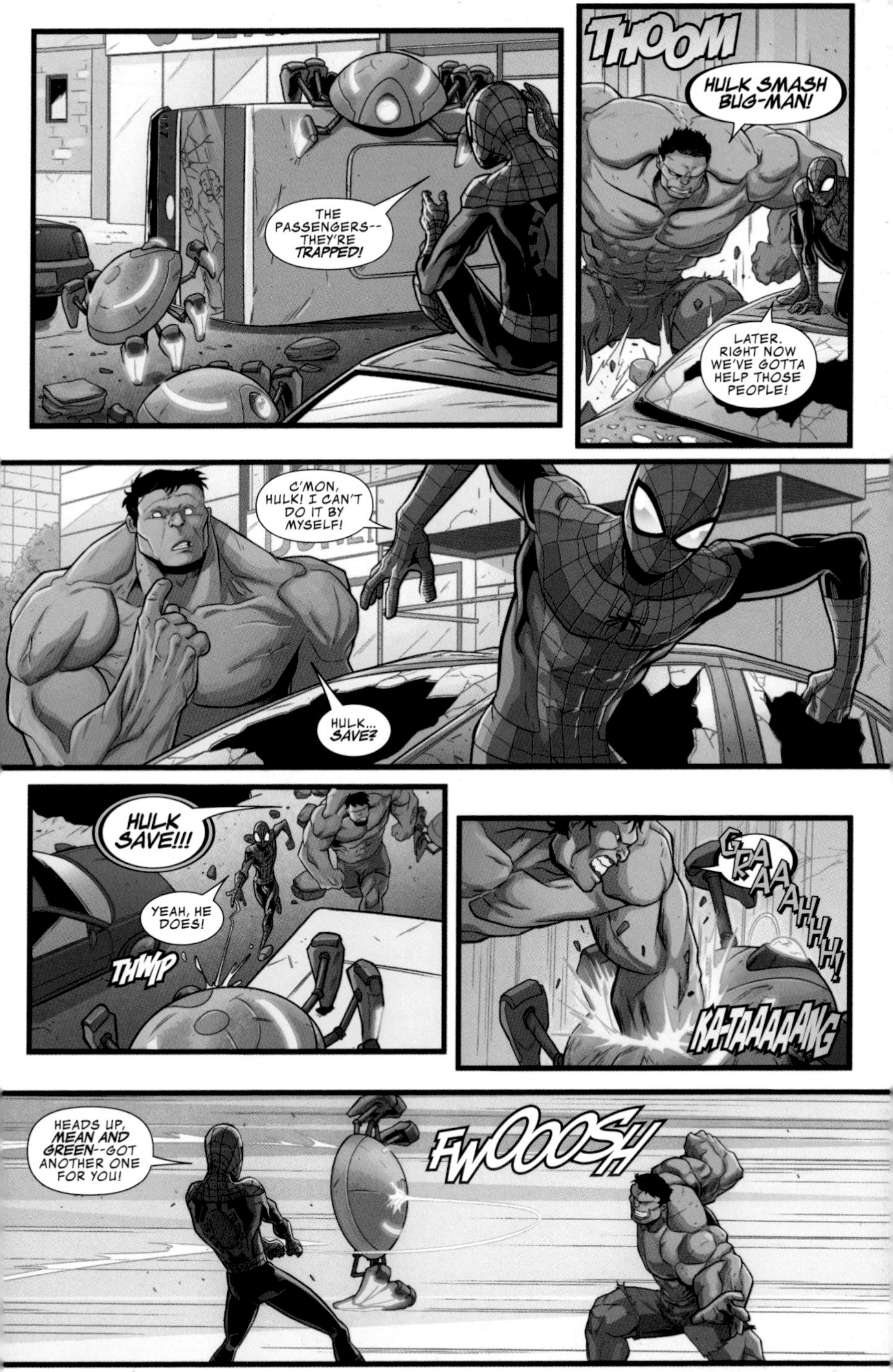
THE PASSENGERS--THEY'RE TRAPPED!
THOOM
HULK SMASH BUG-MAN!
LATER. RIGHT NOW WE'VE GOTTA HELP THOSE PEOPLE!
C'MON, HULK! I CAN'T DO IT BY MYSELF!
HULK... SAVE?
HULK SAVE!!!
YEAH, HE DOES!
THWIP
GRAAAAHHHH!
KA-TAAAAANG
HEADS UP, MEAN AND GREEN--GOT ANOTHER ONE FOR YOU!
FWOOOOSH

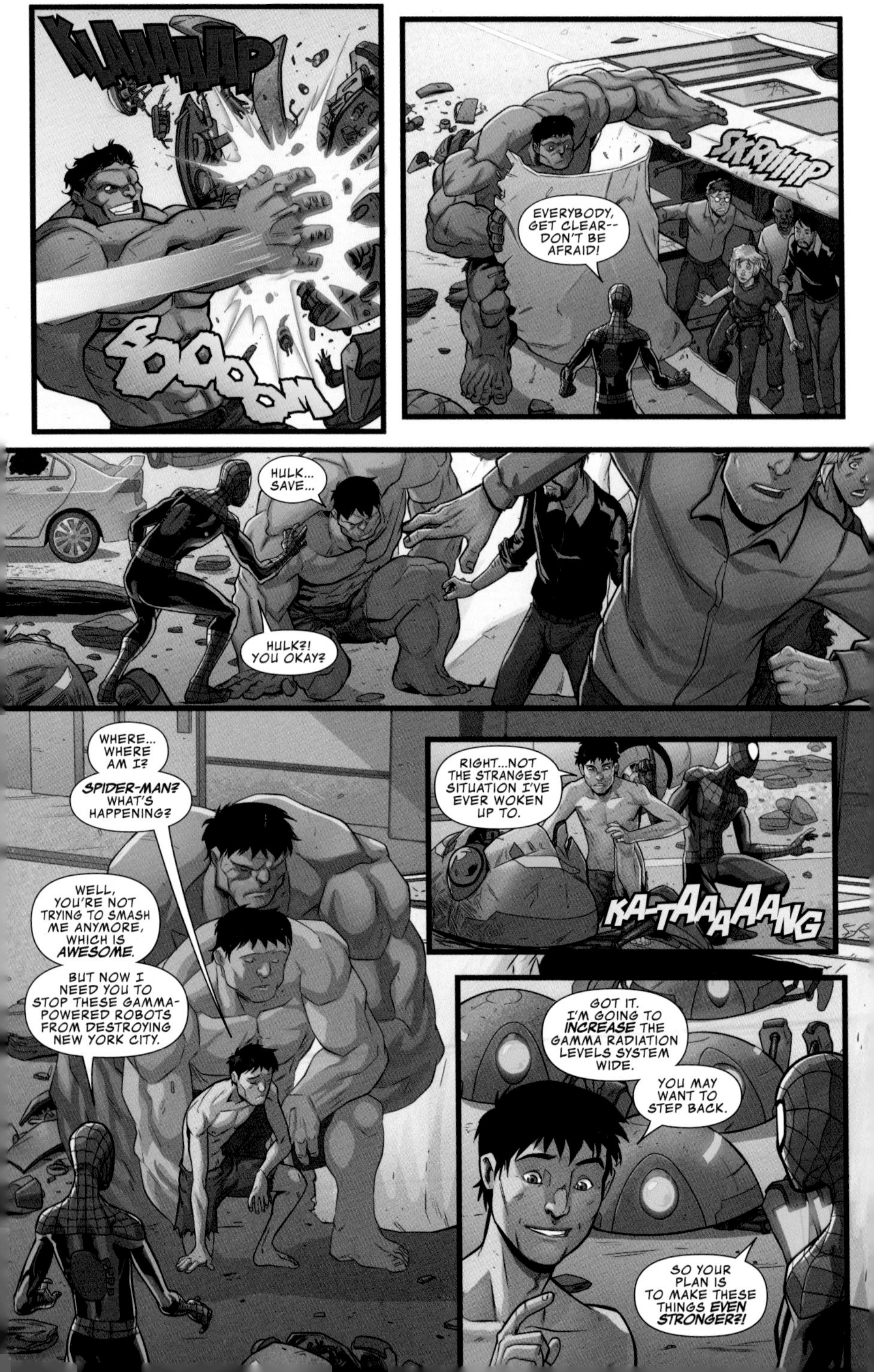
BOOOOM
SKRIIIP
EVERYBODY, GET CLEAR-- DON'T BE AFRAID!
HULK... SAVE...
HULK?! YOU OKAY?
WHERE... WHERE AM I?
SPIDER-MAN? WHAT'S HAPPENING?
WELL, YOU'RE NOT TRYING TO SMASH ME ANYMORE, WHICH IS AWESOME.
BUT NOW I NEED YOU TO STOP THESE GAMMA-POWERED ROBOTS FROM DESTROYING NEW YORK CITY.
RIGHT...NOT THE STRANGEST SITUATION I'VE EVER WOKEN UP TO.
KA-TAAAAAANG
GOT IT. I'M GOING TO INCREASE THE GAMMA RADIATION LEVELS SYSTEM WIDE.
YOU MAY WANT TO STEP BACK.
SO YOUR PLAN IS TO MAKE THESE THINGS EVEN STRONGER?!

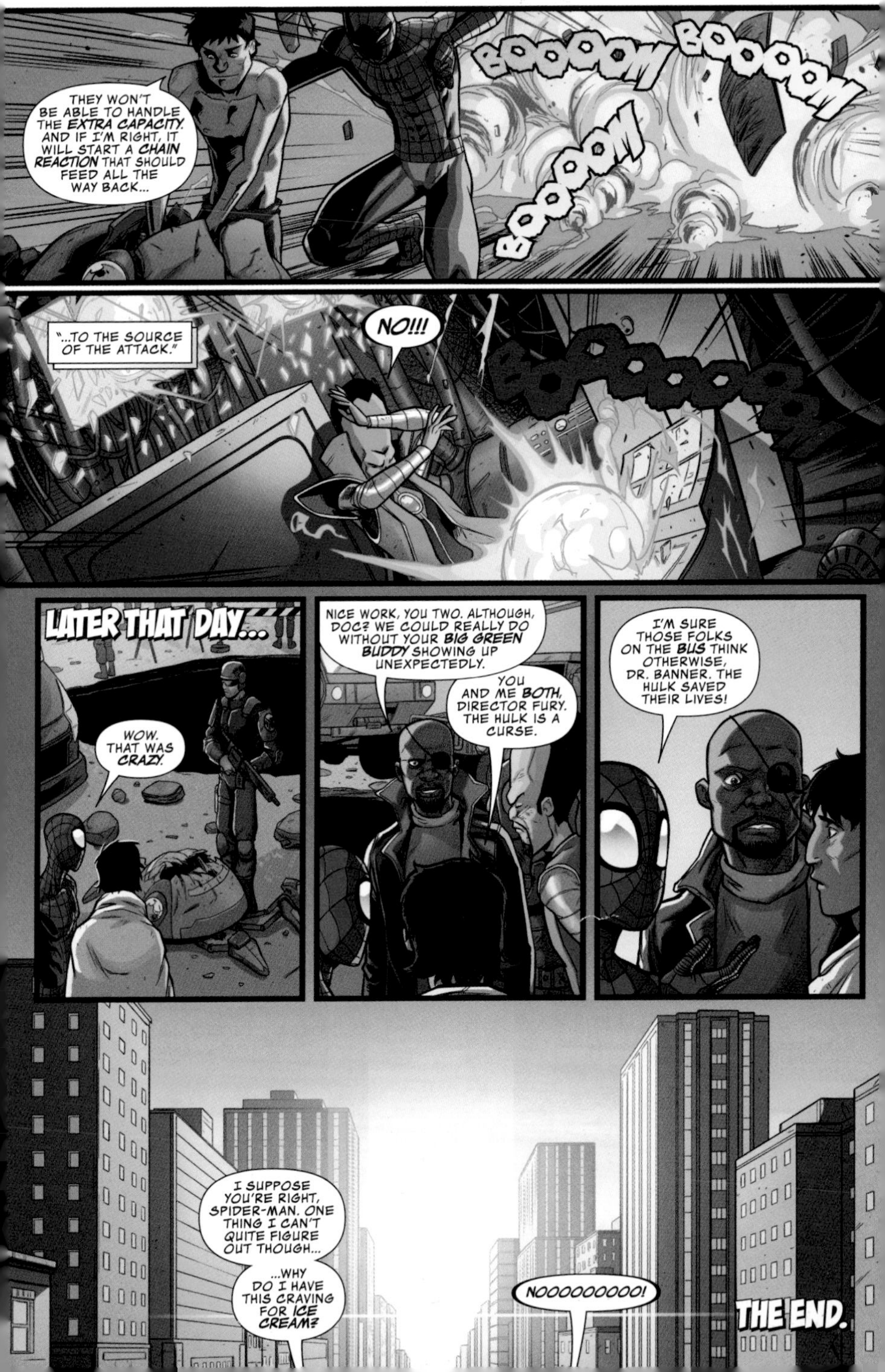
THEY WON'T BE ABLE TO HANDLE THE EXTRA CAPACITY. AND IF I'M RIGHT, IT WILL START A CHAIN REACTION THAT SHOULD FEED ALL THE WAY BACK...
BOOOOM BOOOOM
BOOOOOM
"...TO THE SOURCE OF THE ATTACK."
NO!!!
BOOOOOOM
LATER THAT DAY...
WOW. THAT WAS CRAZY.
NICE WORK, YOU TWO. ALTHOUGH, DOC? WE COULD REALLY DO WITHOUT YOUR BIG GREEN BUDDY SHOWING UP UNEXPECTEDLY.
YOU AND ME BOTH, DIRECTOR FURY. THE HULK IS A CURSE.
I'M SURE THOSE FOLKS ON THE BUS THINK OTHERWISE, DR. BANNER. THE HULK SAVED THEIR LIVES!
I SUPPOSE YOU'RE RIGHT, SPIDER-MAN. ONE THING I CAN'T QUITE FIGURE OUT THOUGH...
...WHY DO I HAVE THIS CRAVING FOR ICE CREAM?
NOOOOOOOOO!
THE END.

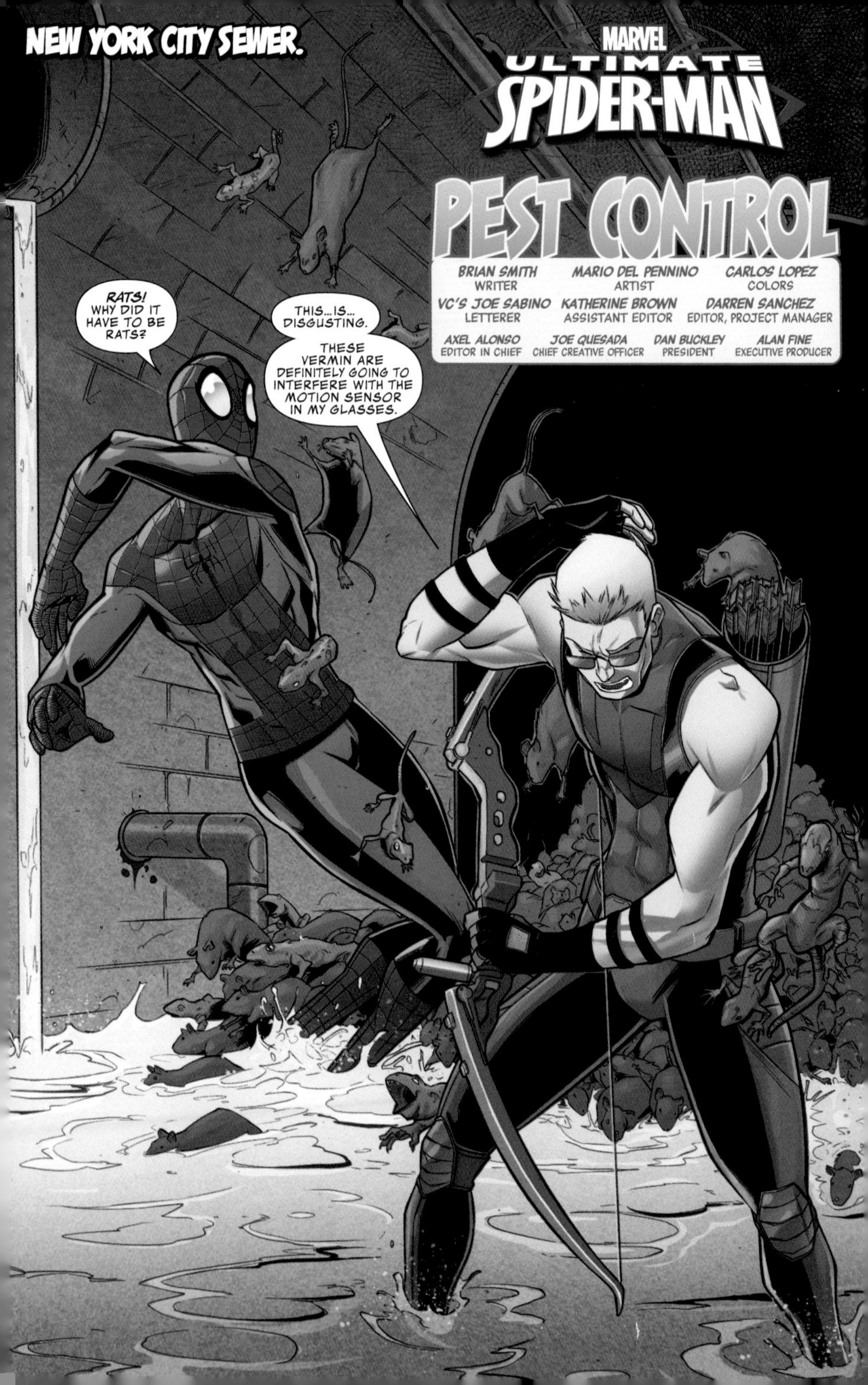
NEW YORK CITY SEWER.
MARVEL ULTIMATE SPIDER-MAN
PEST CONTROL
BRIAN SMITH WRITER
MARIO DEL PENNINO ARTIST
CARLOS LOPEZ COLORS
VC'S JOE SABINO LETTERER
KATHERINE BROWN ASSISTANT EDITOR
DARREN SANCHEZ EDITOR, PROJECT MANAGER
AXEL ALONSO EDITOR IN CHIEF
JOE QUESADA CHIEF CREATIVE OFFICER
DAN BUCKLEY PRESIDENT
ALAN FINE EXECUTIVE PRODUCER
RATS! WHY DID IT HAVE TO BE RATS?
THIS...IS... DISGUSTING.
THESE VERMIN ARE DEFINITELY GOING TO INTERFERE WITH THE MOTION SENSOR IN MY GLASSES.

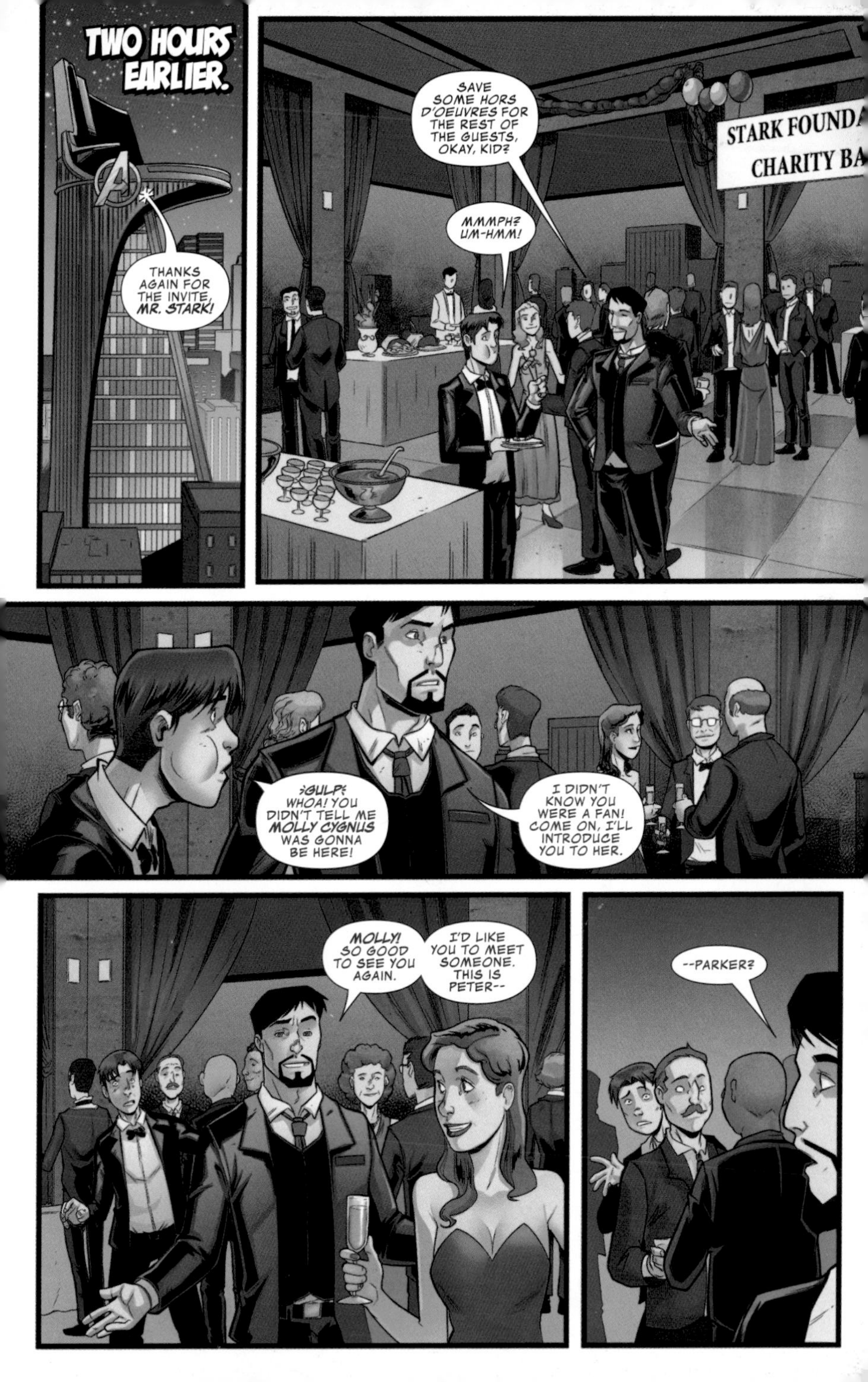
TWO HOURS EARLIER.
THANKS AGAIN FOR THE INVITE, MR. STARK!
SAVE SOME HORS D'OEUVRES FOR THE REST OF THE GUESTS, OKAY, KID?
MMMPH? UM-HMM!
STARK FOUNDA
CHARITY BA
GULP WHOA! YOU DIDN'T TELL ME MOLLY CYGNUS WAS GONNA BE HERE!
I DIDN'T KNOW YOU WERE A FAN! COME ON, I'LL INTRODUCE YOU TO HER.
MOLLY! SO GOOD TO SEE YOU AGAIN.
I'D LIKE YOU TO MEET SOMEONE. THIS IS PETER--
--PARKER?

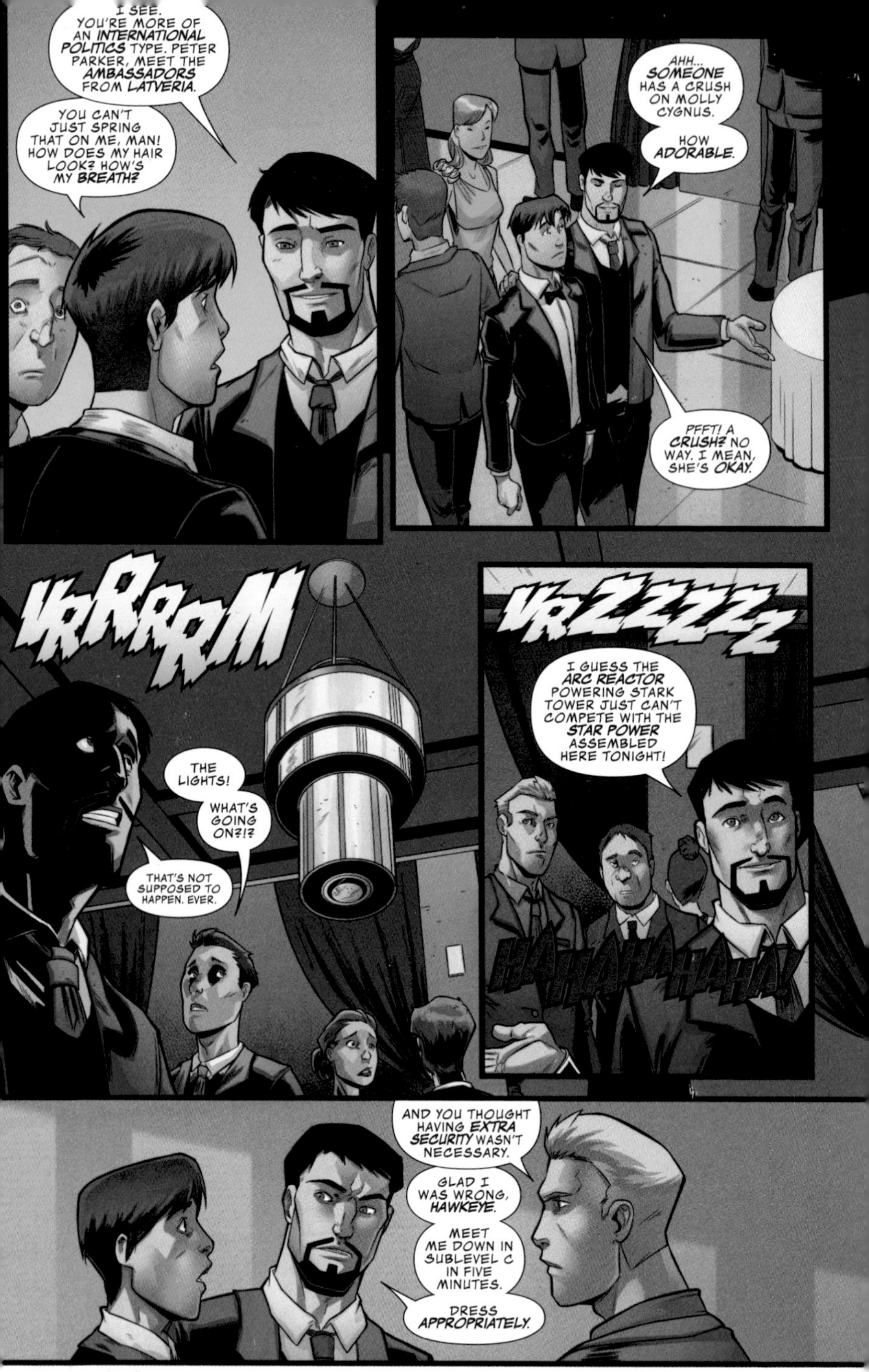

I SEE. YOU'RE MORE OF AN INTERNATIONAL POLITICS TYPE. PETER PARKER, MEET THE AMBASSADORS FROM LATVERIA.
YOU CAN'T JUST SPRING THAT ON ME, MAN! HOW DOES MY HAIR LOOK? HOW'S MY BREATH?
AHH... SOMEONE HAS A CRUSH ON MOLLY CYGNUS.
HOW ADORABLE.
PFFT! A CRUSH? NO WAY. I MEAN, SHE'S OKAY.
VRRRRM
THE LIGHTS!
WHAT'S GOING ON?!?
THAT'S NOT SUPPOSED TO HAPPEN. EVER.
VRZZZZZZ
I GUESS THE ARC REACTOR POWERING STARK TOWER JUST CAN'T COMPETE WITH THE STAR POWER ASSEMBLED HERE TONIGHT!
HAHAHAHAHAHA!
AND YOU THOUGHT HAVING EXTRA SECURITY WASN'T NECESSARY.
GLAD I WAS WRONG, HAWKEYE.
MEET ME DOWN IN SUBLEVEL C IN FIVE MINUTES.
DRESS APPROPRIATELY.

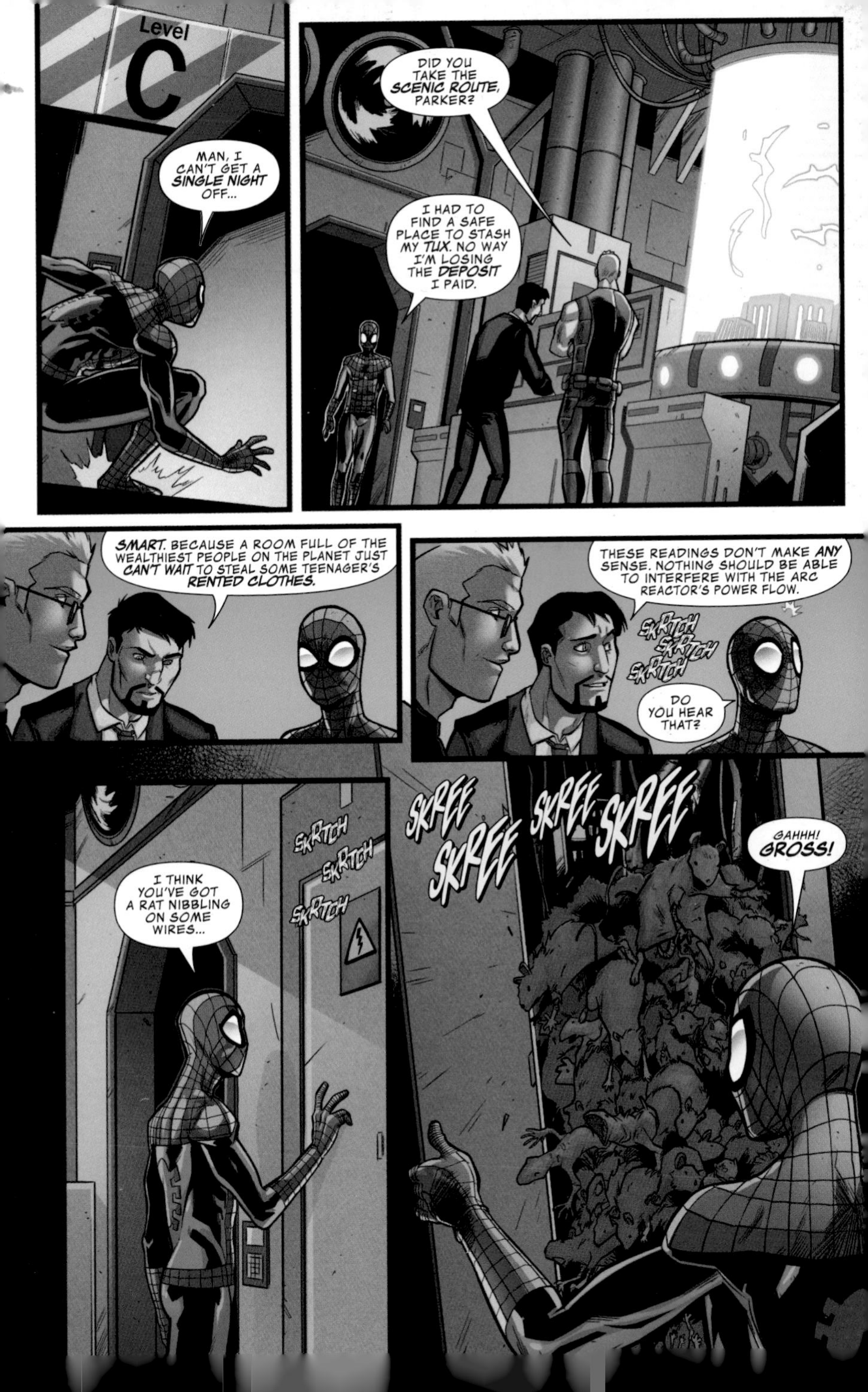
Level
C
MAN, I CAN'T GET A SINGLE NIGHT OFF...
DID YOU TAKE THE SCENIC ROUTE, PARKER?
I HAD TO FIND A SAFE PLACE TO STASH MY TUX. NO WAY I'M LOSING THE DEPOSIT I PAID.
SMART. BECAUSE A ROOM FULL OF THE WEALTHIEST PEOPLE ON THE PLANET JUST CAN'T WAIT TO STEAL SOME TEENAGER'S RENTED CLOTHES.
THESE READINGS DON'T MAKE ANY SENSE. NOTHING SHOULD BE ABLE TO INTERFERE WITH THE ARC REACTOR'S POWER FLOW.
SKRTCH SKRTCH SKRTCH
DO YOU HEAR THAT?
SKRTCH SKRTCH SKRTCH
I THINK YOU'VE GOT A RAT NIBBLING ON SOME WIRES...
SKREE SKREE SKREE SKREE
GAHHH! GROSS!

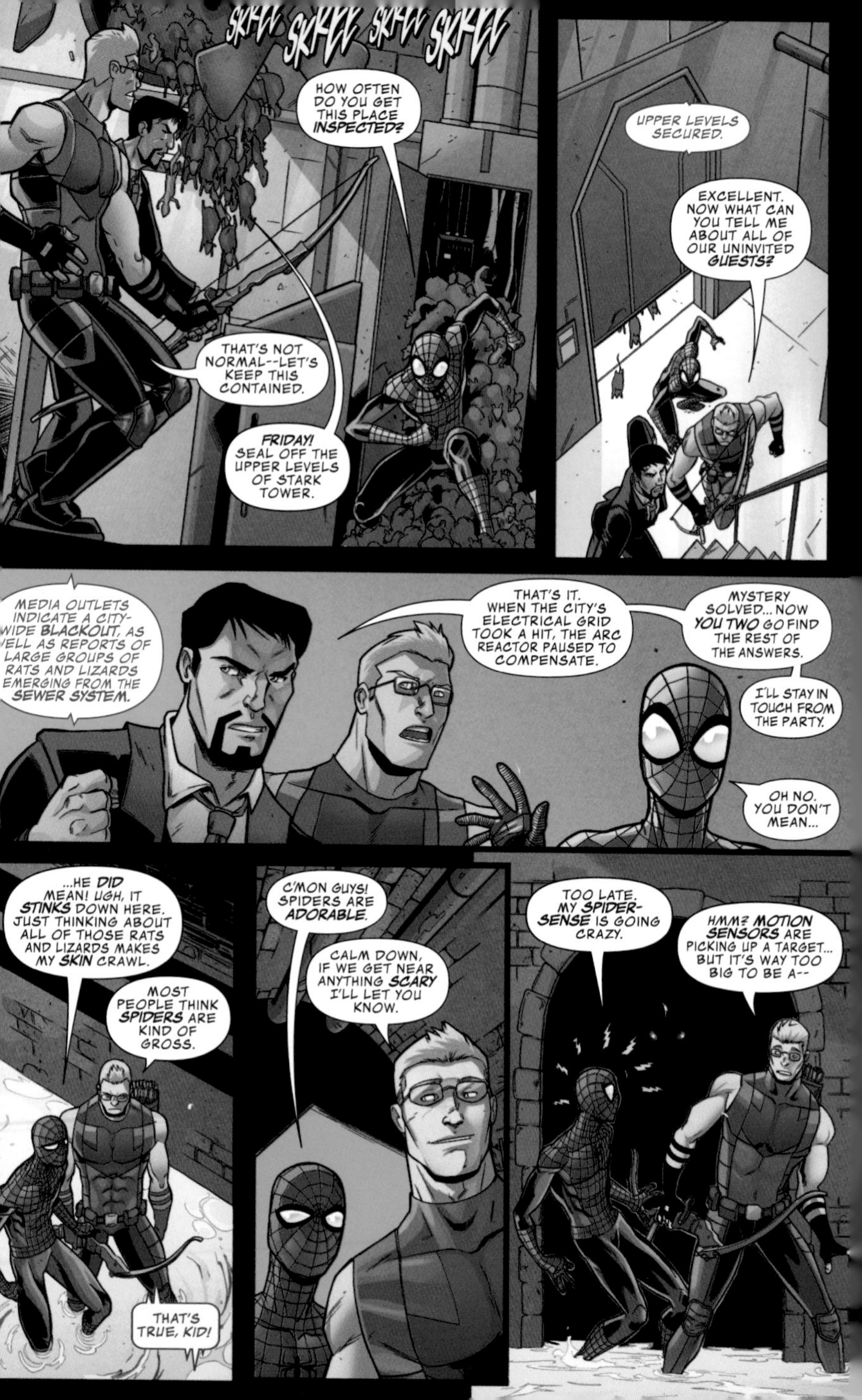
SKREE SKREE SKREE SKREE
HOW OFTEN DO YOU GET THIS PLACE INSPECTED?
THAT'S NOT NORMAL--LET'S KEEP THIS CONTAINED.
FRIDAY! SEAL OFF THE UPPER LEVELS OF STARK TOWER.
UPPER LEVELS SECURED.
EXCELLENT. NOW WHAT CAN YOU TELL ME ABOUT ALL OF OUR UNINVITED GUESTS?
MEDIA OUTLETS INDICATE A CITY-WIDE BLACKOUT, AS WELL AS REPORTS OF LARGE GROUPS OF RATS AND LIZARDS EMERGING FROM THE SEWER SYSTEM.
THAT'S IT. WHEN THE CITY'S ELECTRICAL GRID TOOK A HIT, THE ARC REACTOR PAUSED TO COMPENSATE.
MYSTERY SOLVED... NOW YOU TWO GO FIND THE REST OF THE ANSWERS.
I'LL STAY IN TOUCH FROM THE PARTY.
OH NO. YOU DON'T MEAN...
...HE DID MEAN! UGH, IT STINKS DOWN HERE. JUST THINKING ABOUT ALL OF THOSE RATS AND LIZARDS MAKES MY SKIN CRAWL.
MOST PEOPLE THINK SPIDERS ARE KIND OF GROSS.
THAT'S TRUE, KID!
C'MON GUYS! SPIDERS ARE ADORABLE.
CALM DOWN, IF WE GET NEAR ANYTHING SCARY I'LL LET YOU KNOW.
TOO LATE. MY SPIDER-SENSE IS GOING CRAZY.
HMM? MOTION SENSORS ARE PICKING UP A TARGET... BUT IT'S WAY TOO BIG TO BE A--

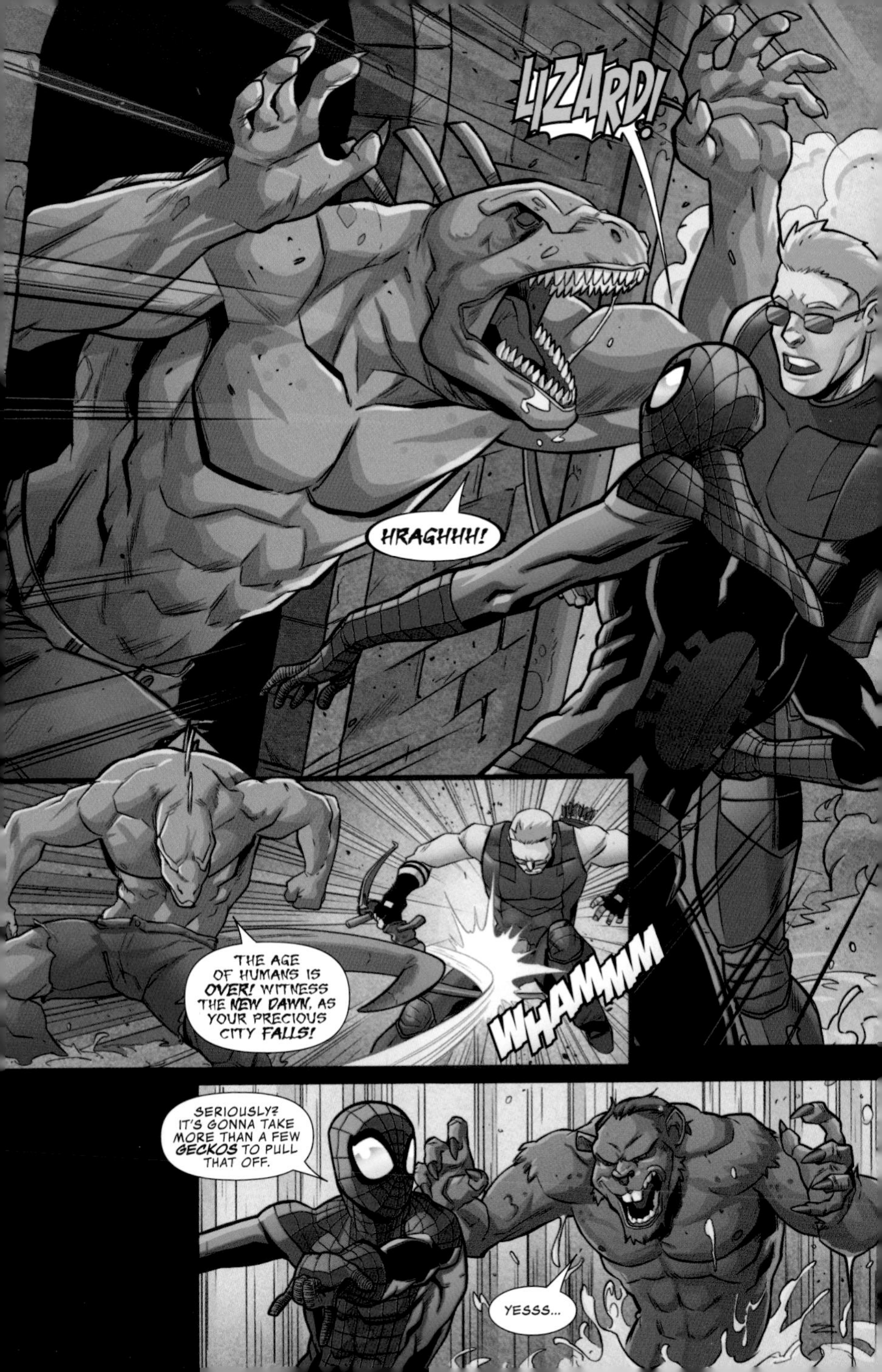
LIZARD!
HRAGHHH!
THE AGE OF HUMANS IS OVER! WITNESS THE NEW DAWN, AS YOUR PRECIOUS CITY FALLS!
WHAMMM
SERIOUSLY? IT'S GONNA TAKE MORE THAN A FEW GECKOS TO PULL THAT OFF.
YESSS...

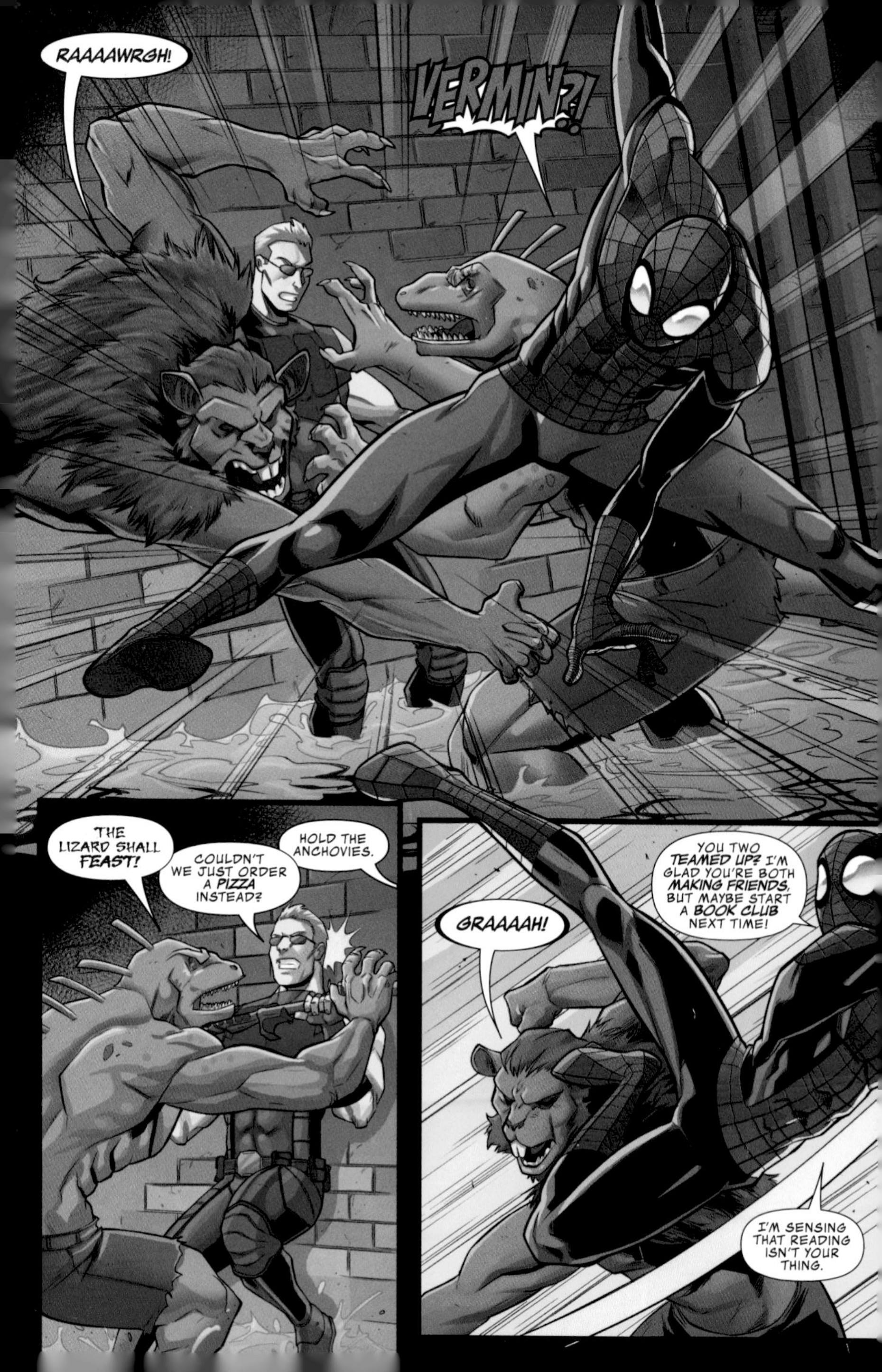
RAAAAWRGH!
VERMIN?!
THE LIZARD SHALL FEAST!
COULDN'T WE JUST ORDER A PIZZA INSTEAD?
HOLD THE ANCHOVIES.
YOU TWO TEAMED UP? I'M GLAD YOU'RE BOTH MAKING FRIENDS, BUT MAYBE START A BOOK CLUB NEXT TIME!
GRAAAAH!
I'M SENSING THAT READING ISN'T YOUR THING.

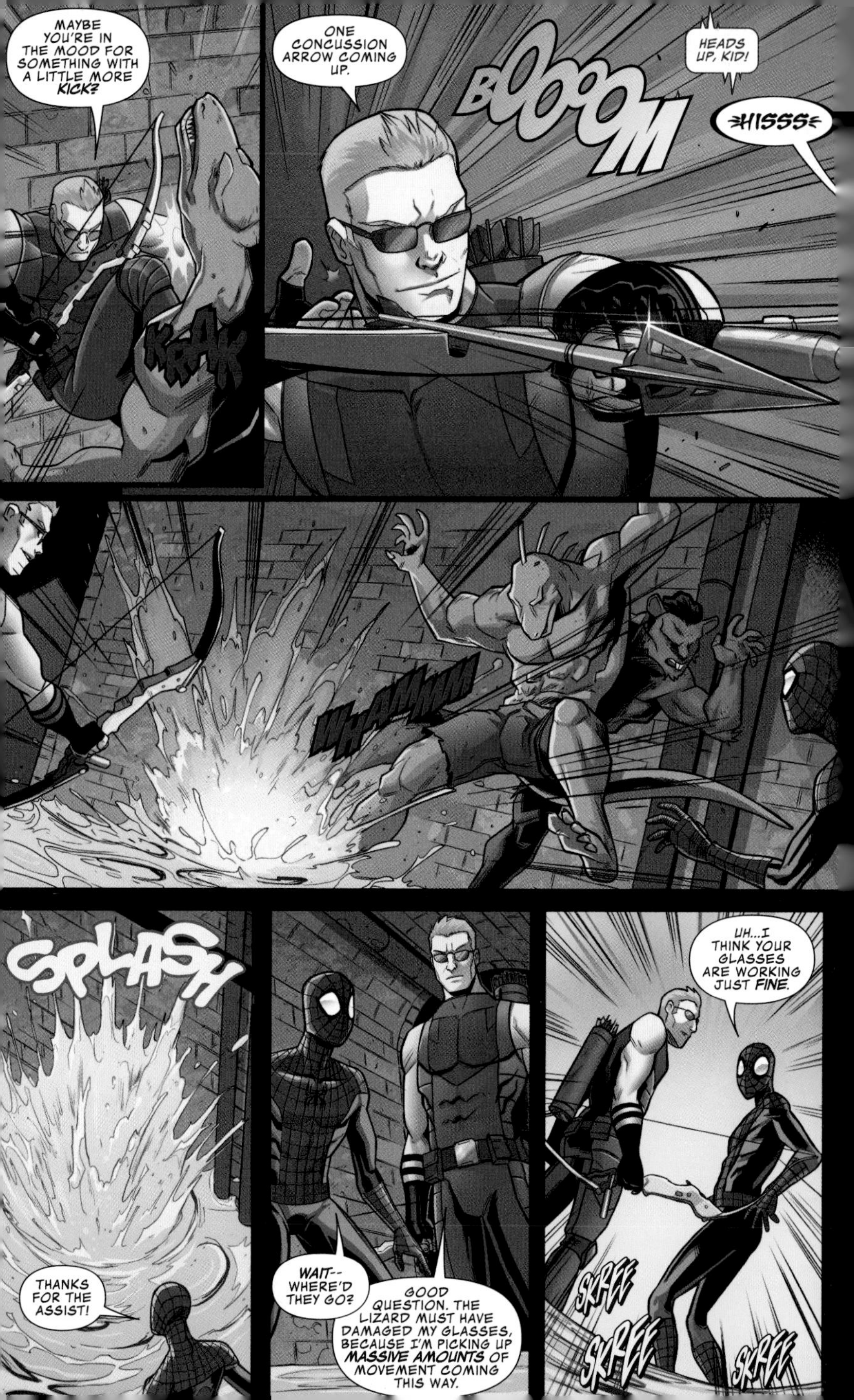
MAYBE YOU'RE IN THE MOOD FOR SOMETHING WITH A LITTLE MORE KICK?
KRAK
ONE CONCUSSION ARROW COMING UP.
BOOOOM
HEADS UP, KID!
HISSS
WHAMMM
SPLASH
THANKS FOR THE ASSIST!
WAIT-- WHERE'D THEY GO?
GOOD QUESTION. THE LIZARD MUST HAVE DAMAGED MY GLASSES, BECAUSE I'M PICKING UP MASSIVE AMOUNTS OF MOVEMENT COMING THIS WAY.
UH...I THINK YOUR GLASSES ARE WORKING JUST FINE.
SKREE
SKREE
SKREE

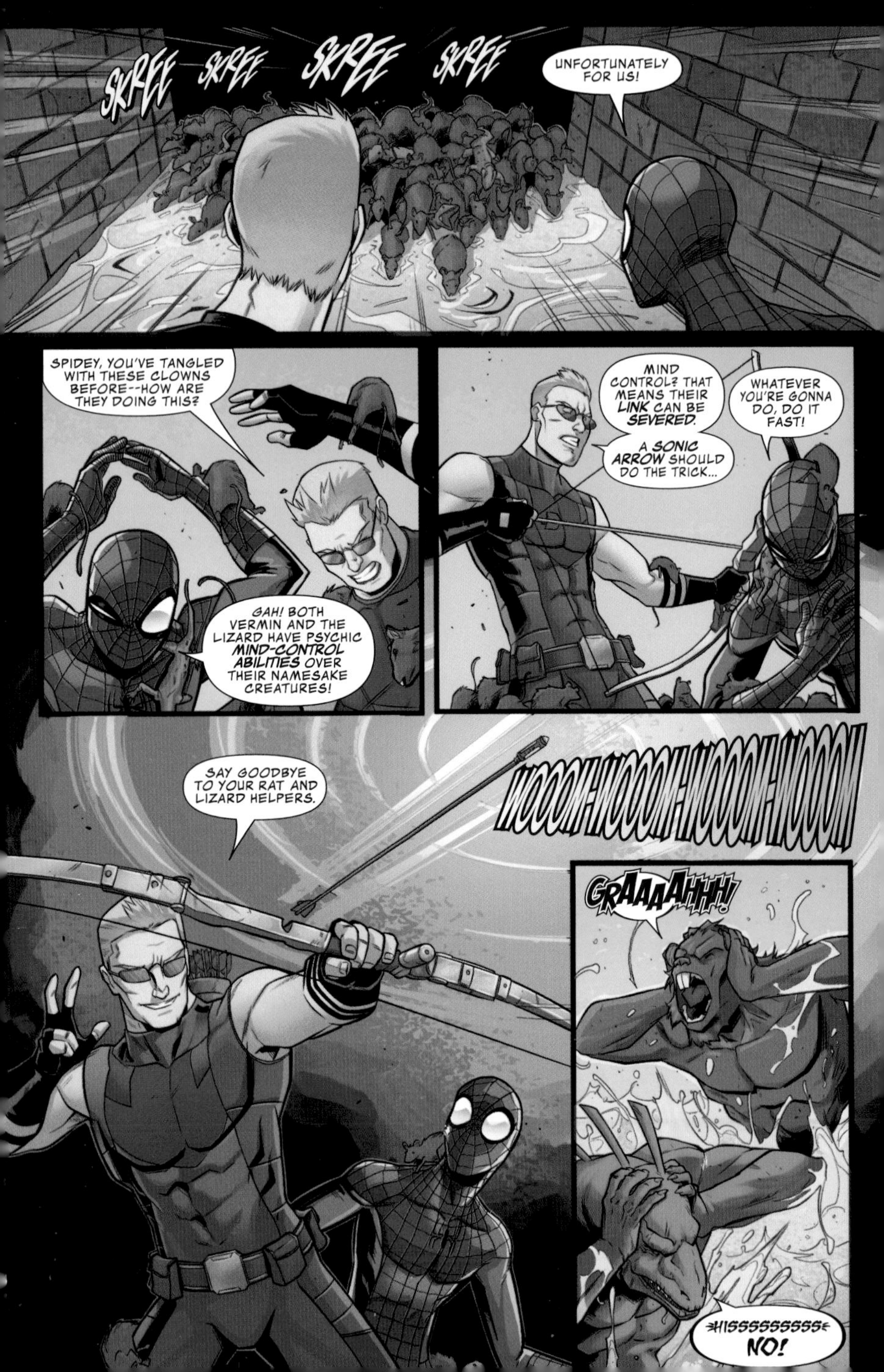
SKREE SKREE SKREE SKREE
UNFORTUNATELY FOR US!
SPIDEY, YOU'VE TANGLED WITH THESE CLOWNS BEFORE--HOW ARE THEY DOING THIS?
GAH! BOTH VERMIN AND THE LIZARD HAVE PSYCHIC MIND-CONTROL ABILITIES OVER THEIR NAMESAKE CREATURES!
MIND CONTROL? THAT MEANS THEIR LINK CAN BE SEVERED.
A SONIC ARROW SHOULD DO THE TRICK...
WHATEVER YOU'RE GONNA DO, DO IT FAST!
SAY GOODBYE TO YOUR RAT AND LIZARD HELPERS.
WOOOM-WOOOM-WOOOM-WOOOM
GRAAAAHHH!
HISSSSSSSSS NO!

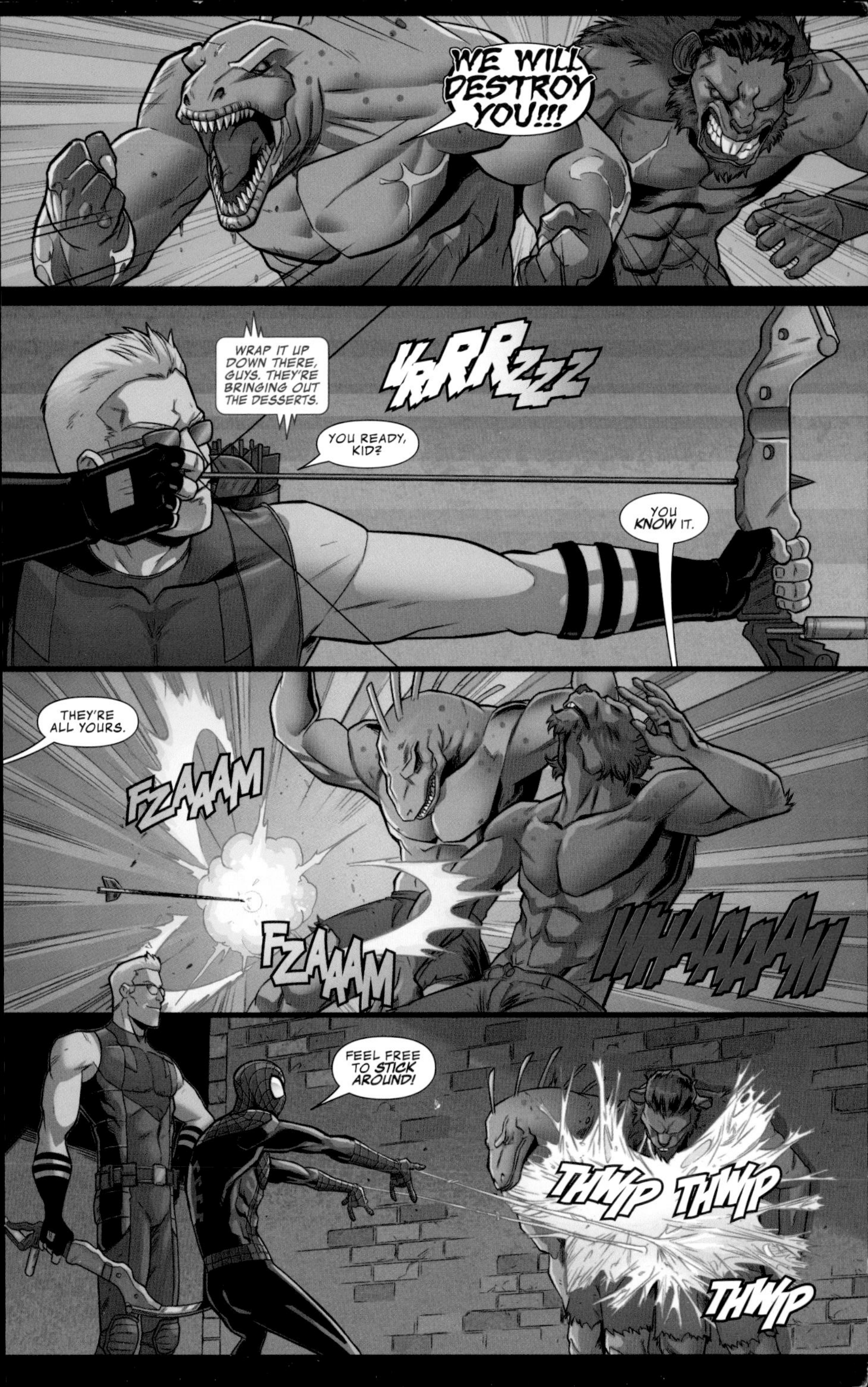
WE WILL DESTROY YOU!!!
WRAP IT UP DOWN THERE, GUYS. THEY'RE BRINGING OUT THE DESSERTS.
VRRRZZZ
YOU READY, KID?
YOU KNOW IT.
THEY'RE ALL YOURS.
FZAAAM
FZAAAM
WHAAAAM
FEEL FREE TO STICK AROUND!
THWIP THWIP
THWIP

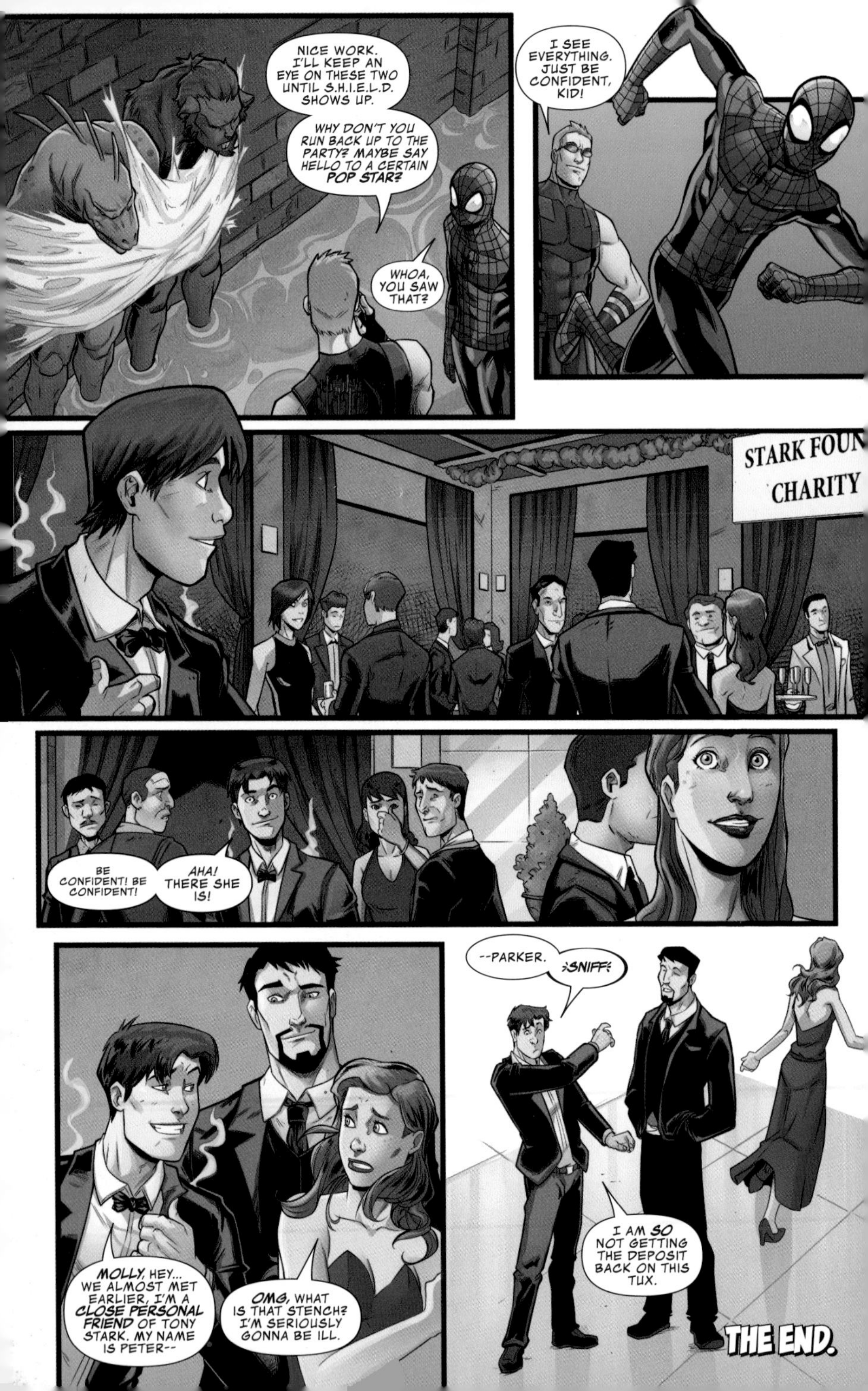
NICE WORK. I'LL KEEP AN EYE ON THESE TWO UNTIL S.H.I.E.L.D. SHOWS UP.
WHY DON'T YOU RUN BACK UP TO THE PARTY? MAYBE SAY HELLO TO A CERTAIN POP STAR?
WHOA, YOU SAW THAT?
I SEE EVERYTHING. JUST BE CONFIDENT, KID!
STARK FOUN
CHARITY
BE CONFIDENT! BE CONFIDENT!
AHA! THERE SHE IS!
MOLLY, HEY... WE ALMOST MET EARLIER, I'M A CLOSE PERSONAL FRIEND OF TONY STARK. MY NAME IS PETER--
OMG, WHAT IS THAT STENCH? I'M SERIOUSLY GONNA BE ILL.
--PARKER.
SNIFF
I AM SO NOT GETTING THE DEPOSIT BACK ON THIS TUX.
THE END.

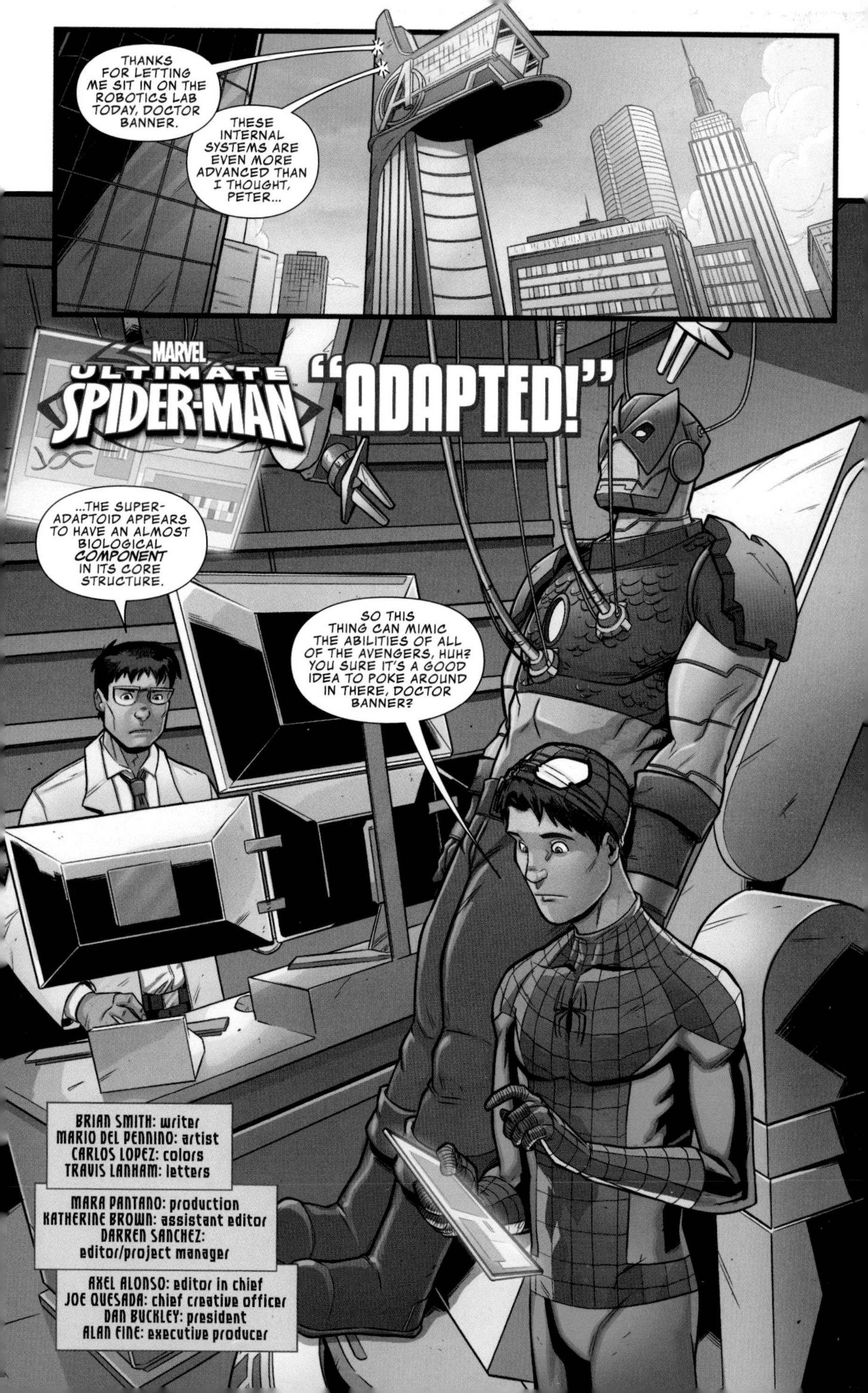
THANKS FOR LETTING ME SIT IN ON THE ROBOTICS LAB TODAY, DOCTOR BANNER.
THESE INTERNAL SYSTEMS ARE EVEN MORE ADVANCED THAN I THOUGHT, PETER...
MARVEL ULTIMATE SPIDER-MAN
"ADAPTED!"
...THE SUPER-ADAPTOID APPEARS TO HAVE AN ALMOST BIOLOGICAL COMPONENT IN ITS CORE STRUCTURE.
SO THIS THING CAN MIMIC THE ABILITIES OF ALL OF THE AVENGERS, HUH? YOU SURE IT'S A GOOD IDEA TO POKE AROUND IN THERE, DOCTOR BANNER?
BRIAN SMITH: writer
MARIO DEL PENNINO: artist
CARLOS LOPEZ: colors
TRAVIS LANHAM: letters
MARA PANTANO: production
KATHERINE BROWN: assistant editor
DARREN SANCHEZ: editor/project manager
AXEL ALONSO: editor in chief
JOE QUESADA: chief creative officer
DAN BUCKLEY: president
ALAN FINE: executive producer

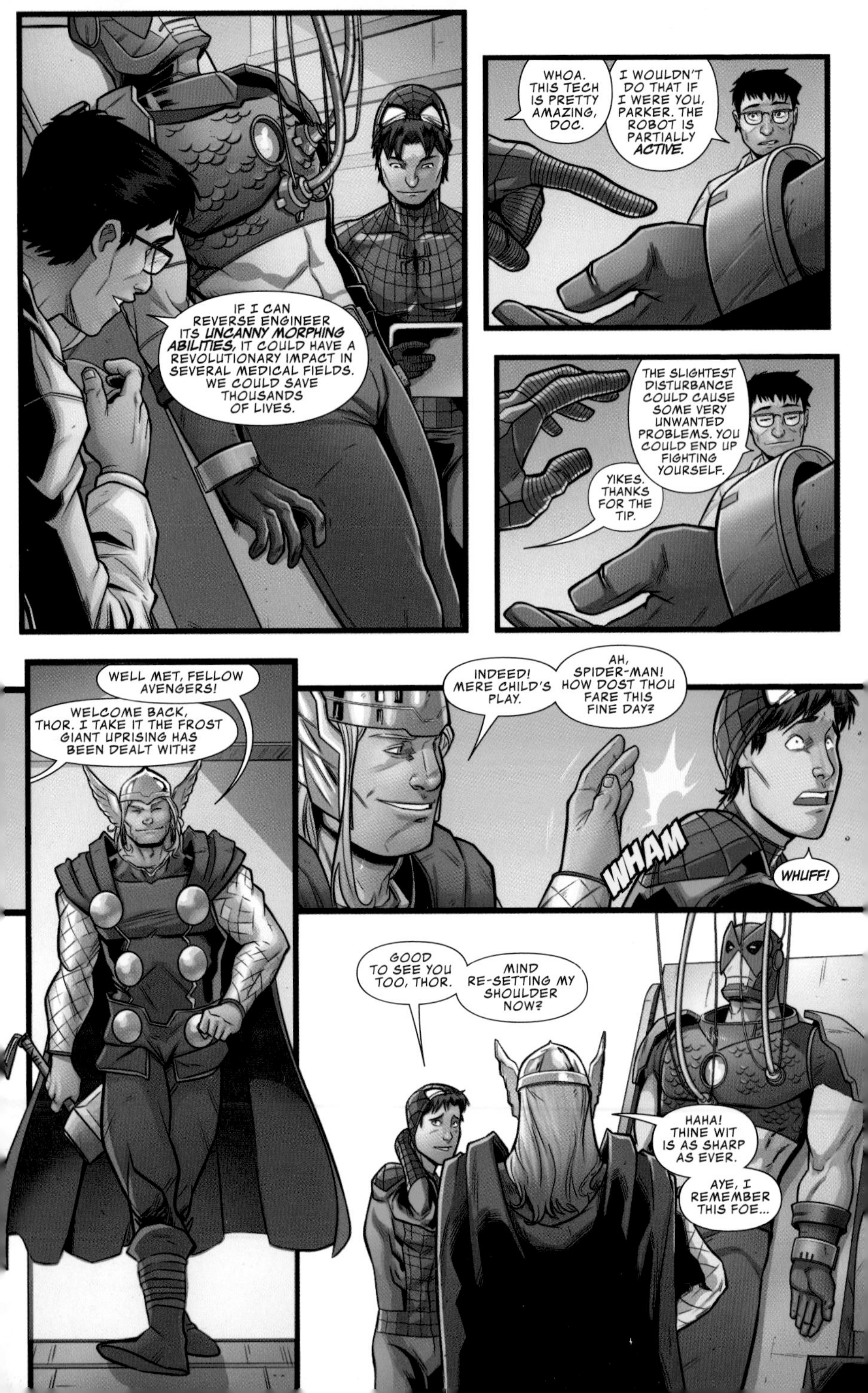
IF I CAN REVERSE ENGINEER ITS UNCANNY MORPHING ABILITIES, IT COULD HAVE A REVOLUTIONARY IMPACT IN SEVERAL MEDICAL FIELDS. WE COULD SAVE THOUSANDS OF LIVES.
WHOA. THIS TECH IS PRETTY AMAZING, DOC.
I WOULDN'T DO THAT IF I WERE YOU, PARKER. THE ROBOT IS PARTIALLY ACTIVE.
THE SLIGHTEST DISTURBANCE COULD CAUSE SOME VERY UNWANTED PROBLEMS. YOU COULD END UP FIGHTING YOURSELF.
YIKES. THANKS FOR THE TIP.
WELL MET, FELLOW AVENGERS!
WELCOME BACK, THOR. I TAKE IT THE FROST GIANT UPRISING HAS BEEN DEALT WITH?
INDEED! MERE CHILD'S PLAY.
AH, SPIDER-MAN! HOW DOST THOU FARE THIS FINE DAY?
WHAM
WHUFF!
GOOD TO SEE YOU TOO, THOR.
MIND RE-SETTING MY SHOULDER NOW?
HAHA! THINE WIT IS AS SHARP AS EVER.
AYE, I REMEMBER THIS FOE...

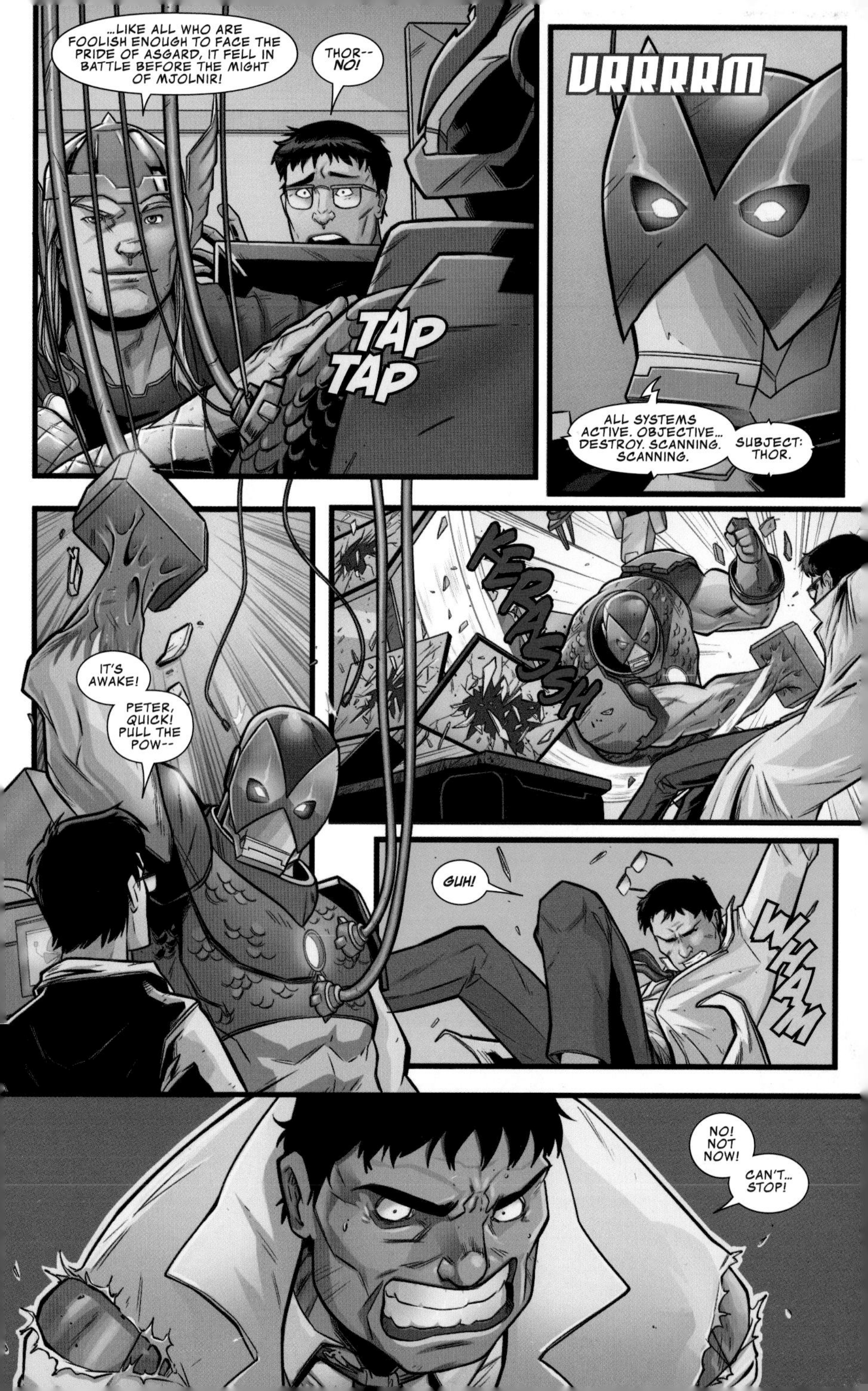
...LIKE ALL WHO ARE FOOLISH ENOUGH TO FACE THE PRIDE OF ASGARD, IT FELL IN BATTLE BEFORE THE MIGHT OF MJOLNIR!
THOR-- NO!
TAP TAP
VRRRRM
ALL SYSTEMS ACTIVE. OBJECTIVE... DESTROY. SCANNING. SCANNING.
SUBJECT: THOR.
IT'S AWAKE!
PETER, QUICK! PULL THE POW--
KERASSH
GUH!
WHAM
NO! NOT NOW!
CAN'T... STOP!

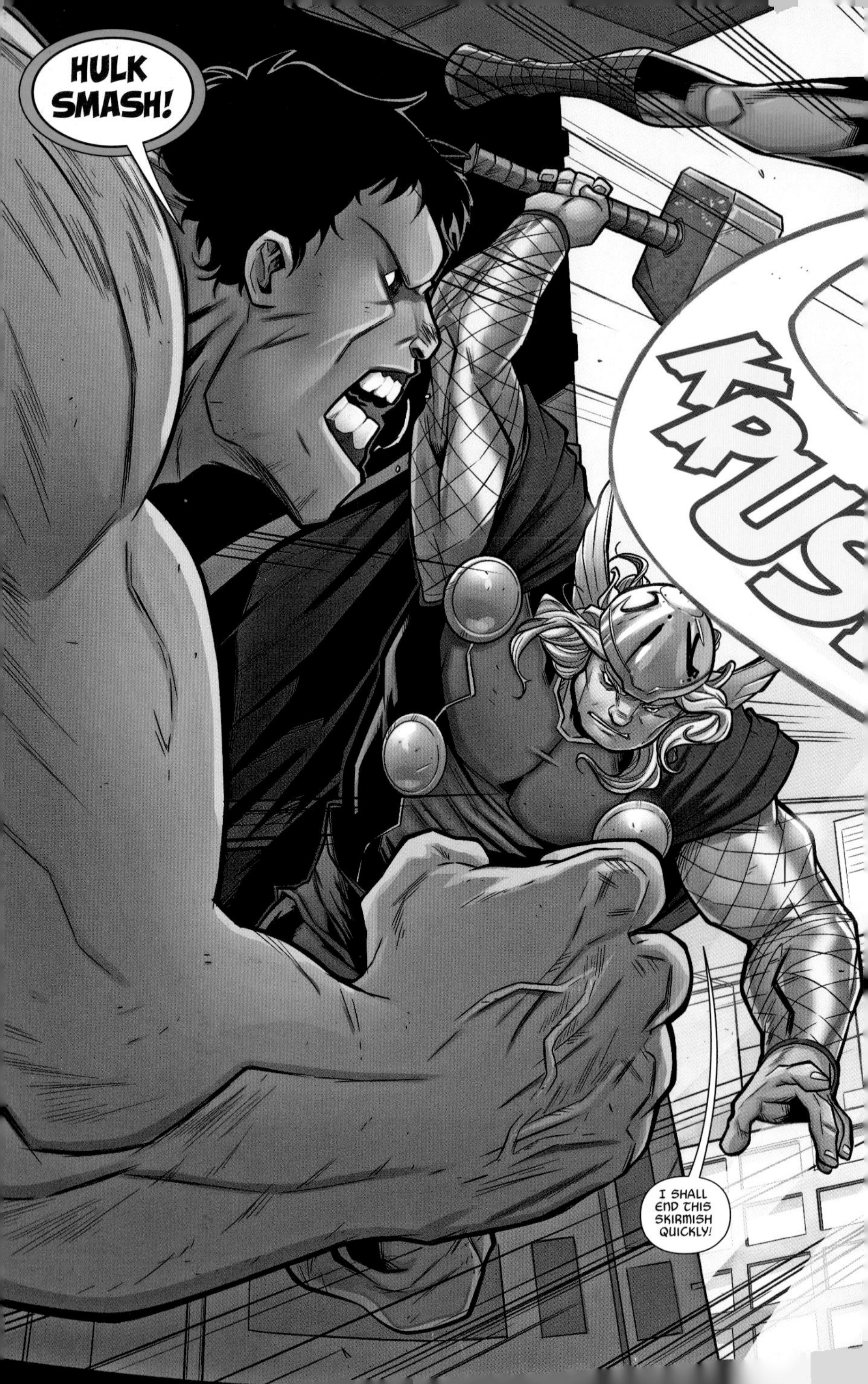
HULK SMASH!
I SHALL END THIS SKIRMISH QUICKLY!
KRUS

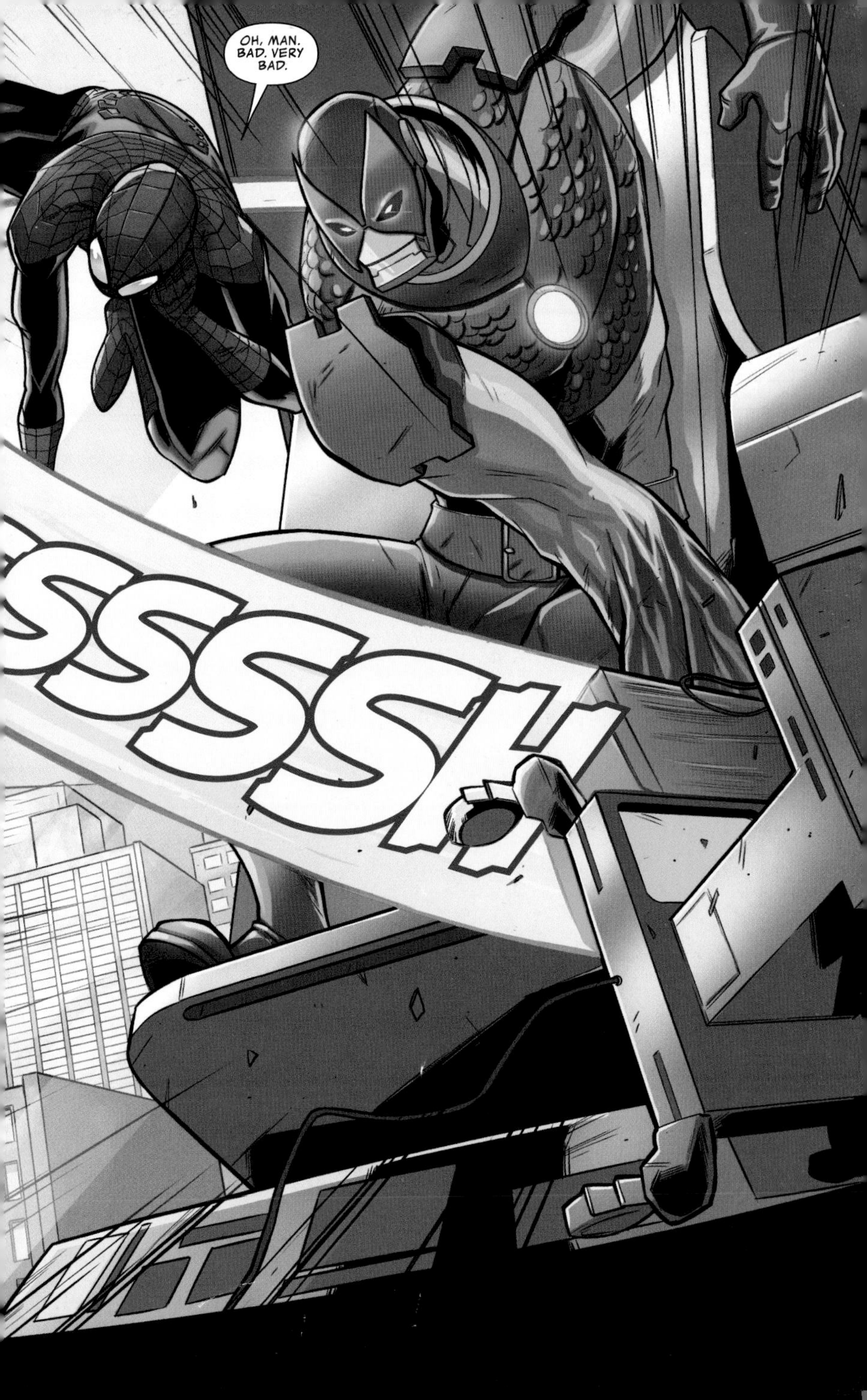
OH, MAN. BAD. VERY BAD.
SSSH!

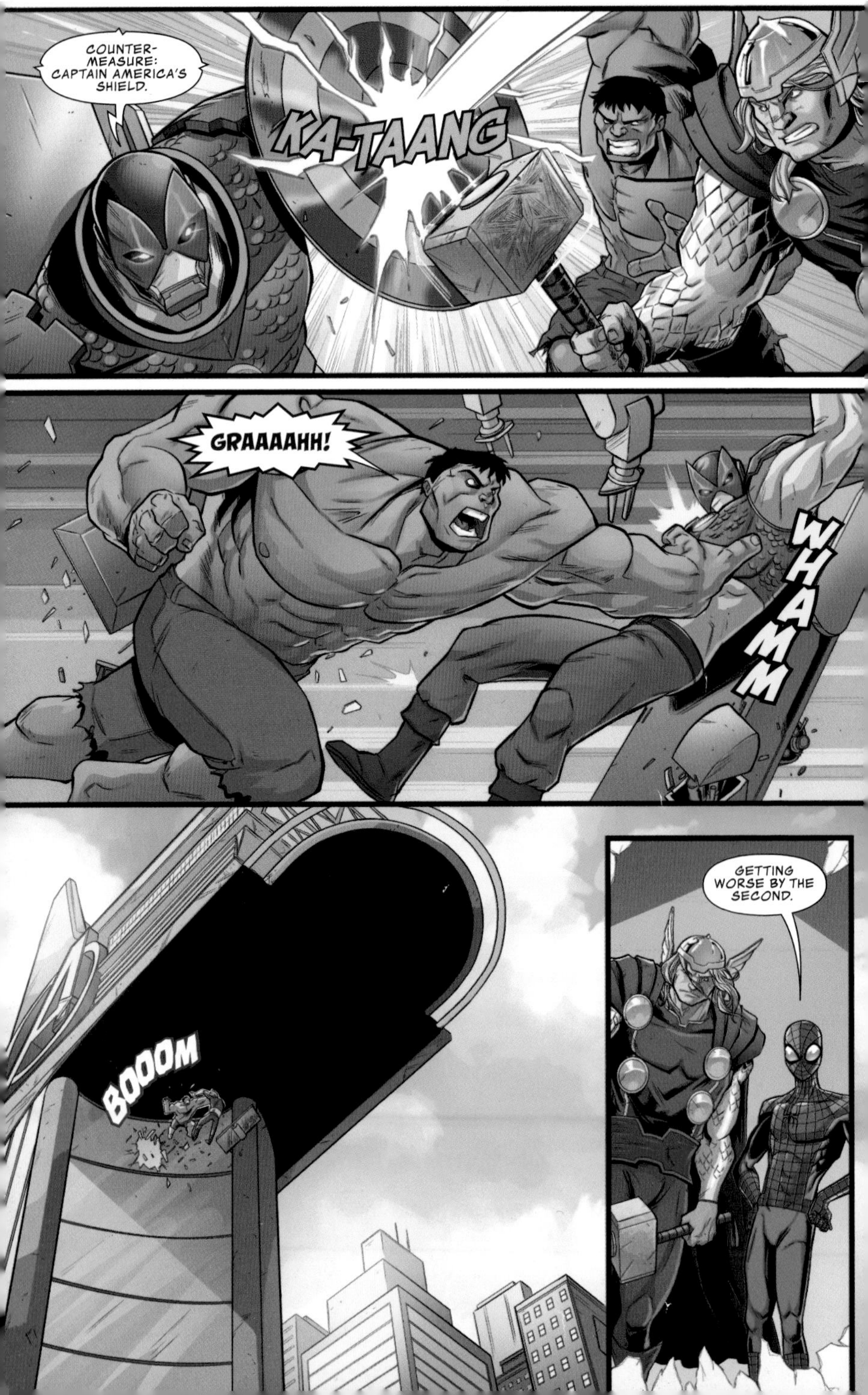
COUNTER-MEASURE: CAPTAIN AMERICA'S SHIELD.
KA-TAANG
GRAAAAHH!
WHAMM
BOOOM
GETTING WORSE BY THE SECOND.

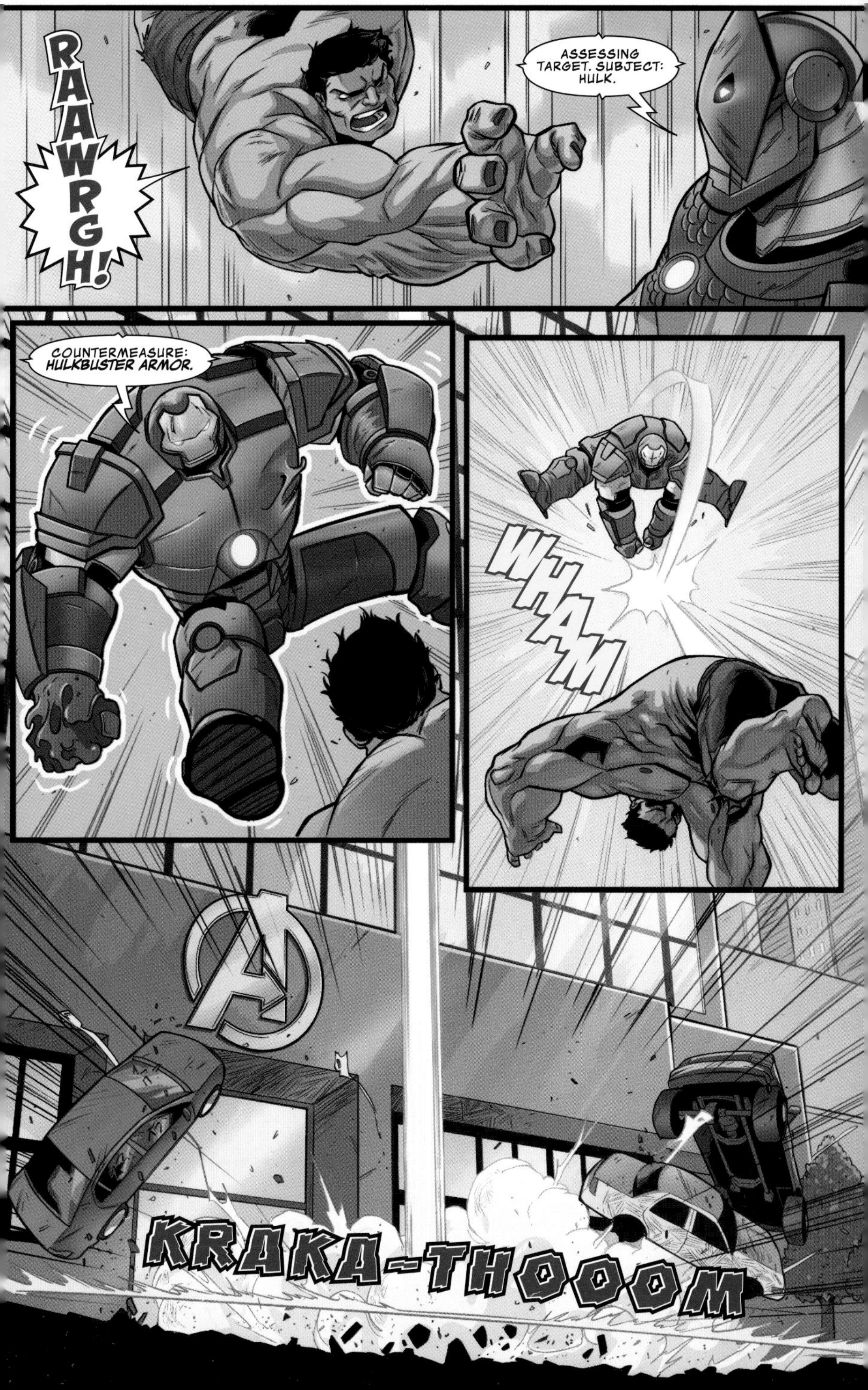
RAAAWRGH!
ASSESSING TARGET. SUBJECT: HULK.
COUNTERMEASURE: HULKBUSTER ARMOR.
WHAM
KRAKA-THOOOM

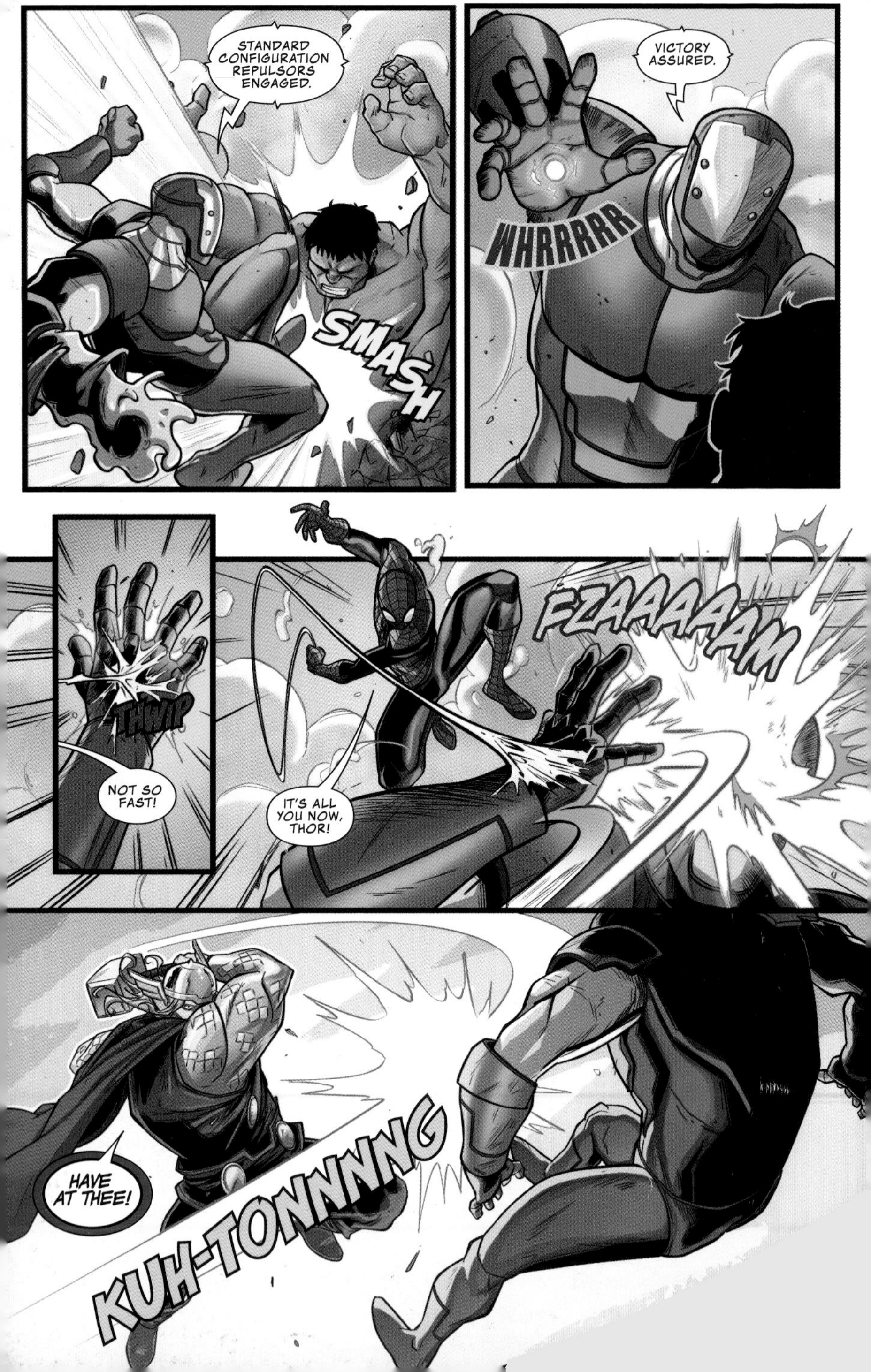

STANDARD CONFIGURATION REPULSORS ENGAGED.
SMASH
VICTORY ASSURED.
WHRRRRR
THWIP
NOT SO FAST!
FZAAAAAAM
IT'S ALL YOU NOW, THOR!
HAVE AT THEE!
KUH-TONNNNG

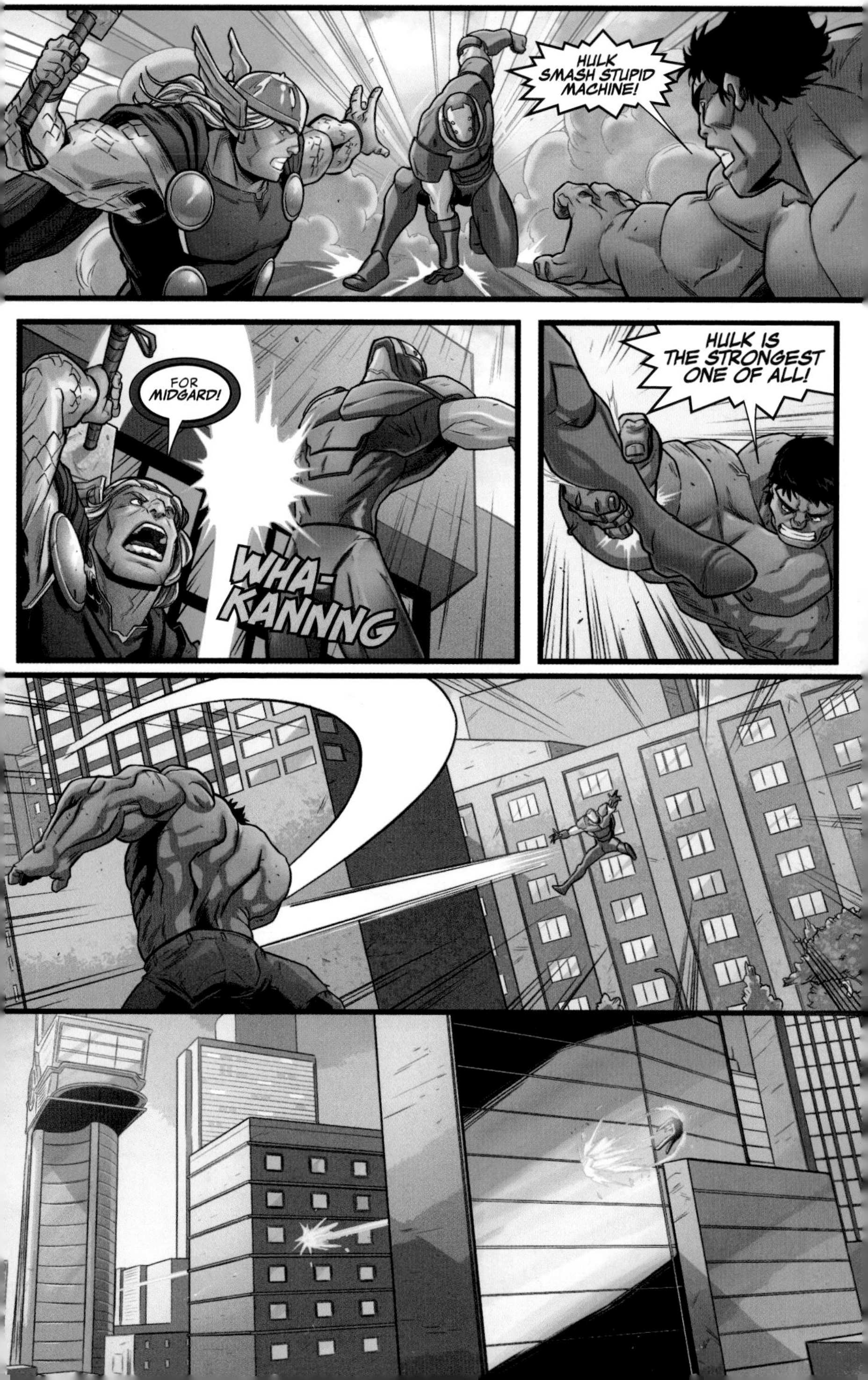
HULK SMASH STUPID MACHINE!
FOR MIDGARD!
WHA-KANNNG
HULK IS THE STRONGEST ONE OF ALL!

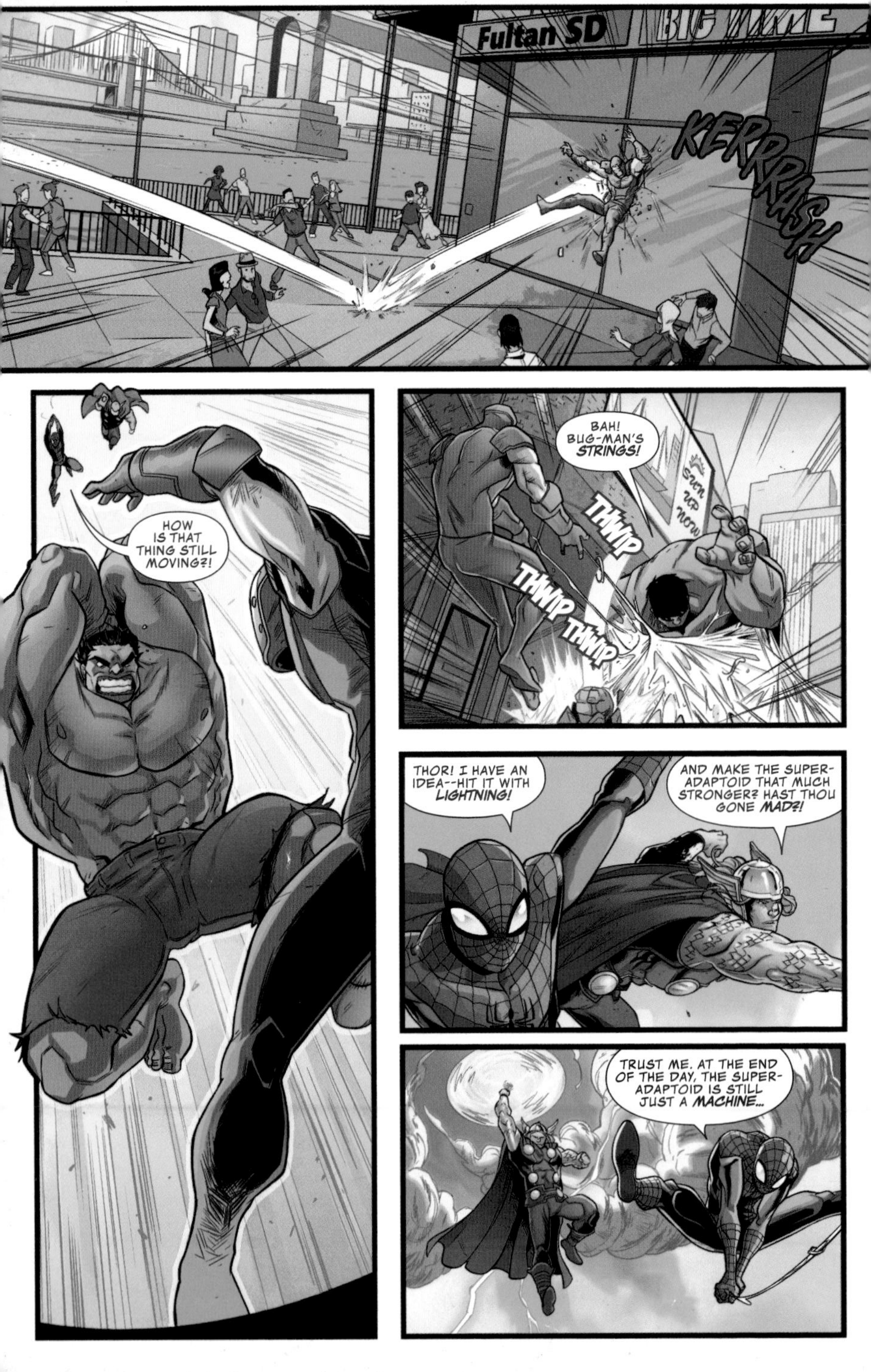
Fultan SD
KERRRASH
HOW IS THAT THING STILL MOVING?!
BAH! BUG-MAN'S STRINGS!
THWIP
THWIP THWIP
THOR! I HAVE AN IDEA--HIT IT WITH LIGHTNING!
AND MAKE THE SUPER-ADAPTOID THAT MUCH STRONGER? HAST THOU GONE MAD?!
TRUST ME. AT THE END OF THE DAY, THE SUPER-ADAPTOID IS STILL JUST A MACHINE...

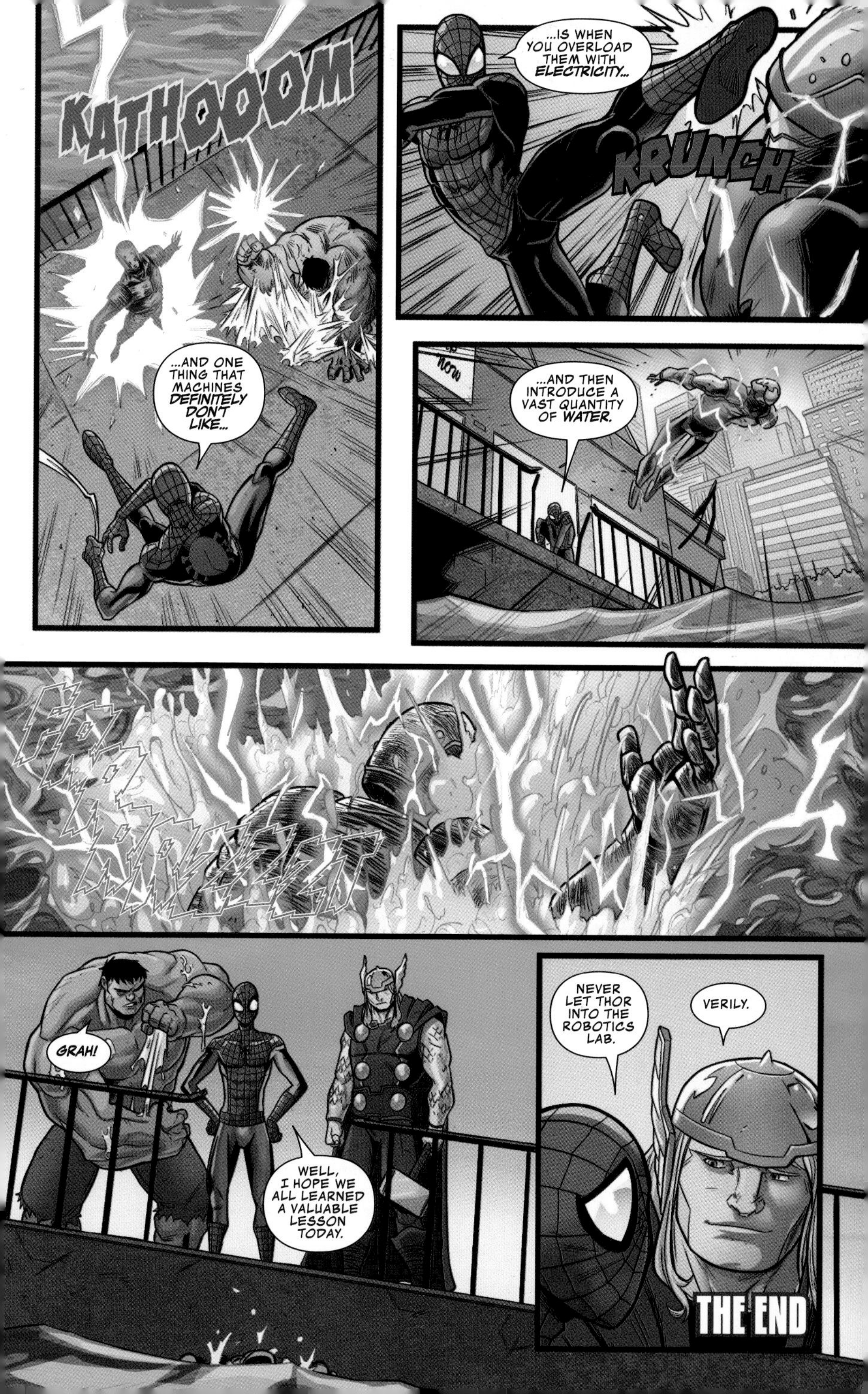
KATHOOOM
...AND ONE THING THAT MACHINES DEFINITELY DON'T LIKE...
...IS WHEN YOU OVERLOAD THEM WITH ELECTRICITY...
KRUNCH
...AND THEN INTRODUCE A VAST QUANTITY OF WATER.
GRAH!
WELL, I HOPE WE ALL LEARNED A VALUABLE LESSON TODAY.
NEVER LET THOR INTO THE ROBOTICS LAB.
VERILY.
THE END

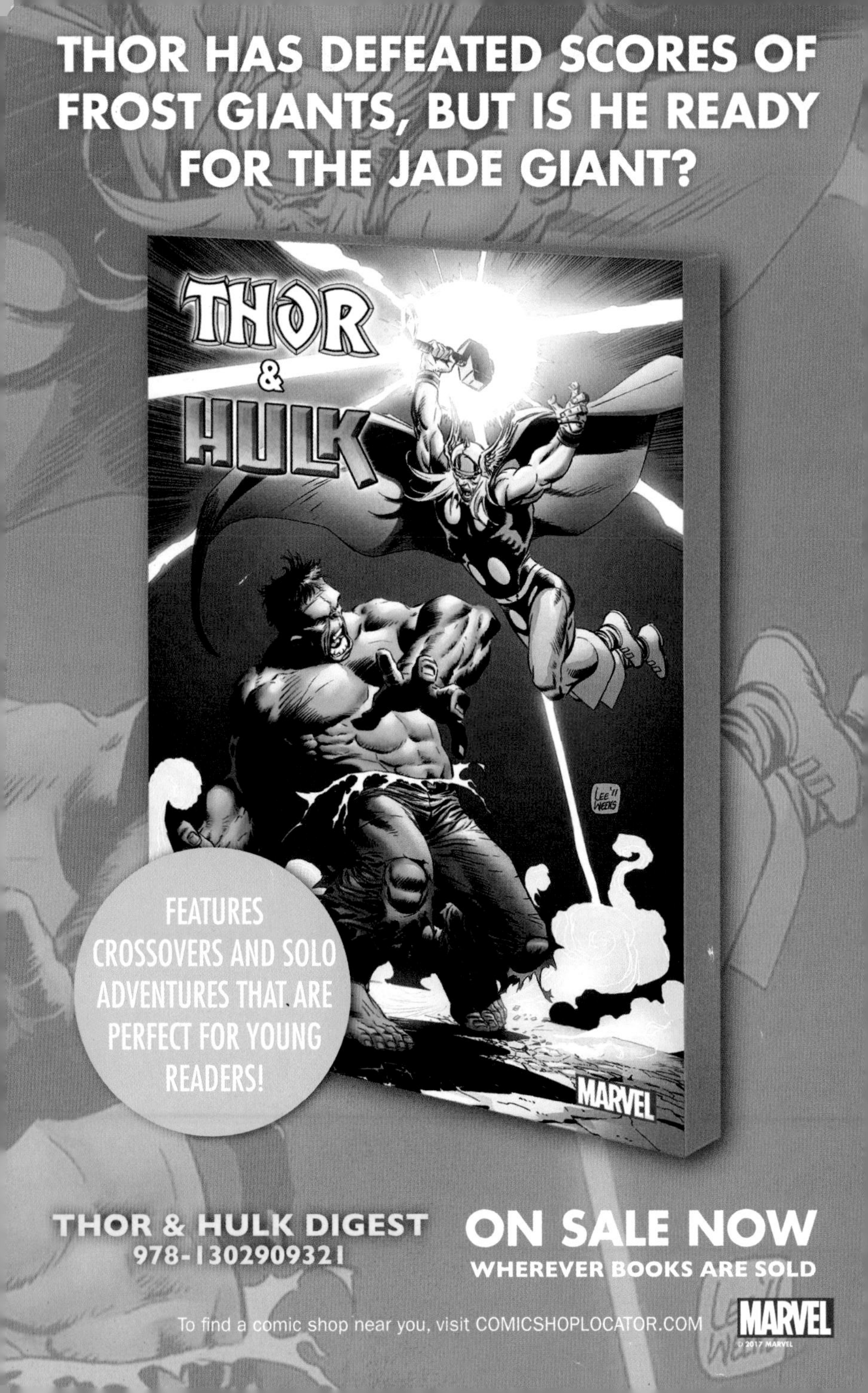

THOR HAS DEFEATED SCORES OF FROST GIANTS, BUT IS HE READY FOR THE JADE GIANT?
THOR & HULK
LEE '11 WEEKS
MARVEL
FEATURES CROSSOVERS AND SOLO ADVENTURES THAT ARE PERFECT FOR YOUNG READERS!
THOR & HULK DIGEST
978-1302909321
ON SALE NOW
WHEREVER BOOKS ARE SOLD
To find a comic shop near you, visit COMICSHOPLOCATOR.COM
MARVEL
© 2017 MARVEL

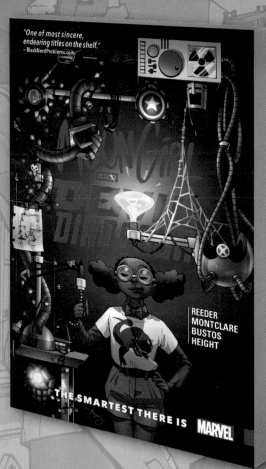